ACTING ONE

ACTING ONE

FOURTH EDITION

Robert Cohen

UNIVERSITY OF CALIFORNIA, IRVINE

Boston   Burr Ridge, IL   Dubuque, IA   Madison, WI   New York
San Francisco   St. Louis   Bangkok   Bogotá   Caracas   Kuala Lumpur
Lisbon   London   Madrid   Mexico City   Milan   Montreal   New Delhi
Santiago   Seoul   Singapore   Sydney   Taipei   Toronto

McGraw-Hill Higher Education

A Division of The **McGraw-Hill** Companies

1 2 3 4 5 6 7 8 9 0 DOC/DOC 0 9 8 7 6 5 4 3 2 1

Library of Congress Cataloging-in-Publication Data

Cohen, Robert
    Acting one / Robert Cohen.—4th ed.
       p.   cm.
    Includes index.
    ISBN 0-7674-1859-X
    1. Acting. I. Title: Acting 1. II. Title.
PN2061.C579 2001
792'.028—dc21   2001030844

Sponsoring editor, Janet M. Beatty; *production editor,* Jennifer Mills; *manuscript editor,* Margaret Moore; *design manager and cover designer,* Susan Breitbard; *manufacturing manager,* Randy Hurst. This text was set in 10/12 Sabon by TBH Typecast, Inc. and printed on acid-free 50# Finch Opaque by R. R. Donnelley & Sons Company.

www.mhhe.com

C O N T E N T S

P R E F A C E

This book is expressly intended for the beginning acting student. The twenty-eight lessons comprise basic material for what could be a one-year or two-year course in acting fundamentals. The amount of time needed to cover them will vary to the degree proficiency is sought or expected, for while the material is presented as an introduction to acting, these are the fundamentals that professional actors spend their lives exploring and perfecting. None of these twenty-eight lessons can ever be fully learned, not even in a lifetime.

Except for a comment in the afterword (L'Envoi), matters of characterization and style are not covered because these are not beginning subjects in acting. Young actors may wish to leap into the classics and into the extremes of farce and tragedy well before they have even begun to master the basics of talking, listening, tactical interplay, physicalizing, building scenes, and making good choices. The fundamentals, however, should be set down first. What is in these pages will hold true for Shakespearean acting, for comedy acting, or for television acting; these lessons should serve as a basis for all advanced acting skills. Get a good handle on these twenty-eight lessons—on the fundamentals of acting—and you will be able to move on to more advanced acting problems with confidence.

On several occasions, I have referred to "the young actor," or "the beginning actor," with the implication that student actors are necessarily young and awkward. I apologize in advance if I hurt anybody's feelings in this regard; there are young and beginning actors who can act with great skill and eloquence. On the other hand, most student actors are somewhat at sea when they go out on stage, and the experienced teacher, or director, or audience member can spot this long before the student can. That's because you can't see or hear yourself while acting, and student actors rarely have the experience to achieve the kind of objectivity about their performance that veteran professionals do. The student actor may *feel* something and be quite satisfied (if not overjoyed) at the intensity of that feeling while still not coming within miles of the intensity a more experienced professional actor would achieve with the same material. It is actually helpful for the beginning actor to remember that he or she is a beginner. It takes the pressure off, and you can try to advance one step at a time rather than taking on the entire artistic community every time you step onto the stage. This book is designed to start that process and carry the beginner into some fairly advanced steps.

The last section of this book, on acting technique, involves some topics not always taught in a beginning acting class. Technique is not always taught because it often proves difficult for young actors to understand how acting can involve emotional and psychological reality and controlled acting "technique" at the same time. It can. Indeed, all fine actors are able to integrate the emotions in a role with a technical ability to perform the role. It is true that some actors (usually American) worry more about feelings, and some actors (usually British or French) worry more about technique, but you do not need to make a choice. There is nothing at all inconsistent between deep and honest emotional responsiveness on the one hand and a superior acting technique on the other. In every section of this book, I have tried to indicate the honest relationships between genuine feeling and controlled acting technique, and between human reality and the art of the theatre.

I have tried to use ordinary terminology throughout this text. Acting books, including some of my own, have often wrestled uncomfortably with semantics; acting discussions are often mired in semantic quarrels of bewildering complexity. This confusion is perhaps understandable since acting has given the world its jargon for both psychology (*role playing, acting out*) and philosophy (*tragedy, persona,* and the like). Therefore I have stayed with words long in the theatrical lexicon (words which themselves are not precisely defined in all cases), except that I sometimes use *goal* when others use *intention* and that I sometimes use the acronym *GOTE* as a memory tool to help you remember the words *Goal, Other, Tactics,* and *Expectation* in the most useful order.

I have also kept this book as free as possible from considerations of theory. Students looking for a more theoretical basis for the lessons in this text might wish to explore them in my *Acting Power* (Mayfield, 1978), which conceptualizes a comprehensive system of acting. In addition, students wishing to extend the lessons in *Acting One* into the areas of style, characterization, and public performance now have available a sequel, *Advanced Acting: Style, Character, and Performance* (McGraw-Hill, 2002), which is devoted to these questions. The interested reader is also directed to my *Acting in Shakespeare* (Mayfield, 1991) for specific lessons and discussions built on acting in the plays of the world's greatest—and most produced—dramatist.

Finally, no one is more aware than I that acting cannot be taught by a book. Acting can most certainly be taught—and the change over the past three decades in American acting has largely been the result of an explosion of actor training nationwide—but the key ingredient in actor teaching is the teacher. I have tried to keep this book open-ended and suggestive rather than narrow and prescriptive so that it might stimulate, not stultify, the crucial work of the classroom. Acting and actor training are individual arts within a collective and collaborative craft process. The actor must find her or his way into the self, as well as into the craft, for the art of the theatre is made out of both ingredients. This book is blind to its readers' individualities; it teaches only as interpreted and implemented by you, the actor, or you, the teacher. I have tried to leave as much room as possible for that interaction, which I value as highly as any in the arts.

I am happy to have had the occasion to once again revise this text. Readers of previous editions will note that I have reorganized the opening of the book, moving to the beginning a fundamental exercise with which I myself begin courses, and that I have added many exercises and discussions throughout the book, particularly in the areas of technique. I have also included, for the first time, some sage acting counsel by distinguished professional actors (and a few directors) that pairs well with the exercises and discussions herein; some of these quotes have been silently condensed a bit, but without altering their sense. These supplement the work by showing that veteran professional actors wrestle with the same questions that beginners do and that "learning to act" is a lifetime process.

I very much appreciate, in the initial preparation of this revision, the individual counsels of Professors Robert Dunkerly at the Community College of Southern Nevada, Mark Radvan at the Queensland (Australia) University of Technology, David Knight at the University of Illinois, Ashley Carr at California State University of Long Beach, Leslie Reidel at the University of Delaware, and C. Tim Quinn at Fresno City College.

I'd also like to thank the reviewers of this edition for their thoughtful comments: Bob Dunkerly, Community College of Southern Nevada; Richard Nichols, Pennsylvania State University; J. Fred Pritt, Ithaca College; Leslie Rivers, California State Polytechnic University, Pomona; and Andrew Ryder, Seattle Pacific University.

Publisher's Note to Instructors

A 35-minute video, "Acting One, Day One, with Robert Cohen" is available. Employing a simple exercise with acting students, Robert Cohen describes and demonstrates the basic principles of goal-directed acting and interacting, as detailed in the text. The video may be purchased from Theatre Arts Video Library at 800-456-8285.

I

Preparation for Acting

CAN ACTING BE TAUGHT?

Yes, of course acting can be taught. In the United States, acting is taught regularly in literally thousands of colleges, conservatories, workshops, and professional studios. Virtually all young actors coming into the profession in the present era have studied acting in some formal manner, and many professional actors continue their training for years beyond their successful entry into the profession. Thus, acting is not only taught, it is also learned.

Of course, reading any certain list of books, or studying with any particular teacher or teachers, or enrolling in any particular training program will not guarantee that you will become a great actor or even a fair one. Fine acting demands a rare combination of talents: intelligence, imagination, psychological freedom, physical dexterity, vocal strength and flexibility, emotional depth, and an ability to learn from mistakes, criticism, and observation. It also requires certain personal prowess, which might appear from time to time as wit, charm, self-confidence, assuredness, honesty, audacity, charisma,

1

passionate intensity, and compelling candor. These characteristics cannot be taught, directly, in anything resembling their entirety: They are acquired, if at all, as much through life experience as by training for the stage.

What can be taught, therefore, is a beginning to the art of acting. This is something more than merely pointing you at the stage and something less than giving you a fully codified set of rules and regulations. It is a method of helping you to get the most out of yourself and to train your acting instrument—primarily your voice and body —into a more workable, more exciting, apparatus. And it is a method that will help you learn from life and apply what you learn to the art of translating life into art: the art of the theatre. Providing this beginning is the goal of this book.

1

Preparing to Act

Relaxation

Every actor knows the importance of relaxation, for it is the necessary starting place for acting. Relaxation is both physical and mental; it allows the body to respond freshly and the mind to create spontaneously. A relaxed actor can do anything; a tense actor is always constrained.

Relaxation cannot be forced, but it can be induced or self-induced. Simple stretching exercises—rolling the head in large circles, bending the body forward and back, and moving the fingers, hands, arms, and legs in figure-eight patterns—are excellent warm-up techniques that both tone body muscles and release physical tensions. Bouncing lightly on the balls of the feet; vigorously shaking the arms, hands, face, and torso; and rapidly shadow-boxing or rope-jumping also limber and relax the body. Virtually all actors develop physical regimens of exercises like these to use before rehearsals and performances, and you should too. Many acting classes begin with such warm-ups; if yours doesn't, you can do your own warm-up beforehand.

Mental relaxation is a matter of putting out of mind the day-to-day affairs of life so that you can concentrate more directly and fully on the problems of acting and on the situation of the characters you will play. Inasmuch as acting is, among other things, a complex mental activity, the more freedom you have from your own daily preoccupations, the more deeply you will be able to involve yourself with your acting situation, even during periods of extreme stress in your personal life. Physical exercise is often a help to achieving this mental relaxation; so are meditation, yoga,

---

⬚ LET YOUR BODY GO

Young actors first work through tension because it's the only thing they know. But it's most inefficient. Do exercises where you let every muscle in your body go, one at a time. Then your body is ready to react to whatever command you give it; your thoughts and emotions will resonate with truth.

LAURENCE OLIVIER, ADVISING THE YOUNG ANTHONY HOPKINS

---

thinking about pleasant images, or "playing" soothing music in your head. One of the best ways of achieving mental relaxation in an acting class is simply to look around you and study what you see. What color are the walls? How many people are in the class? Does your teacher wear contact lenses? Are the other students as nervous as you? Who brought their books to class today? Since most mental tension comes from thinking about ourselves (and how we might be failing to measure up), thinking about other people helps us to relax and put the world in a better perspective.

Relaxation is the starting point for acting, not the ending point. Don't ever confuse relaxation with "not thinking." Relaxation is not stupor; it is a state of openness and receptivity to your surroundings—a state unmarked by extreme preoccupation or worry. Go ahead and think all you want, but don't burrow into your thoughts and dwell on yourself. Relax with your eyes wide open, your senses fully awake, and with the idea of taking in all you can.

◆ E X E R C I S E   1–1

Relaxation

Stand easily, legs slightly apart, with enough room around you to stretch your arms in all directions.

While inhaling, extend your arms fully upward and outward. On your exhale, release your arms totally and let them drop to your sides. Release all the tension in your fingers, then your wrists, then your elbows, then your shoulders.

Repeat the above four times and, starting with the third, go up on your toes as you inhale, let them drop as you exhale. Try to extend your arms and toes farther on each of the last three times, and release your fingers, wrists, elbows, and shoulders farther as well.

Shake out your left leg for three full breaths, then your right leg, then repeat. Roll your neck around from left to right on the repeat.

Hands on hips, shudder your body and release all tension while taking five deep breaths. Avoid hyperventilating.

From the same position, rotate your body all the way to the left and then right three times; then, hands still on hips, bow forward as far as you can, vertebra by vertebra, with your arms hanging to the floor, releasing all tension in your back, shoulders, arms, and fingers as you do so. Hang there for a long moment, taking a deep breath and enjoying the release. Slowly come back up, one vertebra at a time, until you are standing tall and freely erect. Do not compete with the persons next to you! This is a relaxation exercise, not a test of strength, speed, or agility.

Swing twice more to the left and the right, and bow a final time, shuddering your body as you come up.

On a full breath, exhale while saying "HUH, bubba buh, bubba buh, bubba buh!" Do it four more times, a bit louder each time.

On a full breath, exhale while saying "Brekka korex, korex, korex, korex." Repeat three more times, a bit louder each time. (This line, by the way, is an approximation of the "croaking chorus" of *The Frogs* by Aristophanes—a play twenty-five hundred years old!)

Do this line three *more* times, this time croaking each "korex" a tiny bit louder than the one immediately before it, as "Brekka korex, korex, korex, korex."

Exhale on "HUH, bubba buh, bubba buh, bubba buh!" while twisting your body left and right. Continue twisting with "Brekka korex, korex, korex, korex!" Alternate the speeches while twisting and bowing three more times.

Run in place—or jump an imaginary rope—for fifteen breaths.

Go up on your toes and extend your arms fully one last time, then release and collapse gently into a relaxed standing position. You're done.

Trust

Trust is also a precondition for acting. Because acting is something you do with, and in front of, other people, anxiety about those people can eat into your ability to act. Trust, like relaxation, cannot be forced, but you can't sit around waiting for it to arrive, either. Trust is a mutual relationship between you and your fellow actor–students—a relationship marked by giving, sharing, and common concern.

You must take the initiative here, because isolation and apathy invest the first classroom meeting with deadly inertia, and only the determined efforts of you and your fellows will break down the walls of carefully nurtured egotism and suspicion that characterize most groups of arbitrarily gathered strangers. If you can find your acting partner interesting, it will make you interested and interesting; if you find your partner fascinating, it will make you fascinated and fascinating. It is to your advantage to seek out what is admirable and wonderful in your fellow actors, the qualities that will make them prized companions and colleagues and will make you a lively partner dramatically engaged with them.

A word about competition: The theatre is a highly competitive business at the upper levels, which means that you will need companions and colleagues all the more. The intensely personal moments that characterize the greatest performances rarely come forth in a climate of contention or antagonism or through the isolation of seemingly self-sufficient individual actors. Rapport among actors, developed through trusting ensemble work, is the context of fine performance.

Actor trust means, at bottom, that you are comfortable with your fellows and they with you. It is the feeling that you can make a fool of yourself without embarrassment and can be emotionally open without getting stepped on. Acting exposes personal vulnerabilities (good acting does, anyway). An atmosphere of trust ensures that those exposures are not callously rubbed raw—that indeed they will become, if anything, therapeutic rather than humiliating and enjoyable rather than discouraging.

Trust develops first out of self-confidence and out of shared activities among the acting group. Trust exercises and games are often used; even children's games are frequently brought into classes or rehearsals by teachers and directors sensitive to the need for mutual trust. Pure socializing has its important place in the work of actors, both in class and in the professional world. Mutual massage or mutual back rubs are also beneficial, both for trust and for relaxation. An excellent basic warm-up involving both is the following "spine lengthening" exercise adapted from the Alexander technique (see Lesson 18).

◆ E X E R C I S E   1–2

Spine Lengthening

Pair with a partner. One person lies down on a mat, face up, knees raised. The other gently pulls the supine actor's head away from the torso, tilting the chin down slightly at the same time. Going around the supine body, the massaging actor gently pulls one limb at a time away from the torso center, pulling along the limb, and then at the extremities, returning to the head after each limb.

At the end of the massage, the actor is rolled to one side and invited to curl into a fetal position. The actor can then be gently raised to an erect position, his or her head is lifted up and away one last time, and the actors reverse positions. This exercise induces a sense of well-being in addition to relaxation and trust; each actor will feel about two inches taller at the end of it.

Neither trust nor relaxation comes about automatically, and for some people neither will come easily at all. Each of us brings different fears and tensions into our work. In general, the more you can focus away from yourself, and can recognize the uniqueness and beauty of the persons around you, and can respond to the world with wonder rather than with irritation and envy, the more you will be in the creative state that will permit you to act deeply, fully, and with spirit.

Exuberance

Acting—in virtually all of its forms—requires a level of performance energy that more sedentary activities, like writing or studying, ordinarily do not. It also requires, during actual moments of performance, a positive and uncritical attitude so that you can carry through your performance tasks with confidence rather than self-doubt. Putting these two together—energy and positive attitude—we may say that acting requires a level of spirited exuberance, a willingness to make a fool of yourself in public if need be, which is not often seen elsewhere in daily academic life.

Such exhibitionism (as it is sometimes called) does not come easily, and we all come to acting with social conditioning that inhibits public displays of exuberance. No one need immediately start shouting, grimacing, acting-up, and acting-out in public to prove that they are actors, but regular public performance activities, such as singing in a choir or musical, reading aloud in class or in staged play-readings, giving political speeches for class elections, teaching classes, or even speaking in classroom discussions are all useful in developing performance energy and exuberant expression. Here's a simple exercise that helps break barriers as well.

◆ E X E R C I S E   1–3

BAM-POW, Dance, Sing

1. Shadowbox

Make two fists, and bouncing from foot to foot, with one fist (normally the right) held up to protect your chin, jab at an imaginary opponent with the other, extending your arm fully each time. As you do this, shout "BAM!" with every blow.

Continue to bounce from foot to foot, dodging your imaginary opponent's imaginary blows ("Rope-a-dope," Muhammad Ali called this). When you see an (imaginary) opening, hit your opponent with your other fist—a potentially knockout punch known as a cross (a "right cross" if done with your right fist). With every cross, shout "POW!"

Use your "Bams" and "Pows" to cheer yourself on, to frighten your opponent into submission, and to encourage others to cheer for you (which will frighten your opponent even more). Exult in your (imaginary) victory. Attract a crowd.

2. Dance

Balancing on the balls of your feet, step forward on one foot while extending the same arm, wrist forward, in the same direction, letting your fingers follow after the wrist has reached its maximum extension. The movement is identical to throwing a frisbee. At the moment when the fingers follow (or the imaginary frisbee is released), cry "Dance!" Repeat with the other leg and arm, and keep repeating, in alternation, crying "Dance!" with each move.

Continue, switching to the word "Ballet!" As you step on your right foot, go up on your toes on your left foot, and vice versa. Say the word "ballet" in a way that encourages others to appreciate the beauty of ballet (whether or not you find it beautiful).

Continue, switching to the word "L'amour!" (the French word for "love," pronounced "la-MOOR!") and imagining that you are casting beautiful flower petals—as love tokens—at the feet of beautiful persons. Say the word "l'amour" in a way that encourages others to think you a wonderful and imaginative lover (whether or not you think you are).

Exult in your magnificent ballet moves and your beautiful tossing of flower petals.

(Feel like a fool yet? Good; you're doing fine. But in acting, you'll have to do equally ridiculous things—and believe in them! This is just to get you started.)

3. Sing

With your feet planted firmly on the ground, and with one hand on your belly and the other extended before you, sing an aria whose notes you invent and whose sole lyric consists of several repetitions of the word "Aria!"

Exult in your operatic splendor. Hear cries of "Bravo!" in your head.

Continue, switching to "HUH, bubba buh, bubba buh, bubba buh!" Don't just do these exercises; do them *exuberantly*!

Discipline

It goes without saying that an actor must be a disciplined artist. Inasmuch as the theatre is a collaborative art, discipline is essential to the effectiveness of the collaboration. Without discipline, trust disappears. If you can't trust your fellow actor to show up for rehearsal, you can't trust her or him to be sensitive to your feelings.

As a result, theatre artists must be particularly punctual and responsible, must meet all of their obligations on time (and *precisely* on time), and must be fully prepared to expend their energies in the pursuit of high standards of artistic effort. That "the show must go on" is a well-known cliché does not detract from its serious importance in the theatre world. Theatre is not a casual activity, and the intensity of the theatrical experience is made possible only by the dedication and commitment of theatre artists to collaborate fully and responsibly with each other on a continuing basis. Discipline makes you someone who can be counted upon, and it makes you able to count upon the commitment of others. There is no better place to start learning artistic discipline than in an acting class.

Criticism

Every actor, from the beginner to the veteran professional, must learn to come to grips with criticism. There is no way around it. Criticism comes from instructors, fellow students, audiences, directors, the press, neighbors, parents, friends, competitors, and avowed enemies. Some is constructive, some instructive, some destructive, and some entirely beside the point. Some you will find useful; some you will find inane; some you will inevitably find unfair. And let's make no mistake about it: Criticism hurts. Anybody who says it doesn't is either a fool or a liar.

The reason criticism hurts the actor more than it hurts other artists is that the art of the actor comes directly out of the actor himself or herself; therefore, criticism of the actor usually takes the form of criticism of the actor's voice, movement, feelings (or seeming lack of feelings), expression, or personality. Some so-called criticisms of acting published in widely read magazines take the form of vitriolic attacks on the personal appearance or mannerisms of an actor. It is understandable, therefore, that actors in general tend to take criticism personally—and that's why it hurts.

The best way to relate to criticism of your work is to profit from it. As a beginner, you must realize that you have much to learn and that persons with some experience in the theatre can be of great help to you. While well-intended and constructive criticism is obviously going to be the most helpful to you, you can learn from callous criticism as well—as long as you filter it properly. The important things are not to take criticism too personally and not to waste a lot of time defending yourself. In the long run, it means little if the criticism is fair or unfair. If you can learn from it, use it. If you can't learn from it, forget it. All criticism is subjective in the final analysis, and you're not going to please everybody. You should be aiming at steady growth, greater comfort onstage, and greater freedom to go out on one emotional limb after another. Any suggestions or critiques that you can turn to your advantage are not only to be dealt with, they should be sought after with persistence. The finest actors do not try to avoid criticism; they solicit it.

A Playful Attitude

Acting is a serious, but never a solemn, art. While its historic roots may lie partly in religious worship, they lie equally in "play," which includes child's play and acting-out (if not acting-up). In acting, you must develop a healthy balance between disciplined commitment and creative playing, and between studying the reality around you and investigating the imagination within you. Like play, theatre is entertaining—not only for the audience but for you the actors (players) as well. Theatre provides you a very special entertainment, one rooted in deep involvement, energetic effort, and creative improvisation, all within a focused framework. Theatre is mind filling, just like volleyball, chess, and Ping-Pong. Indeed, acting alternates with sports as the chief object of our leisure-time attention; and acting and sports—plays and play—are surprisingly similar activities. For this reason, beginning acting classes—as well as some professional acting ensembles—often begin their work with a few games.

Acting is work, but it is also play. If you forget that, you lose a crucial aspect of this very subtle art.

Freedom

Finally, the actor must learn to be free—free from physical and psychological inhibition—and must learn to enjoy that freedom. The actor must be free to think, feel, touch, and be touched. Above all, the actor's imagination must be unhindered. Relaxation, trust, discipline, and an effective response to criticism all play a part in this—relaxation and trust because they promote uninhibited interaction, discipline because it establishes a limit to gratuitous encroachment of the actor's physical privacy (preventing, for example, unwarranted sexual groping), and a response to criticism that allows the actor to grow, not shrivel, from his or her experience.

The free actor can imagine anything. Fantasy is the actor's playground; unbridled fantasy is the prerequisite to playing Romeo or Juliet, George or Martha. An actor afraid to fantasize, afraid to imagine the unimaginable, is an actor unacceptably bound to a narrow spectrum of emotional life. Plays and scenes may be outwardly mild; inwardly they are usually stormy and violent. The actor's mind must be able to play freely with the inner turmoil of the character: The actor's mind must be open to lust, terror, joy, and exaltation by turns—and must be open to playing the actions that emanate from those mental states.

Acting is emotionally risky. Indeed, one of the joys of acting is in taking those risks. The exercises and suggestions that follow in this book, and experience that will ensue in any acting class, will lead into these emotionally risky areas. An actor obdurately refusing to follow that lead—an actor who, instead, retreats behind a fixed image of herself or himself—is not free to act.

Preparation

You may begin to study acting at any age. Indeed, the study of acting is invariably a prerequisite to the study of other theatre arts, such as directing; it is also a useful preparation for public speaking, politics, law, business, and any profession where self-expression and communication are important. But there are some useful things that you can do or study before beginning to act. Dance, in any fashion, is most helpful to the beginning actor because it teaches a physical mode of performance. Athletics also provides a good background for acting because of the energy it demands and because of the public nature of its exhibition. Singing, poetry reading (and writing), and storytelling are exceptionally helpful because they involve language and performance and getting at the heart of feelings in a constructive way. Reading (novels, plays, and biographies) helps the young actor to understand the complexities of human life, including varieties of human experience not immediately observable in the actor's environment. And of course, theatregoing is a prime preparation for acting: seeing the potentials of performance, and seeing the work of accomplished actors firsthand.

Summary

The precursors to acting—relaxation, trust, exuberance, discipline, the response to criticism, a playful attitude, freedom to act, and prior preparation—do not simply appear on command; nor need you have them in your hip pocket before your first class in acting. They are developed continually in a beginning actor's work, and they need refreshing throughout an actor's career. They will stand you in good stead whether you become an actor or not, for they are also useful preparations for the interactions of daily life, for relationships of every order, whether personal or professional. And they are the sort of basic goals you should check yourself out on regularly as you pursue your studies toward artistic advancement in the theatre or elsewhere.

2

What Is Acting?

◆ EXERCISE   2-1

Pledge Your Allegiance to a Flag*

Imagine there is an American flag on the front wall of your classroom. Pledge allegiance to it. Here are the words:

> I pledge allegiance to the flag of the United States of America, and to the republic for which it stands: one nation, under God, indivisible, with liberty and justice for all.

Go ahead.

* * *

Good. Now repeat the exercise, *very sincerely.* When you finish, as before, don't move or talk; just keep looking at the imaginary flag. Go ahead.

* * *

---

*   This exercise might best be led by an instructor prior to the first assignment out of this book. For a videotape of this exercise, led by the author, contact the publisher.

Keep looking at the flag.

Now imagine the following situation: You are not and have never been an American citizen, nor have visited America, nor indeed have ever been outside your own country, which is across an ocean from America. The country where you have lived your entire life has, in the past years, come under the rule of a tyrannical regime that regularly persecutes—for no reason—people of your race or ethnic origin. This persecution has gotten much worse in recent months. Goon squads are driving through your village arresting people at will. You hear cries of torture from a military post right outside of town. There is no mail, television, radio, telephone, or communications from the outside world, and you are not allowed to criticize the regime to your friends or even your family. And yesterday your little sister was picked up by the goon squad and driven away, screaming for help.

You have decided you must leave your country by any means. You sneak out of your town in the dead of night, with nothing but the clothes you are wearing, and walk toward the distant ocean. Eventually you manage to get on a boat headed to the United States. After a long, miserable crossing, you now, miraculously, find yourself standing on the sand of a beach, facing inland. In front of you is a hill, covered in green grass; on the top of the hill flies an American flag.

You have never seen a real American flag, but you have seen pictures of it. You believe America to be a land of freedom, justice, and democracy, and you decide you will, before proceeding farther, write your own prose-poem offering to become an ally of all Americans. Your prose-poem will declare your allegiance, not only to this cloth symbol of the United States, but also your bond with its democratic government and free citizens.

Still facing this (imaginary) flag, make your pledge to it: However, *the words of your prose-poem just happen to be the identical words of the Pledge of Allegiance cited above.* But these are your own words now, and you are making them up as you say them.

On your own time, and without making any effort to say this prose-poem in unison with anyone else, go ahead.

* * *

Keep looking at the flag.

Now give the pledge one more time: This time, when you come across the four words or phrases described below, think of the possible alternatives —the sort of words you might previously have said under these circumstances, or could otherwise say—before you *choose* the one precise word that is in the pledge as you have twice now given it. These words or phrases are:

"allegiance"   In your former country, you had to pledge your "obedience." But that wouldn't be right here: You're going to be an "ally" of the flag, not a slave to it. On the other hand, what's the single word that means "an ally of"? You don't remember saying this word ever in your life, but you know it: It's "allegiance." So your thinking (in parentheses) that accompanies these first words is something like: "I pledge . . . (not obedience but, ummm . . .) allegiance . . ."

"United States of America"   When you and your friends talked about this country in earlier times, you always said "America" or "USA" or "the US." But that seems a little too informal at this moment, doesn't it, when you are pledging to be an ally of it?

"republic"   What were those definitions of governmental forms we heard about in school? Dictatorship, monarchy, empire . . . no, America is probably a . . . "republic."

"under God"   In your old country, your nation was ruled by the tyrant, and the army, and the rich, and the upper class, or the favored ethnic group. Your new nation, to which you would pledge allegiance, would recognize only one higher power—*if any*—and thus would only find itself "under God."

Pledge your allegiance this time as before, but *choosing*—immediately before you speak them—these four words or phrases from your list of possible alternatives.

On your own time, as before, go ahead.

*   *   *

Keep looking at the flag.

Now you are going to give the pledge one more time, exactly as before, except that this time when you come to the word **"United"** in the country's name you are going to reflect on the fact that what became the United States was originally a group of independent states—and the people in them —that *chose* to unite and that now *you* have chosen to unite with them. As you say the word "United," then, let the people *behind* the flag, who have already united with each other, know that you are coming to unite with them.

And how about the people standing next to you? For the first time, *listen* to them and discover that they, too, seem to be pledging their allegiance—in words that sound amazingly like yours.

You must now realize you are not an isolated escapee from another land but, rather, part of a *group* of emigrants, all fleeing to a country that promises liberty and justice—not just to you, but to *all*.

So—without looking at these other people—start *blending* your voice with the voices around you. *Unite* with them. Make clear to your fellow emigrants—purely by the sound of your voice—that you hear them and that you are willing to help them and gain their help as well, in a united cause.

And when you come to the words **"one nation,"** say this phrase in unison with those around you, making this a united pledge rather than your own solo effort.

And when you come to the word **"indivisible,"** let everybody on the beach know that you will *not let this group be divided again.* The dictator in your home country, by not permitting the freedom of assembly or letting people communicate with each other, kept the citizens isolated: Persuade your fellow emigrants that you will never let this happen again.

And when you come to the words **"for all,"** insist to everyone, both beside you on the beach and three thousand miles behind the flag—that you will work to provide universal freedom and justice for all Americans, including the American you plan to become.

So, starting on your own time, and beginning to listen and blend with the others on "United," go ahead.

* * *

Now one more time.

Bend down and, with the hand you ordinarily throw with, pick up some imaginary sand pebbles from the beach. Stand back up.

This time you are going to make your pledge exactly as before, except that at the words **"with liberty"** you are going to turn around and face the ocean you have just crossed and, beyond that, the country from which you have fled. Thousands of miles from you are the goons that picked up your little sister. As well as the dictator who ordered them to perform those horrific deeds. As well as those friends and family members you left behind.

Send your word **"liberty"** *all the way across the ocean* so that your friends and family can hear it—and can hear that you have made it across the ocean to a land that gives you the liberty to make a pledge such as this one.

Send your words **"and justice"** to them as well—and also to the goons and the dictator and indeed the entire population of your country, so that they will know that justice does still exist in the world, which means that the days of the goons and dictators are numbered.

And with the words **"for all,"** *throw* your sand pebbles all the way across the ocean, so as to blind the goons, and at the same time to float as a signal of hope—angel dust if you will—upon your sister and your captive friends.

Go ahead.

* * *

That's all. The exercise is over.

What was the difference between the first pledging of allegiance and the last?

If you are like the thousands of persons who have participated in this exercise, you will have noticed many if not all of the following changes that occurred.

◆ The speech was more *emotional*. From a mere rote recitation, it moved to an expression of real feeling.

◆ The words were invested with *meaning*. What were at first vaguely understood concepts became specific political or personal principles.

◆ You felt a sense of *connection* with other people, both the real ones next to you and the unseen, imaginary ones planted in the improvisation.

◆ You felt connected *personally* to the words you were saying, which seemed to come not just out of your mouth, but out of your active mind as well.

◆ You felt more *creative,* the creator and not merely the reciter of the text.

◆ You felt *active,* not passive.

◆ You felt your emotions *grow* during the speech, rather than being static.

◆ You experienced *exhilaration* by the end, whereas the first time you had only felt dutiful or even (when asked to pledge "sincerely") a sense of failure.

◆ Technically, your pledge was, in general, *louder,* and by the end it had built to an accelerating crescendo. The same was true for the pledges you heard others saying.

◆ Also technically, the *inflections* (pitch changes), which had always gone downward between phrases (after "allegiance" and "flag," for example) now often went upward, both for you and your fellow students.

This exercise shows exactly *what acting is.*

Acting is taking a memorized text, almost always written by someone else, and investing it with your own personal feelings, intelligence, communicative skills, interest in other people, and personality. All of these are brought out by *living the situation* that the dramatic character—in this case, an immigrant to the United States—experiences.

And, as it happens, the above-bulleted "changes" in your reading from the first to the last pledge all represent what most people call "good theatre" and "good acting": namely, acting that is emotionally vivid, intellectually precise, interpersonally communicative, personally authentic, creative, active, growing, and with variation, momentum, and uplift.

Notice that none of these changes happened when you were simply asked, on the second time through, to "be sincere." Indeed, you probably felt a sense of failure at that request ("Wasn't I sincere the first time?") and again in the pledge that followed, since you were made self-conscious about your level of sincerity (and being sincere basically means not "trying to put on an act," which the "be sincere" command makes you do).

Sincerity, and good acting (and of course *great* acting), comes from fully throwing yourself into a situation, not "putting on an act."

Please note: This exercise is not about your or your author's politics! It is not about America! It is only about *acting*. The improvisation is sheer fiction. The ancestors of some of you came to the United States on slave ships; they moved from relative freedom to unspeakable oppression. Other immigrants have come for pragmatic business or family reasons; other families emigrated thousands of years ago, across the Bering Sea, long before anyone had conceived of "America." And no one can seriously believe that America has provided liberty or justice for *everyone—all the time*. All you are asked to do, in this exercise, is *act the role* of a person who has had, and is having, the described experience. And you are asked to *imagine* that you could throw sand pebbles across an ocean, which of course can happen only in fantasy. Acting, and the imagination that powers it, creates all the bulleted points listed above.

Summary

So, by *experiencing* this improvisation, you have learned—by doing it—the most basic nature of acting. You have taken a memorized text, written by someone else,* and, by accepting, elaborating on, and playing a situation, invested it with your own person. Almost everything in the rest of the book will build upon what you have experienced in this fundamental exercise.

---

* The Pledge of Allegiance was written by Francis Bellamy, a staff writer for *Youth's Companion;* it was first published in the magazine's September 8, 1892, issue. The phrase "under God" was added by Congress in 1954.

The Actor's Approach

ACTING IS A PROCESS INVOLVING CERTAIN TRANSFORMATIONS: A person is transformed into an actor; an actor is transformed into a character. This process is not sudden or magical (although it may at times appear to be both); rather, it is gradual and deliberate.

The actor's approach is the series of steps the actor takes in that process. They are steps of exploring, feeling, trying, and doing; together they form a set of experiences. Every actor, from the beginner to the veteran professional, goes through these experiences. Every actor re-creates the process of acting with every performance.

The actor's approach, therefore, is a process of self-transformation—of moving out of oneself and getting into a role or into a work of art. It is a series of first steps that, like all first steps, are very challenging.

L E S S O N

3

Goal and Obstacle

Fundamental Principle

There is one fundamental principle in acting. It's that the actor must always play toward a goal. This is because characters, who resemble persons in life, are pursuing goals. *The actor acts by pursuing—often vigorously—the presumed goal of the character.*

Sometimes this goal is called the *objective*. Often, in the pages that follow, it is also called the *victory*. Some other teachers use the word *intention*, or *purpose*, or *want*. It doesn't really matter what it is called, as long as you pursue it. This is what makes acting represent life; it's what makes acting lifelike.

There is a corollary to this principle. It's that in a play the goal should be fairly difficult to achieve. This is what makes acting dramatic. "To take a breath" may be a real-life goal, but in everyday situations it is not difficult enough to engage our energies or to be interesting to an audience. If you were under water, however, "to take a breath" would be a goal sufficiently difficult to be dramatic.

Therefore the actor must pursue a *goal* (e.g., "to take a breath") in the context of an *obstacle* (e.g., "you are under water"). You want to marry— a person who is reluctant. You want to overthrow—an adversary who is powerful. You want to win the race—despite your sprained ankle.

The goal is what you—your character—wants.

The obstacle is what stands in your way.

21

GOAL

The actor's intention is the only thing that counts. Everything else is just talk.

WILLIAM H. MACY

You have to try hard to achieve your goal, despite your obstacle.

This ties you to your character and makes your acting both lifelike and dramatic.

♦ EXERCISE 3–1

Reaching

Stand on the right foot; reach as high as you can with your left hand. Reverse: Stand on your left foot and reach with your right hand.

By itself, reaching is not an acting exercise. It is merely a physical exercise, or a calisthenic.

♦ EXERCISE 3–2

Reaching for Goals

Imagine that there is something you greatly desire above your head: a beautiful jewel, or a bowl of strawberries, or "the key to your true love's heart." Now, reach again!

When you are reaching for a goal, your action is purposeful and you are emotionally, physiologically committed. You reach farther, more intently, more energetically. You reach so hard that you pull yourself off balance. You bounce on the balls of your feet. You are not merely following an instruction, you are trying to *do* something. You are intent upon achieving your goal: You want something and you want it badly. All these words— *purposeful, doing, trying, intent, winning, want*—are useful in describing

> **OBSTACLE**
>
> *For an action to be dramatic, it needs a counter-balancing obstacle; so make sure you know what it is.*
>
> JON JORY

the playing for goals. The actor's energetic pursuit of the character's goal is what makes the action of a play acting, not demonstrating; dynamic, not static.

In reaching, you are working against an obstacle: your own physical limitations. You can stretch only so far against the pull of gravity. Now, intensify that obstacle:

◆ E X E R C I S E   3–3

Overcoming an Obstacle

Imagine that you are sick to your stomach and fearful of losing control of your bowels. Reach up as in Exercise 3–2—only the more you reach, the sicker you feel. The more excited you get at reaching for your bowl of strawberries, the more fearful you become that you will publicly embarrass yourself.

In Exercise 3–3, your simple act of reaching has become an emotionally complex experience, even profound. You are acting.

There is no exercise, no acting challenge, that cannot be seen as a confrontation between an obstacle and an actor's pursuit of a goal. The job of the actor is to find and pursue goals in every role, even in every training exercise or calisthenic, and also to find and challenge the obstacles that stand in the way. Finding goals and obstacles sometimes involves research, but it always involves imagination. Frequently, imagination, properly focused, is all that is needed to transform simple, everyday acts into acting.

Imagination is the breeding ground for fantasy, and an actor's fantasy is often the source of his or her most compelling goals and obstacles. What did you think when you read "the key to your true love's heart"? Did you take that literally or figuratively? Would the image of Rapunzel in her tower prison or Tom Cruise in chains have made you reach higher and harder? The actor's job is not just to find goals and obstacles but to create them— and to create them with such vividness and enthusiasm that they can lead to an exciting and clearly defined performance, even in a simple exercise.

Self-Consciousness

If playing toward goals and playing against obstacles are the fundamental principles of acting, self-consciousness is the actor's greatest enemy. Standing up and being observed, being "on display" for the presumably critical eyes of others, is a terrifying prospect to most of us.

◆ E X E R C I S E   3–4

Doing vs. Being

Do the following actions in order. Allow thirty seconds for each numbered command.

1. Stand up in front of the group.

2. Be dignified.

3. Look sexy.

4. Relax.

5. Count the number of men you see.

6. Count the number of women faster than you counted the men. If you succeed, you'll win a prize!

Chances are that the first two minutes of that exercise were agonizing. Being publicly commanded to "be dignified" or "look sexy" fills us with terror; how certainly we will fail! And how can we relax with all those people looking at us? How can we *really* relax—on cue? But counting the men —that's *doing* something; the focus moves away from us and onto the watchers. And counting the women—fast, so as to win a prize (even an imaginary prize)—that's *energetic* doing; that's even almost fun!

The actor cannot simply "be" something or somebody onstage, or simply "look" a certain way, without being acutely self-conscious, unbearably self-aware of being or looking. Nor can the actor be ordered to relax, because relaxing—real relaxing—means not worrying about obeying anybody's orders. The only way for an actor to avoid self-consciousness—and to truly relax—is to do something. And the more actors feel they are doing something important (as, for example, trying to win a prize), the more they relax into the task and think about things other than themselves.

Projection

Self-consciousness is your focus on yourself; projection is your focus on others, on the outside world, and your efforts to project your concerns outside yourself. Projection is also your ability to project your voice, to be heard by others, to *make yourself heard* by others. Projection, therefore, is basically the opposite of self-consciousness; it is the ability to escape the prison of yourself (self-doubt, self-indulgence, selfishness) and to enter into active, productive social intercourse. Every actor must learn this skill quite thoroughly.

◆ EXERCISE   3–5

Resonating

Do the following actions in order.

1. Face the wall and say "ahhhhhh."

2. Recognize that sound is simply the vibration of molecules. Face the wall, say "ahhhhhh," and feel the vibration in your throat.

3. Recognize that sound resonates and that sound may set up sympathetic vibrations in other objects. Face the wall, say "ahhhhhhh," and try to make the molecules in the wall vibrate in harmony with your voice.

The three steps in Exercise 3–5 lead you from self-consciousness to projection. In the first, you are simply making sound. In the second, you are making sound with a purpose: to feel your own vibration. In the third, you are making sound with a purpose that *extends beyond yourself:* In other words, you are projecting your sound purposefully; you are pursuing a goal (trying to make the wall vibrate) and struggling against an obstacle (the firmness of the wall). It does not matter if the wall vibrates or not. (Actually, the wall does vibrate, but there's no way you can measure this.) The point is that you have created and acted upon a goal, using a real object (the wall), your voice, and your imagination.

Did your voice change on the third step? Of course it did. It became louder, more resonant, and more forceful. Chances are that you opened your jaw wider, dropped your Adam's apple lower in your throat, and straightened your posture. You may not know it, but these are exactly what a voice teacher would instruct you to do, and you have done it without thinking about anything except vibrating a wall!

◆ E X E R C I S E   3–6

Resonating (A Continuation)

Pair with a partner and space yourself away from others as much as possible. By turns, say "ahhhhhh" to the partner, with the goal of vibrating your partner's spine with the sound of your voice. With your fingers, feel your partner's spine to see if you can feel the actual vibrations. Try different ranges of your vocal pitch, different kinds of vocal sounds, and different positions of your body. Try to feel the vibrations as much as you can.

In Exercise 3–6, you are projecting sound not to a wall but to another person. Moreover, you are trying to sense the physical effects of that projection. Your concentration has gone entirely from the sound of your voice to the physical effect your voice has on your partner, and now your consciousness is not self-directed but other-directed. This exercise has led you to a moment—however simple—of "pure" acting: person-to-person communication at the most fundamental level.

Some acting moments in plays are precisely this: one character holding, cuddling, or embracing another, saying "ahhhhhh" as a way to lull the other character into relaxing, or into a romantic mood, or to settle the other character's nerves. Or the "ahhhhhh" could be an exclamation, accompanied by a raised sword, as Macbeth draws on Macduff, attempting (as his goal) to frighten him into submission. Not all acting involves lines, but all acting does involve person-to-person communication, at either the verbal or the nonverbal level.

In playing a role, of course, the actor must project more than just sound. Words, gestures, ideas, feelings, commands, personality—these are among the intangibles that the actor must convey to other actors and to the back of the house, that is, the audience. These projections all enter into the stream of communication that every actor both generates and receives; projections are the means by which actors involve themselves with the activity around them—and turn their focus outward, away from self-conscious self-absorption.

◆ E X E R C I S E   3–7

Goals

Do the following tasks. Afterward, define the goal, define the obstacle, and discuss the degree to which your involvement in each task projected yourself into the world outside yourself and dispelled your self-consciousness.

1. Untie and remove your partner's shoes.
2. Find the 126th word on page 56 of this book.
3. Balance this book on your partner's head.
4. Find the wall or piece of furniture or other object that best resonates with the sound of your voice.
5. Find the best pitch of your voice to resonate that which you found in item 4.
6. Neaten your corner of the classroom.
7. Move people from one corner of the classroom to another.

Summary

The actor always plays toward a goal and against an obstacle. Concentration on achieving the goal reduces the actor's self-consciousness; moreover, it demands that the actor *project* by focusing on something or someone. The mutual projection between actors—a person-to-person communication —is the foundation of all acting, even the most complex or most highly stylized.

4

Acting with the "Other"

The Other

In most plays, the actors do not try to resonate walls; they try to have an impact on other people. Usually those other people are the other characters in the play. For the purposes of acting class, the "other" is your acting partner.

Probing deeply into other people is one of the essential tasks of the actor. This does not necessarily mean long talks into the night, social involvements, mutual therapy sessions, or the baring of personal secrets; it certainly does not mean forcing confessions or outside relationships on other actors. It does mean a willingness to look clearly and directly at your acting partner and to take in *the whole person* with whom you are acting.

◆ E X E R C I S E   4–1

Making Your Partner Smile

Pair with a partner. Stand opposite your partner and devote about twenty seconds to each of the tasks that follow. At the end of the list, change roles and repeat the exercise.

1. Study your partner's eyebrows.

2. Make your partner smile.

THE OTHER

I work very much with other people; I don't do a performance alone, and I want the other person to react with me and be honest with me. I need that desperately.

ESTELLE PARSONS

3. Study your partner's mouth.

4. Make your partner laugh.

5. Ask yourself: What makes my partner laugh?

6. Make your partner laugh *loudly.*

7. Study your partner's eyes.

8. Ask yourself: What does my partner see, looking at me?

9. Make your partner take you seriously.

10. Smile.

11. Take your partner's two hands.

12. See the four-year-old child your partner once was.

13. See the corpse your partner eventually will be.

14. Make your partner smile.

(While you're trying to make your partner smile, your partner should simply be studying your face, with the goal of trying to figure out how your mind works.)

When you try to make your partner smile, or laugh, or take you seriously, you are not merely "doing something"; you are doing something to (or with) someone else. That is, you are participating in an interaction. All acting is interacting with other persons (even monologues, which are discussed at the end of this lesson).

Your acting partner is a person. He or she was an infant once and is as mortal as you are. Your acting partner (like you) is a sexual person, a fearful person, a caring person, and a person who has profound desires. In other words, your acting partner is not just "your acting partner." He or she is an individual and, potentially, a source of great inspiration for you.

The more fully you contact your acting partner, the more fully you will be acting. Acting is something you can never do entirely in isolation or entirely by yourself. In order to "live" onstage, you must first make the other characters, your acting partners, "live" in your mind. Your communication—your acting—will ultimately depend as much on them as on you and on the intensity with which you make yourself believe in them and care about them.

Interactive Dynamics

The actor's awareness of others is not merely a matter of dispassionate observation. Stage relationships that are properly dramatic must suggest a potential for dramatic change: usually the potential for love, on the one hand, or the potential for physical or psychological violence. These potentials are the dynamics of relationships. Because this potential for love or violence is always present, we say that the actors are vulnerable. Exercise 4–2 is a simple way of approaching actor-to-actor vulnerability.

◆ E X E R C I S E   4–2

Vulnerability

Pair with a partner and designate one of you to be A and the other B. Memorize and quickly "rehearse" this contentless scene. (A contentless scene is one in which the words, by themselves, do not clearly reveal any specific characters or plot; it is a scene that has no specified dramatic content.)

A: One.

B: Two.

A: Three.

B: Four.

A: Five.

B: Six.

A: Seven.

B: Eight.

A: Nine!

B: Ten!

"Perform" the scene while imagining each of these situations:

1. You have reason to believe that your acting partner may be planning to murder you and that he or she may have a concealed weapon.

2. You were separated from a beloved sibling when you were three years old, and you have reason to believe that your acting partner is that sibling.

3. Person A has reason to believe (1) above, and Person B has reason to believe (2).

4. Person B has reason to believe (1) above, and Person A has reason to believe (2).

Vulnerability, a crucial component of all acting, means that you are aware of the other actor as a complete person, and that you are also aware of *the potential good or harm that can come from the relationship* between you.

Interactive dynamics suggest that relationships are not merely static arrangements between agreeable people but are evolving interplays of mutuality and independence, attraction and separation, desire and fear. The person you meet in the cafeteria today *could* be your life companion twenty years from now; the person you are rehearsing a scene with *could* pull out a revolver and shoot you. The normal human impulse is to ignore such remote potentials. The actor's impulse, in an acting situation, should be to make them vivid, to create the dynamics of the relationship wherever possible and appropriate. Even a scene as content-free as "one, two, three . . . ten" can become a vivid and exciting drama if you explore the potential for both love and violence that might be imagined as existing between characters A and B and the vulnerability of the actors to those potentials.

◆ E X E R C I S E   4–3

Discovery

Pair with a partner and designate an A and a B. "Play" the following interchange. Try to discover as much as possible about your partner by studying his or her tone of voice, expression, and changes in breathing pattern, and by speculating on his or her possible thoughts or fantasies.

A: Can I see you on Monday?

B: How about Tuesday?

A: How about Wednesday?

B: How about Thursday?

A: How about Friday?

B: How about Saturday?

A: How about Sunday?

B: OK, then, Sunday.

Don't make any effort to give clever readings, and don't worry about your own delivery of the lines. Concentrate entirely on your partner and finding out what you can about him or her.

Try this alternate scene, too, with the same instructions:

A: I know you will.

B: I know I won't.

A: I know you will.

B: I know I won't.

A: I know you will.

B: I know I won't.

A: I know you will.

B: I know I won't.

The dialogs in this exercise were chosen because they can be memorized instantly. Memorized dialog from scenes that you work on later also can be used in this exercise, if you wish to return to it.

The Character

Here's an important question that may have occurred to you already: When you make your partner smile, or when you imagine your partner as a long-lost sibling, or when you ask your partner if he or she can see you on Sunday, is your partner a classmate, or an actor, or a character? Philosophers may answer that question in a variety of ways, but for you there is only one answer: *Your partner is always a character.* The moment an acting exercise begins, it exists within a theatrical context. At that point, all participants are characters, and all behavior is acting, or "playing."

This is a liberating answer. It means that the interactions between your partner and yourself take place within an overall context in which you have already agreed to "play," or to interact as characters. Therefore you can experience your feelings fully; you can experience the depth of love, lust, violence, and ambition within a dramatic context (even in an exercise or improvisation) without committing yourself in any personal (outside of class) way. Indeed, you can explore the extremities—and profundities—of feelings within the "playing" arena and return to your more private personality when the exercise (or play or improvisation) is over. The ability to see your classmates as characters—which extends to seeing your best friend as Iago and your worst enemy as Romeo—is the ability to free your feelings so as to act vividly and intensely with other people.

Tactics

Tactics are the strategies of human communication; they are the active ingredients of dynamic interactions. Most of the tactics of everyday life are simple and benign, generated more by spontaneous impulse than by conscious plan. Smiling, for example, encourages agreement and tolerance; raising the level of the voice, on the other hand, encourages compliance. Some tactics are used to seek the support of other characters; some to silence their opposition.

In the effort to achieve goals and overcome obstacles, the actor continually tries to put some pressure on the other actors—who are, of course, characters in the play or scene. This pressure is real; it may be the seductiveness of a raised eyebrow, the menace of a clenched fist, or the bedazzlement of a brilliantly articulated argument, but it is a pressure felt by the other actors and by the audience alike. Your power in playing tactics will determine your authority and magnetism on stage.

◆ E X E R C I S E   4–4

Using Tactics

Pair with a partner. Imagine that the nonsense word *beetaratagang* means "Get out of here!" in some foreign language. Imagine that the nonsense word *cleridipity* means "Come over here" in the same language. Take turns playing the following situations.

1. Order your acting partner away by saying "*beetaratagang!*" to him or her.

2. Urge your acting partner to come toward you by saying "*cleridipity*" to him or her.

3. Send your partner away with "*beetaratagang*" and then draw him or her back with "*cleridipity.*" Reverse.

To communicate with your partner, use body language, tone of voice, inflection, gesture, facial expression, threats of physical force, seductive and inductive postures—everything you can think of *except* physical contact.

Full contact with an acting partner depends on your willingness to engage in genuine emotional interaction with another person: to frighten, to encourage, to alarm, and to entertain your acting partner. The desire to achieve your goal, coupled with a willingness and ability to translate that desire into effective person-to-person behavior, creates the baseline of your acting performance. Your ability to make "*beetaratagang*" so unsettling as to force someone to go away, or to make "*cleridipity*" so evocative as to induce someone to approach you, is a primal acting ability, coming wholly from you and not from a text or a dramatic staging or interpretation.

◆ E X E R C I S E   4–5

One Two Three Four Five Six Seven

This exercise is intended to deepen your concentration and extend your repertoire of communication tactics. Trying is more important than succeeding in these tasks.

Without touching your partner, and using only the words "one two three four five six seven" on each task, try to elicit the following actions or feelings from your partner.

1. Make your partner sit down next to you.

2. Make your partner kneel before you.

3. Make your partner feel sorry for you.

4. Make your partner happy.

5. Make your partner nervous.

6. Make your partner aroused.

7. Make your partner feel chilled.

Monologues

How do you act with the "other" when there seems to be no other? In, for example, a monologue, soliloquy, or one-person show, where you are alone onstage with no one else—physically at least—listening to you? You might say you are talking "to yourself" or "thinking aloud" in these cases, but that's not a very dramatic solution, nor is it particularly true to life.

Before mulling this over further, try the following exercise, in which you invent an imaginary other to act with.

◆ E X E R C I S E   4–6

Inventing the Other

Do Exercises 4–4 and 4–5 without a partner, but with the following "others" that you create in your imagination:

1. As a "rehearsal" where you practice how you would frighten a bully away by saying "*beetaratagang!*" to him or her. Practice it out loud and to a variety of imagined bullies, big and small.

2. Speak to an imagined god-figure (Zeus, let's say, or Buddha, or the Judeo-Christian-Islamic "God") in whom you believe, or at least can imagine you believe. Try to bring this deity into your physical presence by saying "*cleridipity*" or "one two three four five six seven." Vary the deity: Replace Zeus with Venus, then Satan, then a revered ancestor or role model of your own. Such an exercise is, in fact, essential for playing characters (Oedipus or Dr. Faustus, for example) who worship or fear higher powers.

3. Imagine you learn that your hated uncle has murdered your beloved father. You know you will have a chance to confront him in court. Rehearse pointing your finger at him and crying these words of public accusation: "Bloody, bawdy villain!" Rehearse the line several times, trying to find the most persuasive tone.

4. Imagine a god-figure hovering above or around you as you contemplate a life-threatening adventure. Pose this dilemma to the god: "To be or not to be, that is the question." See if the god—by word or silence or gust of wind—answers you in any way or gives you any hint as to your best course to follow. Repeat several times, imagining the god-figure in different forms.

5. Speak to an imaginary audience that you cannot see (as would be the case onstage, with stage lights in your eyes). Try to get them to answer this question:

> "What is a man,
>   If his chief good and market of his time
>   Be but to sleep and feed?"

See if—and how—they answer you. They won't answer, but keep trying to get them to do so, repeating your question three or four times.

The speeches in numbers 3, 4, and 5, as you probably know, are from soliloquies spoken by Shakespeare's Hamlet. All dramatic speeches, even monologues and soliloquies, are spoken to "someone" else, even though that someone may be nonpresent at the time, dead, otherworldly, or imagined. This subject is taken up more fully in Lesson 28. If you're interested in tackling such a speech now—for an upcoming audition, for example—you might skip ahead to that lesson.

Summary

Acting is not something you do by yourself; invariably it is something you do to, with, and for at least one other person. Most of what the audience eventually sees in an acting performance is a *relationship* between characters—a relationship created by you and your acting partner. In order for that relationship to be a dramatic one, it must be dynamic. The actors must be vulnerable to one another. A potential for good or harm—preferably for both—must be clearly implied by the relationship, and the actors, through the use of interpersonal tactics, must put pressure on each other to change or improve their relationship.

L E S S O N

5

Beginning to Act

Contentless Scene

In the preceding pages we have introduced several foundations of acting: goals, obstacles, vulnerability, projection, and the person-to-person contact and tactical interplay that characterize dynamic relationships. These fundamentals can all be explored in a series of contentless scenes—so called because they are devoid of fixed plot or characterizations.

A contentless scene can be memorized quite rapidly—usually in about ten minutes. In a group situation, actors should pair up and memorize their parts aloud, one person of each pair memorizing part A, the other person memorizing part B. During memorization, no attempt should be made to create an interpretation with the lines or to "fix" readings or inflections of individual lines; the lines are to be learned simply by rote.

When the scene has been memorized, the actors should then switch partners so that each A will be paired with a B with whom they have not rehearsed or spoken this dialog. The contentless scenes may be performed many times, switching partners each time, so that each time the scene is produced, it is produced without prior rehearsal between the two paired actors.

◆ EXERCISE 5-1

Contentless Scene I

Perform this scene without rehearsal or planning of any kind. For each performance, however, use one of the seven situations on the list below.

Scene: "What did you do last night?"

A: Hi!

B: Hello.

A: How's everything?

B: Fine. I guess.

A: Do you know what time it is?

B: No. Not exactly.

A: Don't you have a watch?

B: Not on me.

A: Well?

B: Well what?

A: What did you do last night?

B: What do you mean?

A: What did you do last night?

B: Nothing.

A: Nothing?

B: I said, nothing!

A: I'm sorry I asked.

B: That's all right.

The Seven Situations

1. A is a parent; B is a teenager. The scene takes place at the breakfast table; B eating a bowl of cereal, A entering.

2. A and B (different sexes) are a young married couple. Last night, after an argument, B left the apartment. It is now the following morning. A is washing dishes. B returns.

3. A and B (same sex) are roommates. Both have been involved with the same boy (or girl) during the past few weeks, both are still interested in pursuing the relationship, both are somewhat suspicious of the other's secrecy. They meet while returning to their room after a night's absence.

4. A and B (different sexes) are classmates who have been romantically interested in each other for some time. They meet in a cafeteria by accident, and A sits down next to B.

5. A and B (same sex) are auditioning for an important role. It is rumored that the director plays sexual favorites in casting. A and B meet at the bulletin board to await the announcement of callbacks.

6. A and B are siblings. B has recently been released from a psychiatric unit after a suicide attempt. After B has stayed out all night, A finds B in the waiting room of a bus depot.

7. A and B are friends. B has recently been released from a psychiatric unit after maniacally attacking a friend with a butcher knife. A, aware of this, comes upon B in an isolated spot.

When many variations on contentless scenes are performed, with the actors switching partners each time, several things become evident.

The content of the scene is created entirely by the given situation and the actors: The words become instruments of the action, not the dictator of plot, character, or behavior. Thus the acting becomes a way of creating a spontaneously changing relationship—and the plot develops entirely out of what happens between you and your acting partner.

The scene is happening in real time; that is, it is being *experienced* while it is being performed. One often talks, in acting, about "creating the illusion of the first time."* In Exercise 5–1, "the first time" is no illusion; you are indeed experiencing the interchange for the first time, live and unrehearsed.

You will find that there is nothing you can do in Exercise 5–1 to succeed "on your own." Whatever happens in the contentless scene depends not on you or on your acting partner, but on what happens between the two of you. Person-to-person contact, tactical interplay, projection, and vulnerability are demanded by the exercise itself. In these situations, feelings come to you naturally.

The scene is unpredictable. One of the problems in the theatre is that scripts, by nature, are predictable: The last act has already been written and rehearsed when the curtain rises on Act 1. Exercise 5–1 helps you avoid— for a time at least—the problem of making a predictable scene look unpredictable: The scene *is* unpredictable, and neither you nor your acting partner knows, at the outset, how it is going to end. Such a condition keeps you alert, involved, and mentally active throughout the scene, often to an extraordinary degree.

---

* The notion, first expressed by nineteenth-century American actor–playwright William Gillette, that acting should appear unrehearsed, that each speech should be delivered as though the character was uttering the words "for the first time."

Intensifiers

Exercise 5–1 can be repeated almost indefinitely, inasmuch as there are hundreds of possible situations and thousands of implications that will make every rendition fresh and different. The exercise can also be intensified by adding obstacles to the situations.

◆ E X E R C I S E   5–2

Intensifying

Replay the dialog in Exercise 5–1 using one of the seven situations, plus one of the obstacles on the following list. Repeat the exercise by varying both situations and obstacles.

1. Your acting partner has been known to carry a revolver.
2. You feel sick to your stomach.
3. The odor in the room is noxious.
4. You suspect your acting partner is dying.
5. Your acting partner is partly deaf.
6. It is very cold.
7. Your acting partner seems sexually frustrated.
8. Your acting partner seems especially flushed.
9. You do not feel that you can stand up without losing control of your bowels.
10. You feel that if you speak loudly, you will start crying.

The intensifiers are not things that you play or that you have to show in any way. Indeed, they are actually obstacles that you will have to struggle *against:* against showing them and against their standing in your way. The struggle against obstacles makes you perform more intensely; when speaking to a partly deaf person, for example, you must speak louder and with clearer articulation. Obstacles cannot be so great that they inhibit action altogether (that is why we specify a *partly* deaf person), or so insignificant that you can forget about them entirely. They must be bold enough to make you work harder, and difficult enough to make your quest dramatically interesting.

Physicalizers

Sometimes extraordinary changes occur in scenes simply when the locale is changed or when the actors are asked to carry on some sort of underlying action, such as jogging. Physicalizing a scene frequently brings out subtler undertones and more poignant transitions; it also gets the acting "into the body" more than simply sitting and talking.

◆ E X E R C I S E   5–3

Varying Locale or Action

Replay the contentless scene in any of these physicalized variations:

1. While jogging
2. While setting the table together
3. While lying down at the beach
4. B lying in bed, A seated at foot of bed
5. While playing basketball
6. While arm wrestling
7. While dancing to music
8. While doing push-ups
9. While eating a real banana
10. While giving a backrub, one to the other

Invent your own variations!

◆ E X E R C I S E   5–4

Contentless Scene II

Memorize the following dialog. Then, using the new dialog, repeat Exercises 5–1, 5–2, and 5–3.

Scene: "I'm going away."

A: Hi!

B: Hello.

A: You all right?

B: Yes.

A: Are you sure?

B: Yes, I'm sure. A little headache, that's all.

A: Oh, good. You want some aspirin?

B: No. Don't be so helpful, OK?

A: You are upset.

B: Good Lord!

A: OK, OK. I thought you might want to talk.

B: About what?

A: About anything.

B: I'm going away.

A: What do you mean?

B: I'm going away, that's all.

A: Where?

B: Not far. Don't get excited.

A: When?

B: Now. *[Starts to leave]*

The situations in the previous scene will work here, but you can invent dozens of other situations as well.

Summary

The contentless scene—in which the dialog is essentially ambiguous, trivial, or both—provides an opportunity to explore the playing of goals, tactics, and relationships in a fresh, improvisatory manner, without planning or rehearsing. The personal interaction can be intensified by establishing obstacles to the basic goals. Physicalizing the scenes may bring out subtle meanings and pointed moments that are valuable in an acting performance.

6

Tactics

Punishment and Reward

To the actor, goals are more than just wishes or daydreams. They are what the dramatic character actively wants to win, gain, acquire, or achieve. Acting, by definition, is *action,* and it is *active.* We in the audience do not want to see you simply thinking about your goals, we want to see you working hard to achieve them.

Characters pursue their goals just as real people do, by employing *tactics.* They argue, they persuade, they threaten, they seduce, they inspire. They try to influence other characters in the play to support them and to discourage other characters from opposing them. Indeed, this is why drama is *dramatic.* Tactics are the moment-to-moment work of truly dramatic acting. Tactics drive and define the basic interactions of the play.

Do we use tactics in our own lives? Most of us would like to believe that we don't, that we simply live and let live without trying to manipulate our friends and acquaintances. But as we saw in Lesson 4, this is not the case. When someone is talking to us, we smile to invite more talking or look skeptical to shut the fellow up. We frown at a disobedient child and raise our voices to make sure our instructions are followed. Or we squat humbly at the feet of a celebrated guru and beam upward to indicate the respect that may draw forth a word of wisdom. These are interpersonal tactics, and we use them whenever we are in the presence of others.

Dogs, cats, and two-month-old babies use tactics too; any thinking species with needs and wants uses tactics to seek and achieve its moment-to-moment goals and victories. Acting requires that the actor learn how to play tactics forcefully, winsomely, and engagingly.

There are basically two kinds of tactics: those that threaten and those that induce—punishment and reward, in other words. Tactics that threaten say, "Do what I want or I'll make your life miserable." Tactics that induce say, "Do what I want and you'll be happier for it." Raising your voice is a threatening tactic, smiling an inductive tactic; both are common in everyday life and on the stage that mirrors life.

Playing Tactics

When you play tactics on stage, you *really* play them. When your character is trying to threaten another character, you try to threaten your acting partner. On the other hand, if your character is trying to encourage warmth from another character, you make every effort to induce that warmth from the actor who is your partner.

But remember this ground rule: The actor must never physically or sexually abuse another actor during an exercise, a scene, or an improvisation. Any acting involving physical force, combat, or overt sexual behavior must be rehearsed and talked through until both actors are fully comfortable with it. It is often useful to have a general understanding of what constitutes sexual abuse in an exercise situation, as this definition may vary depending on the age, experience, and cultural milieu of the actors involved.

◆ E X E R C I S E   6–1

Frighten Your Partner

Pair with a partner. Using one of the phrases below, try to *actually frighten* your partner.

1. Shut up!

2. Get out of here!

3. Leave me alone!

4. Go to hell!

5. Go on, kill me!

Study your partner's expression. Has color or animation drained from his face? Does she seem to be trembling or fidgety? Are his eyes widening? Remember, it's not essential that you *succeed* in achieving these results, only that you *try* to achieve them—and that you *really* study your partner to find out whether you have in fact succeeded or failed (in which case, try harder!).

◆ E X E R C I S E   6–2

Building Intensity

Using the phrases in Exercise 6–1, again trying to frighten your partner, repeat each phrase three times, building your intensity each time, as in "Shut up! Shut up!!! SHUT UP!!!!!" You might even add a mild oath to the last invective, as "Shut up! Shut up!!! SHUT UP, DAMMIT!!!!" Try to increase your intensity in several ways—not just by increasing your volume (although that will be part of it), but by a more vigorous pronunciation, an increasingly commanding (and threatening) physical presence, and a deepening emotional commitment to your goal.

◆ E X E R C I S E   6–3

Try to Make Your Partner Cry

Repeat Exercise 6–2 with a different partner, and try to make a tear well up in your partner's eye. Again, don't worry if this doesn't happen; the point is not to succeed, but to try. Plays are filled with characters who don't succeed at their goals; actors only need to make the effort of the character—the genuine effort. Trying to make your partner cry gives your tactic a physiological reality; it gives you a very specific and human psychophysical goal to pursue, and you will succeed—as an actor—merely by pursuing that goal convincingly. But really try. And try hard.

Trying to make the other actor cry is one of the strongest goals an actor can pursue, inasmuch as it brings to the surface thoughts and emotions, often repressed from childhood, that unlock a great deal of subconscious behavior. Our earliest tears stem from pain, rage, and fright—often the fright induced by a seemingly omnipotent parent—and any improvisation or dialog that brings back those primal situations can be an immensely stimulating acting discovery. Trying to make somebody cry brings out qualities of behavior that are rarely seen in the classroom, and it liberates much of the inherent power of the performer.

◆ E X E R C I S E   6–4

Movement and Contact

Repeat Exercise 6–3 several times, adding physical gestures and movements that intensify the pursuit of your victory. Use *agreed-upon* physical contact: a soft shove on your partner's shoulder or shoulders; seizing your partner's wrist; or slapping your partner's arms and torso. Be sure to use the physical business simply as a means of adding force and emphasis to your lines—not as a way of making your partner cry by inflicting real pain. The threatening tactics of an actor are psychological only; physical violence, onstage, is *always* simulated.

You will quickly tire of threatening or frightening exercises, which can be sustained only for a very short time in any event. Ordinarily they should be alternated with inductive exercises, such as the one below.

◆ E X E R C I S E   6–5

Encourage Your Partner

Pair with a partner. Using one of the phrases below, try to encourage your partner to come closer to you, to sit down, or to engage in behavior that you suggest would be enjoyable.

1. Come on over here.

2. Sit down next to me.

3. I want to talk with you.

4. I have something I think you'd like.

5. Please . . .

6. [Make something up yourself.]

Repeat Exercise 6–5, building on your original phrase with improvised elaborations. Use your body, your intonation and inflection, the sound of your voice, and the manner of your gesture and expression to induce calm, trust, and amusement in your acting partner. Work to make your partner *smile* or *laugh*. As a physicalizer, take one or both of your partner's hands in yours. Try to coax your partner into a genuine rapport with your desires.

Induction tactics (which tend to *induce* behavior rather than threaten noncompliance) are the common stuff of everyday human interaction, much more common than threats both in life and on the stage. When well played, they give an actor magnetism and charm, just as threatening tactics, when well played, lend an actor a commanding forcefulness.

Both threatening and inductive tactics are efforts on your part to influence the behavior and ideas of the other actor—to interfere with the other actor's state of tranquillity or direction. By playing tactics, the actor creates a character who is trying to shape the scene, the only kind of character that is dramatically interesting. Characters in plays are never merely observers. Even those characters who describe themselves as observers, such as the title character in John Van Druten's *I Am a Camera,* are active in interpersonal engagements. Characters in plays are all interpersonally active: They are always trying to influence, to overthrow, to impress, to seduce, to win over, to suppress, to engage somebody. This is why tactics are so important to the actor: They are the actual "happenings" onstage; they are what is going on between the characters—and therefore between the actors.

Alternating Tactics

Tactics are almost never monolithic on stage; most of the time they alternate —often with mercurial speed—between threats and inducements. Actors who can switch between hair-raising forcefulness and ingratiating charm in an instant—actors such as Al Pacino, for example—are widely admired for encompassing this range of interpersonal effectiveness, which is dramatically thrilling because it suggests an almost explosive unpredictability.

◆ E X E R C I S E   6–6

Mixing Tactics

Pair with a partner. Improvising with phrases from Exercises 6–1 and 6–5 (or similar phrases), create a sequence of varying tactical approaches to your partner. For example:

1. *[threatening]* Get out of here! I said get out of here! *[inductive]* Will you get out of here? Come here. Come on over here. Please? *[threatening again]* Please! Oh, shut up! Shut up! Dammit, John, shut up!

2. *[inductive]* John, come up here. Come on, sit down. I want to talk to you. Will you take off your shoes? Come on, take off your shoes. *[threatening]* I said, take off your shoes. Dammit, John, take off your shoes! *[inductive]* Please? Everything will be OK, I promise. Come on.

Alternate threats and inducements as a way of *increasing the pressure* on your partner. Employ the art of surprise; shift tactics suddenly and without warning.

You should try this exercise in three successive stages:

♦ First, with your partner saying the word *no* between each of your phrases.

♦ Then, with your partner just nodding *no* each time.

♦ Finally, with your partner remaining wholly impassive each time—but still not acceding to your demand.

Learn to vary your tactics—and to try harder—not only when your partner specifically turns you down (i.e., says no), but when your partner remains impassive. In the latter case, you have to "read in" the obstacle yourself. This will prove important in more complicated acting assignments later on.

The Middle Ranges

Making someone cry and making someone laugh are at the extreme ends of tactical behavior; in the middle there is making somebody listen, making somebody care, making somebody proud, or worried, or happy, or agreeable. These are the middle ranges of acting, and this is where most of an actor's time is spent.

♦ E X E R C I S E   6–7

Eliminating the Extremes

Pair with a partner and designate one of you as A, the other as B. Memorize and play the following scene, escalating steadily from inductive tactics at the beginning to threatening ones at the end:

1. A: I know you will.

   B: No, I won't.

2. A: I know you will.

   B: No, I won't.

3. A: I know you will.

   B: No, I won't!

> **OUTWARD-DIRECTEDNESS**
>
> *In "real life" the mother begging for her child's life, the criminal begging for a pardon, the atoning lover pleading for one last chance—these people give no attention whatever to their own state, and all attention to the state of that person from whom they require their object. This outward-directedness brings the actor in "real life" to a state of magnificent responsiveness and makes his progress thrilling to watch. On the stage, similarly, it is the progress of the outward-directed actor, who behaves with no regard to his personal state, but with all regard for the responses of his antagonists, which thrills the viewers.*
>
> DAVID MAMET

4. A: I know you will!

   B: No, I won't!

5. A: *[Pulling out all the stops]* I know you will!!

   B: *[Ditto]* No, I won't!!

Repeat several times, each time intensifying the escalation by adding facial expression, gesture, and whole body movements.

Now, with the pattern of five exchanges fairly set in your mind, repeat but do not escalate the last (fifth) exchange; in other words, hold the last exchange down to the level of the fourth.

The first and fifth exchanges in Exercise 6–7 are the extremities; the second, third, and fourth are the middle ranges where most acting occurs. The extremities must always be there, in the actor's mind at least, for they define what's finally at stake in a scene or play. But most acting exchanges take place at the level of forceful—but not extreme—tactical interaction. Working on the middle levels and on the continuum from powerful induction to electrifying threats, actors explore and develop their tactical range.

The exercises in this lesson should be considered "études," or studies, that allow you to explore a mere fraction of acting, but an important fraction: those moments, usually at the climax of a scene, which require you to be deeply committed to succeeding in some cause or other—and trying to succeed by influencing the feelings and behavior of your acting partner. When these études are put into a play, with all your power at their service, they become the key moments in your performance.

Summary

There are two basic types of tactics: those that threaten and those that induce. A successful actor learns how to play both types strongly and in rapid alternation. There is also a broad middle range of tactics between the extremities, which are in process most of the time—although the extremities are always latent in the actor's mind. Tactics are *real* interpersonal behaviors, designed to influence other people; they should be played on stage as intensely as in real life and should aim at creating real reactions (including physiological reactions) in the other actors. Playing tactics forcefully, intensely, and physically brings to the surface human emotions—both from you and from your acting partner—and creates vivid and dynamic acting relationships.

L E S S O N

7

Expectations

Expecting Victory

Expectation is at the leading edge of an actor's performance; the character must not only *try* to achieve a goal or victory, he or she must *expect* to achieve it. This expectation may be irrational—but that is the character's irrationality, not the actor's. You have read the script beforehand, but your character has not; therefore your character can expect victory even if victory is not going to be the end result.

Thus, when trying to make your acting partner cry, you must *expect* your partner to cry; that is, you must expect that if you try as hard as you can, you will emerge victorious. This expectation creates the energy of performance—and pulls energy out of you that you could not otherwise "push" simply by trying to be "energetic."

Expectation gives rise to several "E" words: *energy, excitement, electricity,* and *enthusiasm,* all of which characterize the high-voltage performances that have the capacity to stimulate an audience. Audience empathy, in fact, comes almost entirely from the audience's identification with the character's expectations. This is surprising at first glance. We tend to think that audiences identify with a character's suffering, and beginning actors often play self-pity in the mistaken notion that this will stimulate a sympathetic audience reaction. But the audience can identify only with a character's expectations and enthusiasms. The excitement of a deaf and blind Helen Keller's learning to understand the word *water,* for example, creates the tremendous emotional response to William Gibson's fine play, *The Miracle Worker;* it is not our pity for Keller's handicap that generates this feeling. Character expectations carry the audience along, pulling them into the action and sweeping them up into the emotions of the play. A character's enthusiasms are the points of audience contact; they determine the elation we feel when the character succeeds and the poignancy we share when the character fails. Expectation provides the context of the character's behavior for the audience and the impulse for the behavior for the actor who plays it; enthusiasm, which is itself theatrically compelling, provides the excitement of dramatic conflict.

Conversely, a character who is resolutely unenthusiastic—who has no expectations of success—is relegated to a purely functional role in the drama and will inevitably appear to be uninvolved no matter how sensitively and carefully the role is otherwise performed. Audiences cannot—or will not—identify with predetermined losers, nor do they often find such people believable as realistic characters. For the fact is that virtually everybody sets out on difficult courses with at least some expectation of success (even an irrational expectation), and that expectation makes people, including dramatic characters, interesting, lively—and sometimes heroic.

◆ E X E R C I S E   7-1

Playing Bored

Memorize the following line: "I am bored, bored, bored." This is Masha's famous line in Chekhov's *Three Sisters*. The situation: Masha, the married sister, is one of several at a gathering of family and friends in a small provincial town. She is speaking to no one in particular—or to everyone in general.

Now play the line to your class.

How did you play the line in Exercise 7-1?

Did you try to "act bored"—to convey boredom, to demonstrate what it's like to be bored, to imitate what you would consider the attitude of a bored person? That would be wrong, as it would ignore the fundamental principles we have been talking about and substitute some sort of "demonstration" for the dynamic interplay of goals, obstacles, tactics, and expectations.

What is Masha's goal? Surely to get *un*bored: to stimulate someone to entertain her (or to fall in love with her—which is what happens). Perhaps Masha wants to call attention to herself, or to make a joke out of her boredom, or to parody the decadence of her society (to parody the kind of characters one finds in Chekhov!), or to liven up the party. Any of these goals would provide Masha—and the actress playing her—an opportunity to inject energy, excitement, and enthusiasm into her self-described "boring" social life. And it would also make us realize all the more just how tragically boring Masha's life really is.*

Positive Goals

There are hundreds of possible interpretations of the line "I am bored, bored, bored"; but the best ones all lead to Masha's effort to do something positive, to stimulate something desirable. If she is bored (and who knows —perhaps she isn't telling the whole truth!), her reason for saying she's bored is not to admit that fact but to *change* it, to act upon her environment rather than give in to it. And to do so now! We speak only in order to change things, to improve things, not simply to confirm reality. We are under no obligation to speak at all; if we do speak, it is to have some impact on our world and on the people who surround us.

So what is Masha's expectation? Experiment with any of these five possibilities and then play her line again to real or imaginary guests in your/her house:

1. You want to liven up the party.

2. You want _____ to fall in love with you.

3. You want your sisters to acknowledge your intellectual superiority.

4. You want everyone to laugh.

5. You want to make fun of _____.

♦ E X E R C I S E   7–2

Enthusiasm

The following speeches lend themselves to the exploration of positive expectations and enthusiasms—sometimes obviously and sometimes only after a

---

* Even the Russian tradition—solid since Stanislavsky—of playing this line in a doleful manner has been broken since I first wrote these words. I was happy to see that Lynn Redgrave, in a 1991 production directed by (Soviet) Georgian director Robert Strura, stormed about the room and all but jumped on the furniture when uttering this line. It is perhaps for this reason that, later that year, Georgia voted to secede from the USSR.

bit of searching. Memorize each short speech, find a positive goal to pursue, and imagine some wonderful result that you can enthusiastically expect to occur. Say the line to either a real or an imaginary person or persons.

1. "Oh heavens, how I long for a little ordinary human enthusiasm— that's all. I want to hear a warm thrilling voice cry out 'Hallelujah! Hallelujah! I'm alive!' I've an idea. Why don't we have a little game? Let's pretend that we're human beings, and that we're actually alive. Just for a little while. What do you say?" (Jimmy Porter, in John Osborne's *Look Back in Anger*)

2. "Use your head, can't you, use your head, you're on earth, there's no cure for that!" (Hamm, in Samuel Beckett's *Endgame*)

3. . . . ."He anxious to sell the land, Doaker. He don't want to be bothered with it. He called me to him and said cause of how long our families done known each other and how we been good friends and all, say he wanted to sell the land to me. Say he'd rather see me with it than Jim Stovall. Told me he'd let me have it for two thousand dollars cash money. He don't know I found out the most Stovall would give him for it was fifteen hundred dollars. He trying to get that extra five hundred out of me telling me he doing me a favor. I thanked him just as nice. Told him what a good man Sutter was and how he had my sympathy and all. Told him to give me two weeks. He said he'd wait on me. That's why I come up here. Sell them watermelons. Get Berniece to sell that piano. Put them two parts with the part I done saved. Walk in there. Tip my hat. Lay my money down on the table. Get my deed and walk on out. This time I get to keep all the cotton. Hire me some men to work it for me. Gin my cotton. Get my seed. And I'll see you again next year. Might even plant some tobacco or some oats." (Boy Willie, in August Wilson's *The Piano Lesson*)

4. "I don't want realism. I want magic. I don't tell the truth. I tell what ought to be truth. And if that is sinful, then let me be damned for it!" (Blanche, in Tennessee Williams's *A Streetcar Named Desire*)

5. "I'm not a leader of men, Willy, and neither are you. You were never anything but a hard-working drummer who landed in the ash can like all the rest of them. I'm one dollar an hour, Willy! I tried seven states and couldn't raise it. A buck an hour! Do you gather my meaning? I'm not bringing home any prizes any more, and you're going to stop waiting for me to bring them home!" (Biff, in Arthur Miller's *Death of a Salesman*)

6. "You've finally got the game of life licked, don't you see that? Then why the hell don't you get pie-eyed and celebrate? Why don't you laugh and sing Sweet Adeline? The only reason I can think of is, you're putting on this rotten half-dead act just to get back at me! Because you hate my guts!" (Hickey, in Eugene O'Neill's *The Iceman Cometh*)

7. "Oh, did you believe my courage would never come back? Did you believe that I was a deserter? That I, who have stood in the streets and taken my people to heart, and talked of the holiest and greatest things with them, could ever turn back and chatter foolishly about nothing in a drawing room? Never, never, never, never: Major Barbara will die with the colors. Glory, Hallelujah!" (Major Barbara, in George Bernard Shaw's *Major Barbara*)

8. "It's three hours since you've met and known and loved each other. Kiss each other quickly. Look at him. He hesitates. He trembles. Happiness frightens him . . . How like a man! O, Irma, kiss him, kiss him! If two people who love each other let a single instant wedge itself between them, it grows—it becomes a month, a year, a century; it becomes too late! Kiss him, Irma, kiss him while there is still time, or in a moment his hair will be white and there will be another madwoman in Paris." (The Madwoman, in Jean Giraudoux's *The Madwoman of Chaillot*)

9. "My ears have yet not drunk a hundred words
Of thy tongue's uttering, yet I know the sound;
Art thou not Romeo, and a Montague?"
(Juliet, in William Shakespeare's *Romeo and Juliet*)

10. "No/ I don think you was tryin' to tell me I'm some kinda fool/ but/ ya gotta understand/ I ain't never gointa college/ I ain't gonna be no vet or a doctor or a nurse even/ shit/ I probably couldn't even make it as a administrative assistant's assistant/ but I can ride/ & I wanna be the best I can/ I ain't got much left as a woman/ you right/ I ain't got mucha family/ do you think that mean I ain't s'posed to want nothin' mo' out my life?" (Cassie, in Ntozake Shange's *Daddy Says*)

11. "Bless me anyway.
     I want more life. I can't help myself. I do. I've lived through such terrible times, and there are people who live through much worse, but. . . . You see them living, anyway.
     When they're more spirit than body, more sores than skin, when they're burned and in agony, when flies lay eggs in the corners of the eyes of their children, they live. Death usually has to *take* life away. I don't know if that's just the animal. I don't know if it's not braver to die. But I recognize the habit. The addiction to being alive. We live past hope. If I can find hope anywhere, that's it, that's the best I can do. It's so much not enough, so inadequate, but. . . . Bless me anyway. I want more life." (Prior, in Tony Kushner's *Perestroika*)

If you know these plays, you know that few of these characters are considered optimistic! Jimmy Porter is virtually defined by his anger, and

EXPECTATION

I played a game with myself when I gave that speech that I could really persuade everyone, all the extras, to vote for our slate.

GREGORY PECK, REFERRING TO HIS ROLE
IN THE FILM *OTHER PEOPLE'S MONEY*

Blanche by her desperation; author Beckett is widely known for his pessimism (or even nihilism), and Williams, Miller, and O'Neill are hardly upbeat in their portrayal of mid-twentieth-century American life. Nonetheless, these characters—certainly in these speeches—all express an excitement and an expectation for a better life, somewhere. It's up to you to find not their despair, but their enthusiasm and their excitement.

Learning to play speeches positively, with expectations of some concrete and specific victory in mind, is a strong step away from grievous actor problems—most particularly self-consciousness and a tendency to play toward self-pity, empty sarcasm, sentimentality, and pious moralizing. No action can be convincing onstage—and no actor can be sufficiently confident in his or her role—without an expectation of success in the action's outcome, without an *excitement* at the prospect of success. Creating that expectation—which the script does not always confirm at the play's conclusion—is the actor's job, and often the actor's most delicate job.

♦ EXERCISE   7–3

Try the Impossible

Try to jump twenty feet in the air. (That's right, you can't do it. But try.) Now try to jump twenty feet in the air, expecting to succeed! Think of the prizes you are going to win! Think of the cheering crowds! The adulation! The rewards! The romantic opportunities! You can do it! Do it again! Again! AGAIN!!

What happens in this progressive escalation of expectation in Exercise 7–3? Did the expectation of victory (even of an impossible victory) give you a greater tone, strength, and vivacity? Did you jump even higher? Did you enjoy the exercise more? Did you get more of your body into play? More of your emotions? Were you less self-conscious?

EXPECTATION

You can't play a loser, so don't ever do it. You've always got to play it like a winner. You can never give up. That was the lesson to me as an actor in Fargo. *The subtext of every scene you do has always to be "I can solve this. There is an answer and I will find it."*

WILLIAM H. MACY

Chances are that you answered "yes" to all those questions. Positive expectation and enthusiasm have brought far more out of you than merely following a stage direction. It was your *imagination* that made you jump higher, act more energetically, feel more deeply, and perform more vividly. And the same process is at work in a subtle and complex performance of a dramatic role.

Eye Contact

Where do you look when you act? There is no single answer to this, but in general the best place to look is right at your *acting partner's eyes.* That is because in a strong dramatic scene you are seeking a goal with or from your partner, who is the "other" character with whom you interact. Direct eye contact with your partner, therefore, is the best way to see if you are on track to win your goal, because it's the surest way to read your partner's innate responses. Eye contact also expresses your confidence—your positive expectation—that you are indeed going to achieve what you seek. It is, moreover, an effective tactic in gaining your partner's trust and/or respect. The distinguished actor Michael Caine even advises actors to refrain from blinking ("Blinking makes your character seem weak") so as to intensify the acting power that direct eye contact provides.

 TWO VIEWS ON EYE CONTACT

Reacting is why one only wants to work with good actors; it's tennis, and you have to react to that ball coming back! And your eye's always got to be on what's coming back to you, and you have to react to that.

EILEEN ATKINS

You never know what [your character's] going to be until the day you walk onto the set and look into the other actor's eyes.

MERYL STREEP

You needn't look at your partner all the time, of course, and sometimes it's wholly appropriate to look at someone or something else—as, for example, to imply to your partner "Stop bothering me with your problems." But you should always look at *something* or *someone* while acting, not just look "away" or study the floor. Looking at the floor, even unconsciously, makes clear you are pursuing no goal, using no tactic, and have no positive expectations. It is, in fact, a nervous acting tic, implying only that you'd rather be anywhere but on stage acting this scene. Looking at the floor between lines, or when you're unsure of yourself, may be a hard habit to break (particularly because you're not always aware when you do it), but you should ask your teacher or fellow classmates to alert you when they see it.

◆ E X E R C I S E   7–4

Tactics and Expectations

Go back to the exercises in Lesson 6 and repeat them with escalating expectations of victory and full direct eye contact with your partner. You will probably find that the exercises are more fun to do, less "clinical," and less like exercises.

If you have been through the experience of rehearsing plays through to performance, you may recall a director begging the cast for more "energy" in the last days before the play's opening. "Louder! Faster! Funnier!" is the classic (and old-fashioned) directorial plea. But you can't simply pump energy into a play like air into a tire: If a tire leaks, it'll stay flat no matter what's pumped into it, and so will a play. The truest theatrical energy comes not from a director's desperate exhortations but from the actor's eager portrayal of the character's expectations and his or her consequent efforts to bring these expectations to fulfillment.

Summary

Positive expectation, on the actor's part, lends his or her portrayal a necessary excitement and energy. Not all characters succeed, of course, but they must be shown to expect success and even to be enthusiastic about their prospects, if their actions are to excite audience interest and empathy. Even the most despairing of dramatic characters must have this quality of positive expectation, for it is only when their expectations are dashed that their pathos can be shared.

8

GOTE

A Basic Method

The foundations of an actor's approach have been set out in the preceding lessons; admittedly, there's a good deal to keep in mind at one time.

GOTE is an easy-to-remember acronym that stands for and brings together the four basic principles. GOTE, therefore, represents a basic method for approaching an acting assignment. The letters individually stand for

Goal

Other

Tactics

Expectation

Let us go over these terms with an eye to their interdependence and mutual relationship.

Goal is the character's principal quest, which the actor assumes: Everything on stage must be seen, first and foremost, as a character pursuing a goal. Elsewhere the word may be called *victory, objective, want, intention, action,* or *purpose,* and these words may also suffice, when they refer to the same thing.

In brief, the actor becomes the character primarily by pursuing, as vigorously as possible, the character's goal. Moreover, the goal should be something quite specific and outgoing: not just "I want to find self-fulfillment," but "I want to be King of Denmark" or "I want to marry Romeo." If you did the Pledge of Allegiance exercise in Lesson 2, your goal might have been any of the following: to secure freedom, to acquire allies, to win friends, to return and save your sister, to join a republic, to disable the goon squad you left behind, or any variation of each and all of these.

The *other* is the person (or persons) with whom, for whom, or from whom you seek your goal. There is *always* an other in acting; no goal can be achieved simply by yourself. Thus Hamlet cannot simply say, "I want to be King of Denmark," and have a crown appear above his head; nor can Juliet say, "I want to be happily married," and then marry happily. Not in good theatre, anyway. In drama all the victories must be hard-earned and must be achieved through interpersonal struggle. There are simply no good plays about characters learning the multiplication table or developing a personal philosophy without an interpersonal struggle.

The other in a scene, therefore, is what makes achieving goals difficult. Often the other is your chief *obstacle:* another "O" word. The struggle to overcome obstacles—particularly when those obstacles are other persons and other persons' pursuit of *their* goals—creates much of the dynamics of acting, the work of acting. The struggle to overcome obstacles onstage should make you sweat.

So, in acting, the goals that are worth pursuing must be achievable only with the compliance or defeat of other characters. To the extent that these other characters are sympathetic, your character may be seen as inspirational. To the extent that the other characters are obstacles, your character may be seen as heroic. To the extent that the other characters are complex, your character may be seen as profound. The nature of your actions—and of your acting—will be determined by your confrontation with the other who stands between you and your goal.

Putting together the confrontation of goal and other, you will ask of every given scene or exercise:

1. What is my goal?

2. Who is/are the other person(s) who affect my gaining it?

   a. How can they help me?

   b. How can they hurt me?

   c. How are they my obstacle?

3. How can I demand/induce/encourage their help?

4. How can I overcome the obstacle they pose?

5. What should my tactics be?

Tactics are the character's means of trying to achieve goals; they are what gives acting its "guts."

Tactics—and trying to achieve goals through them—make acting "real" for the actors and make actors indistinguishable from characters, at least from the audience's point of view. That is to say: Jane trying to get Jim to fall in love with her is absolutely indistinguishable from Juliet trying to get Romeo to fall in love with her, when Jane is playing Juliet and Jim is playing Romeo. The lines are Shakespeare's, but the tactics are your own; tactics will come out of your life experience, not out of the script.

As we saw in Lesson 6, tactics can be divided between those that threaten and those that induce; they can be divided also into extreme tactics and a broad middle range of subtler tactics. A good actor will be able to move fluidly and purposefully from tactic to tactic in pursuit of victory. Tactical strength and tactical versatility are what make acting, by turns, forceful, seductive, visceral, and dramatic. Actors work all their lives on expanding and developing their tactical range.

Expectation, the last word on the list, gives tone, spring, and excitement to the dramatic pursuit of goals and quest for victory. It also lends every dramatic action at least a touch of enthusiasm, which can prove deliciously infectious. Too often actors choose to pursue goals in an academic way, as perhaps may be implied by the overly clinical word *objective.* It is not that your character just "wants" or "desires" something; people have all sorts of petty wants and desires that are rarely worth dramatizing. Look at any fine play, and the chances are that the author created characters who not only desire goals but crave them—characters who are excited and enthusiastic about their eventual success; characters who, deep in their hearts, are sure (even mistakenly sure) that they will win in the end. *Expectation, excitement, enthusiasm,* and even *energy* are "E" words that make a memory package: They define characters who have not only wants, but passions as well. You are playing one of those characters. The victory you seek is not just an ordinary whim; it is the prime goal of your life, and it is within your reach if you try hard enough. Go for it! NOW!

Get Your Character's GOTE

These "first six lessons"* have outlined a method of approaching any role. Approaching the role does not necessarily mean performing the role to everybody's satisfaction—much less to the demands of this highly regarded art—but it is the starting point for professional and beginner alike. Before a role can be played, it must be approached: It must be understood and created in *acting* terms. What makes the character not just an invention of the

---

* *The First Six Lessons* is the subtitle of Richard Boleslavsky's justly famous book, *Acting* (New York: Theatre Arts Books, 1933).

GOTE

[Acting is] very clearcut. You have to answer four questions: Who am I speaking to? What do I want from them? How am I going to get it? and What is standing in the way of what I want? But it's not just answering them—you have to answer them incredibly specifically.

JASON ALEXANDER

playwright, but a living, breathing, feeling, caring, *acting* person? Characters act. In order to play a character, you must play the character's actions—and in order to play that character brilliantly, you must create those actions in vivid detail and with believable intensity.

Getting your character's GOTE, which means creating those actions in the context of goals, obstacles, tactics, and expectations, is the key to putting yourself into the role and to approaching the character with the full resources of your acting instrument (your voice and body) and your personal history, intelligence, and emotional resourcefulness.

How do you get your character's GOTE? Studying the script is, of course, the first step. But using your imagination is the more important second step—more important in that most of the "answers" aren't answers at all but, rather, creations. Most of the GOTE aspects are only *implied* by the script—and determining which implications are the correct ones is a highly subjective and imaginative task. Study gives the main lines of a character's desires, but imagination fleshes them out. Indeed, that is one of the particular characteristics of drama, which, unlike narrative fiction, creates action only through spoken words and physical movement, not through thought revelations or extended third-person descriptions, except in rare cases.

Often the play is silent about matters crucial to the character. What does Hamlet really want from Ophelia? What are Cordelia's feelings and desires toward King Lear? The actor's *choices*—governed but not restricted by the actor's research—will determine the character's behavior.

◆ E X E R C I S E   8–1

The GOTEsheet

The GOTEsheet is a starting point for analyzing any role. Using your imagination, take a blank piece of paper and answer the following questions about a dramatic character from a play you know. Reread the play first, with the questions in mind, and answer *as the character would:*

1. Basic information about the character

   Name:

   Sex:

   Age:

   Marital status and history:

   Educational level:

   Economic/social status:

2. Goal: What do I really want? When do I want it?

3. Other: From whom (in the play) do I want it? Who in the play can help me? Who in the play can hurt me? Who is an obstacle? Why? What are my deepest fears?

4. Tactics: How can I get it? How (and whom) can I threaten? How (and whom) can I induce?

5. Expectation: Why do I expect to get it? Why does it excite me? What will I do when I get it?

You may answer impressionistically or in lists, but answer vividly, not academically.

Now, memorize, rehearse, and play a scene, trying to implement your answers to these GOTEsheet questions.

Summary

GOTE is an acronym for *goal, other, tactics,* and *expectation;* in combination, these are the four coordinates of the actor's approach to any role. The GOTEsheet is the actor's basic list of questions whose answers will create the foundation for approaching a specific character.

III

The Actor's Tasks

PART THREE SUGGESTS PRACTICAL METHODS FOR PREPARING AN acting role for presentation, either in a scene for class or in a play. Naturally your instructor (in a class) or director (in a play) will provide some specific policies, advice, and guidance in your work; nonetheless, it is finally up to you to develop a fundamental working method for preparing a role on your own.

Scenes are the basic medium of acting. The two-person scene, from three to eight minutes in length, drawn from any play (or adapted from other sources), is the basic exercise for the acting student. It involves, in microcosm, virtually all the acting skills a play involves and yet can be prepared in a relatively short time with little or no cost.

This section deals primarily with scenes to be presented in class, although some discussion is devoted to scenes in plays, where the method may be somewhat different.

L E S S O N

9

Preparing a Role

Finding Your Role

The first step in beginning any kind of scenework, either in class or in performance, is finding a role. Sometimes this may be done for you, as when you are cast in a play or assigned a role (and perhaps a partner) in class. On other occasions you will be in charge of selecting a role yourself—and probably also selecting the play or other material it comes from, as well as an acting partner to play it with. Every class and every instructor has certain rules and limits as to what sorts of scenes you should choose. In general, however, and absent instructions to the contrary, you should

1. Choose roles of your own sex and close to your own age.

2. Choose roles in which you can clearly see something at stake, emotionally, for the character you will be playing.

3. Choose roles in which something is happening in the scene itself—as opposed to roles in which characters are talking about something that has already happened.

4. Choose roles in which you can identify with the character's struggle or dilemma.

5. Choose roles in which the characters and situation interest you personally.

Finding Your "Character"

Do not, for this assignment, try to create "a character" different from yourself. Simply put yourself into the role. "Character," says actress Fiona Shaw, is the "combustion of yourself with events. Put yourself in the situation and you'll discover your character." Her advice is appropriate not only for this lesson but for every exercise in *Acting One*.

You should also try to choose roles in scenes set in periods and styles that you understand well and with characters whose backgrounds you can identify with. And, given the opportunity, you should try to select scene partners of both sexes over the course of several scene assignments.

Editing a Scene

Sometimes it is necessary to edit a scene, to cut it down in length, or to combine two short scenes into a longer one, or to delete references within the scene that are unrelated to the immediate matters at hand. Sometimes a little rewriting, if permitted by the instructor, may be useful for eliminating a minor character in the scene.

Sometimes you can adapt a scene from a novel or short story by transcribing the dialog and omitting the narrative. Some outstanding contemporary, realistic scenes for young people can be obtained this way, as many more novels than plays are published in any given year, and novels today tend to include extensive dialog. In adapting a novel for classroom scene use, you might consider yourself a practicing screenplay adapter, for this is how many films begin.

Once a script is fully edited, you and your partner must obtain exact duplicate copies. You should also agree on the context of the scene: What is the basic relationship of the characters—as they both understand it to be—and what is happening in the scene as both characters understand it? These basic understandings should be just that—basic—one or two sentences that define only the outer boundaries of the scene. For example, "A and B are husband and wife. A is trying to get B to confess her adultery; B is trying to make A get dressed to go to a party." You and your partner should read the scene once or twice together. Then memorization should commence.

Memorization Methods

Memorizing is "donkey work," according to Alec McCowen, who once memorized the Gospel according to Saint Mark for a spectacularly successful one-man presentation. But if pursued diligently and immediately, this donkey work goes hand-in-glove with the actor's understanding of the role so as to provide the firmest possible basis for richly experimental and emotionally charged acting. Memorization is sometimes a difficult task, and it invariably gets more difficult as you get older. Young children memorize almost immediately; two or three times through a script, and eight-year-olds will have their parts memorized; two or three more times through and they will have everybody else's parts memorized as well. Conversely, older actors frequently find memorization an absolute horror; many, indeed, give up the theatre for film and TV, where they can use cue cards in lieu of memorizing and can (to a certain extent) ask for retakes if they "go up" (forget their lines).

You must learn your lines exactly, even for a simple scene performed in class. There are several reasons for this. First, that's the only way your partner can be secure about coming in on cue. Second, learning your lines exactly gives you a confidence in your role that you can never have if you're fishing for the exact way to say something. Third, such rewriting as you do when you paraphrase your lines invariably weakens your role; you will tend to reduce your role to a commonplace character, rather than rise to the level created by the author's words. Fourth, by paraphrasing, you will probably defeat the author's sense of timing and diminish the power of the play's builds, climaxes, and rhythmic effects. Fifth, you will look bad in the eyes of those who know the play, who will feel you haven't come up to the level of the character even if they are unaware of the specific line changes you have made. The slightest paraphrases of Shakespeare, for example, will make the acting seem profoundly "off" even if the source of the deviation is not apparent. And finally, you are simply insulting the author and the theatre itself by your laziness! So learn the lines verbatim.

Many actors prefer to learn their lines in rehearsal, going through their parts "on book" (with script in hand) until the lines are embedded in their memory. This common practice invites certain problems. While going through a part on book, you are not acting; you are reacting to the book, not to the situation, and your main contact is not with the actors but with the script. You may well pick up patterns and readings in this "running through" that have nothing to do with the interactions between you and your partner but, rather, with your immediate idea of what is "theatrical" about your part.

Try sitting down and memorizing your part first. By doing so, you will also be studying your part from your own character's point of view, not jumping to conclusions about what is the most theatrical way to play the scene. You can also develop your GOTEsheet as you memorize, studying the part while you are learning it.

Begin by underlining or highlighting all your lines.

Start reading the text; read aloud for your own part, to yourself for the other character's part. Start with a quarter page or so, and go back to the

THREE VIEWS ON LINE LEARNING

I think it best to learn the lines before rehearsals start. Actors who like to start from scratch don't even notice what you are doing because they have their faces buried in their scripts. Whereas you, from the start, can look at them, speak to them, listen to them, and be surprised by them, and this element of surprise is one of the most valuable things that can happen.

PETER BARKWORTH

I never study lines. I find out in the process of working what my function is in a particular play or movie, who that person is, what they're all about and I learn by reading. I read the script over and over again. I've never really sat down and taken a line and said, "This is the line I have to say."

CICELY TYSON

It's sluggish work. I hate it. I always try to synchronize what I'm saying with what I'm doing or not doing; the pattern of movement and words: one prompts the other. I used to do it by being cued, and have somebody else read the other speeches while I'd walk around. But I've found other things in recent years: I'll write the words out so they become visual, or I'll put difficult speeches on the tape recorder—my own speeches—and listen to them. I'm not trying to memorize a way of delivery; I'm simply trying to memorize the words, using all the senses I can. I try to sop up everything: the visual sense, the aural sense, the actual saying of the words, the repetition of the words, and so on.

HUME CRONYN

beginning each time you complete this small section. Soon you will have your first few lines in your memory. Get a postcard or index card and cover up your first line. Read (to yourself) the line before it (your cue line), and recite your line from memory. Move the card down and read (to yourself) the next cue line or lines. Recite your next line from memory. Gradually go through the script, an hour or so at a time, lowering the card as you memorize more and more lines; eventually, you will have the text committed to memory.

At this point your memorization is still shallow; it will probably not stand up to an intense rehearsal. This is OK; there's no problem with struggling with your lines when your character is struggling to win his or her goals. Your memorization will "lock in," however, as you rehearse the scene, and it will lock in together with the specific goals and tactics of your character as you develop them. But don't stop learning your lines after you first go through the scene off book. Go back to the script and learn them again—learn all of those you haven't mastered exactly. Record your cue lines on a tape recorder, and run your lines with the machine. Or get a friend to run lines with you. Run your lines aloud while driving, cycling, jogging, or showering. Run your lines with your acting partner, without trying to rehearse the actual staging. Write your lines out, by memory, in long-hand or at the computer.

Cues

Always learn your lines with your partner's cues. There are usually two cues for each line: the action cue and the line cue. The *action cue* is what prompts you to speak; the *line cue* is the actual line you come in on. For example:

EDDIE: You gonna marry him?

CATHERINE: I don't know. We just been . . . goin' around, that's all.
  What've you got against him, Eddie? Please, tell me. What?

EDDIE: He don't respect you.

(Arthur Miller, *A View from the Bridge*)

The *action* cue for Eddie's last line is "What've you got against him?" The *line* cue is "What?" Eddie's line is prepared in response to the action cue; it is held until the line cue.

Sometimes there are certain lines that seem to stick; an actor has memorized the part, but one or two lines don't seem to come when cued. In this case the actor should study the cue (both action cue and line cue) and look for the precise linkage in the character's mind that triggers the response. Some linkages are obvious and rarely cause problems:

KRISTIN: Government rations are small but sure, and there's a pension for the widow and children.

JEAN: That's all very fine, but it's not in my line to start thinking at once about dying for my wife and children. I must say I had rather bigger ideas.

KRISTIN: You and your ideas! You've got obligations too, and you'd better start thinking about them.

JEAN: Don't you start pestering me about obligations.

(August Strindberg, *Miss Julie*)

This dialog is easy to memorize, for the action cues contain the germinal words of the responses. The following dialog is more difficult to memorize:

NICK: Everybody drinks a lot here in the East. Everybody drinks a lot in the Middle West, too.

GEORGE: We drink a great deal in this country, and I suspect we'll be drinking a great deal more, too . . . if we survive. We should be Arabs or Italians . . . the Arabs don't drink, and the Italians don't get drunk much, except on religious holidays. We should live on Crete, or something.

NICK: And that, of course, would make us cretins.

GEORGE: So it would. Tell me about your wife's money.

(Edward Albee, *Who's Afraid of Virginia Woolf?*)

This is caustic dialog, representing the half-clever repartee of heavy-drinking faculty colleagues at a late night party. It is difficult to memorize because it contains elliptical phrases, artificial constructions, and apparent non sequiturs, or illogical jumps. But there are some tricks to help you learn George's part, which is the particularly difficult one here.

George's analysis of the drinking habits of Arabs, Italians, and Cretans may be made simpler by picturing, in your head, a map of the Mediterranean, since all of these cultures bound this sea, and since George, a history professor, would be thinking of specific locales when he speaks; thus the line has more continuity than may be perceived at first glance. And George's apparent out-of-nowhere leap to "Tell me about your wife's money" may be memorized by associating Nick's "that would make us cretins" remark with the fleeting thought "Anybody who would crack a joke like that must be a member of the idle rich." Or simpler yet, the transition may be memorized by picturing a cretin counting out money, an image that henceforth will be triggered by hearing Nick's "cretin" line and will, in turn, trigger George's "money" line. This, by the way, is not merely an acting gimmick. The character of George (inasmuch as we think of him as a real person) would himself go through some sort of mental gymnastic to make the jump. The goal of playing a character like George is to show that these leaps from "out of nowhere" are, in fact, from "out of somewhere": out of his individual and possibly peculiar mind. You are not only playing George's lines, you are playing George's *thinking* process—his *coming up with* his lines.

Studying the Part

Learning the lines of a role will teach you a great deal about the part that is not immediately apparent. Mainly, it will make clear to you the *logic* of your character's position and how the lines develop not out of an author's whim but, rather, out of a character's thinking process. Learning a long speech—out of George Bernard Shaw, for example, where the speeches can go on for pages—seems at first a formidable task, but as you start to work on it, the structure of the speech begins to assert itself in your mind. By learning the speech you begin to understand the speaker, and to understand why the words are in their particular order, and how the lines of thought, or argument, or reaction, develop in the character's mind. You may be amazed with the speed with which you can learn a long, well-crafted speech and the speed and conviction with which you can deliver it within a short period of time.

While you are memorizing your part, you begin to study it. What are your character's goals? How will other people—particularly the other person or persons in the scene(s) with you—help you to achieve that goal? How are they your obstacles? What sort of tactics can your character use? What sort did he or she grow up with? What is he or she afraid of? Excited by? How vivid are his or her expectations? How wild are his or her fantasies? How can you find the expectations of the character? The enthusiasm? These are questions to be answered first and last by you, the actor. Studying is the private part of actor preparation, and it is important, in a nondirected scene, that you first study your part by yourself and not with your acting partner. Your acting partner, no matter how clever or experienced, is not your acting consultant. Indeed, he or she, in the guise of his or her character, is most likely your *obstacle*. Don't confuse yourself, or diminish yourself, by trying to forge an agreement with your partner as to how your scene should play. The best acting scene will be the result of a dramatic *confrontation* between you and your partner—with both of you seen as individually ambitious (and yet vulnerable) characters. Your individualism must be nurtured in private: hence the importance of your private study in approaching your part.

So get your character's GOTE and integrate your memorization of your part with the filling out of your GOTEsheet. Strategize on behalf of your character! Make your character's plans! The GOTEsheet responses, your character's plans, do not come out of rehearsal as much as they come out of you and from your own imagination. Try to prepare a part such as Laura or Jim in the exercise that follows.

◆ E X E R C I S E   9–1

The Gentleman Caller I

Following is the Gentleman Caller scene from Tennessee Williams's modern classic *The Glass Menagerie*. In this play, set in the late 1930s, Laura Wingfield lives with her mother and brother in an urban tenement apartment.

Laura, a young woman, is described by the author as "exquisitely fragile," at least in part because a childhood illness has left her with one leg slightly shorter than the other. The author cautions, however, that Laura's physical defect "need not be more than suggested on the stage." In the play, Laura's mother begs her son—Laura's brother—to invite a co-worker to the family home for dinner, in the hope the guest would become a "gentleman caller" for her daughter. And thus Jim O'Connor, an up-and-coming young businessman, arrives one evening for dinner. Laura immediately realizes Jim is a boy she knew and liked in high school, and she can barely speak during the meal. But afterward, Jim follows Laura into the living room, carrying the candelabrum and a glass of dandelion wine, and they have the conversation that follows. In this famous scene (only the first part of which is included in this exercise), the characters' deepest thoughts are expressed mainly indirectly, and dialog only suggests their profound feelings, fears, and desires.

1. Study the scene and prepare the role of Laura or Jim, depending on your gender. Assume both characters are your actual age (as they could be— their age is unspecified in the play).

2. Underline your actual *lines* in one color. Underline your *line cues* in a second color and your *action cues* (where they are different from the line cues) in a third.

3. Analyze the *logic* of your speeches and imagine the thoughts that connect them. Make notes of the *thought linkages* that connect your lines with each other, and with the other character's lines. Make notes toward a GOTEsheet for your part.

4. *Memorize* your part, using the thought linkages to help you connect the individual lines.

5. Complete your GOTEsheet.

6. In a subsequent class, pair with a partner and play the scene without rehearsal, just as you played the contentless scene (Exercise 5–1). You or your instructor will need to bring to class a pillow, two drinking glasses, and something to represent a candelabrum.

7. Switch partners and play it again. Repeat.

The scene

(Note: All stage directions are by Williams.)

JIM: Hello there, Laura.

LAURA *[Faintly]*:   Hello. *[She clears her throat.]*

JIM: How are you feeling now? Better?

LAURA: Yes. Yes, thank you.

JIM: This is for you. A little dandelion wine. *[He extends the glass toward her with extravagant gallantry.]*

LAURA: Thank you.

JIM: Drink it—but don't get drunk! *[He laughs heartily. Laura takes the glass uncertainly; she laughs shyly.]* Where shall I set the candles?

LAURA: Oh—oh, anywhere . . .

JIM: How about here on the floor? Any objections?

LAURA: No.

JIM: I'll spread a newspaper under to catch the drippings. I like to sit on the floor. Mind if I do?

LAURA: Oh, no.

JIM: Give me a pillow?

LAURA: What?

JIM: A pillow!

LAURA: Oh . . . *[She hands him one quickly.]*

JIM: How about you? Don't you like to sit on the floor?

LAURA: Oh—yes.

JIM: Why don't you, then?

LAURA: I—will.

JIM: Take a pillow! *[Laura does. She sits on the floor on the other side of the candelabrum. Jim crosses his legs and smiles engagingly at her.]* I can't hardly see you sitting way over there.

LAURA: I can—see you.

JIM: I know, but that's not fair, I'm in the limelight. *[Laura moves her pillow closer.]* Good! Now I can see you! Comfortable?

LAURA: Yes.

JIM: So am I. Comfortable as a cow! Will you have some gum?

LAURA: No, thank you.

JIM: I think that I will indulge, with your permission. *[He musingly unwraps a stick of gum and holds it up.]* Think of the fortune made by the guy that invented the first piece of chewing gum. Amazing, huh? The Wrigley Building is one of the sights of Chicago—I saw it summer before last when I went up to the Century of Progress. Did you take in the Century of Progress?

LAURA: No, I didn't.

JIM: Well, it was quite a wonderful exposition. What impressed me most was the Hall of Science. Gives you an idea of what the future will be in America, even more wonderful than the present time is! *[There is a pause. Jim smiles at her.]* Your brother tells me you're shy. Is that right, Laura?

LAURA: I—don't know.

JIM: I judge you to be an old-fashioned type of girl. Well, I think that's a pretty good type to be. Hope you don't think I'm being too personal— do you?

LAURA *[Hastily, out of embarrassment]*:   I believe I *will* take a piece of gum, if you—don't mind. *[Clearing her throat]* Mr. O'Connor, have you —kept up with your singing?

JIM: Singing? Me?

LAURA: Yes. I remember what a beautiful voice you had.

JIM: When did you hear me sing? *[Laura does not answer.]* You say you've heard me sing?

LAURA: Oh, yes! Yes, very often . . . I—don't suppose—you remember me—at all?

JIM *[Smiling doubtfully]*:   You know I have an idea I've seen you before. I had that idea soon as you opened the door. It seemed almost like I was about to remember your name. But the name that I started to call you— wasn't a name! And so I stopped myself before I said it.

LAURA: Wasn't it—Blue Roses?

JIM *[Springing up, grinning]*:   Blue Roses! My gosh, yes—Blue Roses! That's what I had on my tongue when you opened the door! Isn't it funny what tricks your memory plays? I didn't connect you with high school somehow or other. But that's where it was; it was high school.

This scene is famous more for what the characters don't say than what they do. Study how the characters reach out to each other through smiles, physical gestures, and tentative efforts at humor and enthusiasm—"Comfortable as a cow!" Study the author's stage directions and particularly his punctuation: dashes indicating pauses and exclamation points indicating excitement. As you play the scene with different partners, try moving in different ways: As Laura, do you want to hide your physical defect? Or do you want Jim to see it so as to be more sympathetic to you? As Jim, do you want to impress her with your vigor? Or with your sensitivity to her feelings? Do you want to amuse her with your fancy talking—or overcome her shyness by your provocations?

In playing these parts without rehearsal, and with different partners, you will see how your character's thinking, feeling, and behavior are affected by the behavior of the actors playing opposite you. Don't try to simply repeat your part the same way every time; allow yourself to vary your behavior according to what's happening between you and your partner. And, yes, let the scene really "happen" in real time between the two of you. Study your acting partner and his or her reactions to your expressions. Try to get to know your acting partner better, simply by rehearsing the scene together. You may not succeed—but it will make the scene much more interesting.

You will probably want to explore this scene further. Find the play at the library and read it. Learn the entire scene and rehearse it with one or more partners.

Summary

The first step in presenting a scene is to choose, edit, and memorize material. During memorization, you will begin studying the part and preparing your GOTEsheet analysis—as you explore the logic of your character's thinking and the connection of your character's speeches with each other and with the "action cues" that prompt them. A memorized and studied scene can be presented without rehearsal and with different partners, revealing a good deal about the spontaneous behavior that may be part of the scene's situation and interaction.

10

Rehearsing

Rehearsals

Rehearsals are the opportunity to practice and develop the dramatic confrontation between your character and your acting partner's character.

Rehearse originally meant "re-harrow"—that is, to plow the field again. The French word for rehearsal is *répétition*. Thus rehearsal is a process by which you repeat your parts until they are learned—and until the lumps are broken down.

In a play production, rehearsals are under the control of the director. Ordinarily the early rehearsals involve lectures or discussions on the play's meaning, the production concepts, and the development of the play's staging. In preparation for a classroom acting scene, ordinarily no individual controls the rehearsal; therefore you and your partner must develop a working method together.

Undirected Rehearsals

Your first task in an "undirected" rehearsal is to establish a rehearsal schedule and exchange addresses and telephone numbers for staying in contact between rehearsals. Once scheduled, no rehearsal time should be changed except for reasons of emergency (or mutual convenience). If possible, your schedule should include at least one rehearsal in the space where your scene will be presented; if that is impossible, then rehearse at least once in a similar space. Also, at least one rehearsal should involve all the props you will use and the clothes you will wear in the scene. Ordinarily, this will be the last rehearsal.

Usually you will begin your first rehearsal by "running lines" with your partner. This means sitting or standing apart from others and saying your (memorized or partly memorized) lines to each other as directly as possible.

Don't "try" to act. On the other hand, don't try to maintain a complete monotone. Inevitably, as you run lines, you will begin to slide into the scene, to slide into acting. This "sliding" will show you the continuity between yourself and your character and help you to discover yourself, quite naturally, in your role.

As soon as you can comfortably run lines without looking at your script, discard it and, without consideration yet of staging the scene, begin to run lines in a variety of imaginary locales. Run your scene while seated at a lunch counter, or while jogging, or while lolling on a sofa. Do the scene while washing the (real) dishes, or while eating a (real) salad, or while changing your (real) outer garments. As you do this, even though the actions may be irrelevant to the content of the scene, the lines will become more natural to you, and you will find yourself, by necessity, studying your partner very freshly each time. As you rehearse in this manner, the relationship between you and your acting partner—as characters in the scene—will grow and deepen of its own accord.

Between rehearsals, you will naturally want to talk about the scene. How much should you discuss or analyze what's happening? The perhaps surprising answer: not much. Analysis may diminish the freshness of the scene and superimpose a director–actor relationship onto your character–character one. Analysis tends to forge a "playing agreement" that may defeat the dramatic confrontation your scene is supposed to portray. Try to find out more about your scene and your characters by rehearsing rather than by analyzing. Do your best thinking about the scene *while it's going on.*

Above all, never try to direct your partner and never allow your partner to direct you. No matter how experienced you feel you are, or how well you think you understand your partner's role, or how well you know "how the scene should play," your job is to act your role to the fullest, not to play both roles at the same time. As an actor, you will shape the scene *from within,* not from the outside. When actors try to direct each other, the scene inevitably becomes self-conscious, and the emotions and rhythms become fixed rather than free-flowing. An acting scene is not a directed performance, and it should not try to look like a directed performance; its goal is to bring out the most intense, honest, vivid, and dramatic interaction between the two of you. No one will mind, at this stage in your work, if the outward form does not resemble the Royal Shakespeare Company production.

> REHEARSALS
>
> *Rehearsals are not to get it right straightaway, they're to do it wrong and then find another way of doing it, and see which serves the play better and serves the character better.*
>
> JANET SUZMAN

Between rehearsals you should talk about the context of the scene. How old are we (characters)? How long have we known each other? Where did we go to school? Where did we first meet? How rich are our parents? What are we wearing? Where do we work? And so forth.

You can also tell your acting partner which of his or her behaviors stimulate you emotionally: "You really frighten me when you look at me that way," or "I get very charged up when you do that." With such remarks you can encourage your partner to do the kind of things that "get to you" and will, in turn, make your own performance more exciting.

Remember, you want your acting partner to surprise you. You also want your partner to get under your skin, to annoy you, to interest you, to unnerve you, to frighten you, to attract you, or to disgust you. Intellectual analysis, well-intentioned and brilliant though it might be, will tend to level out the emotions and eliminate the surprises in your scene. Rehearsal, remember, is "harrowing." It should plow up the field, not smooth it down.

At this point, you can also begin to talk of the staging elements of your eventual presentation. Where should the scene be set? What props should be used? What should you wear? These are decisions you must reach together, preferably after some experimenting during rehearsals. Gradually you will add these elements to the rehearsal process.

Between rehearsal periods—and sometimes during short rehearsal breaks—you should go over your GOTEsheet by yourself, adding to and changing or refining your character's goals as the rehearsals seem to suggest. The rehearsal period is an opportunity for experiment, and nothing that comes out of the study should be treated as sacrosanct—particularly if it does not prove stimulating or effective in rehearsal. During rehearsal you will certainly want to try out various tactics: Which ones work best on your acting partner? If he or she proves impassive to your threats, or immune to your charms, don't simply complain: Try new threats or new charms, and keep trying until you find tactics that actually work. Sure, you can "direct" your partner outside the scene and force him or her to fake the sort of response you want—but how much better it is to find the action that will provoke a real response. If you find your partner difficult, all the better; it will simply make you work harder within the scene, which will translate as acting intensity.

Acting, like life, is not easy; and acting that represents life should not be easy. The most common fault of beginning actors is to try to stage-manage a scene by agreement ("I'll raise my fist and you run toward the door," "I'll smile and you throw your arms around me and give me a kiss") rather than really working hard to make their intended character victories come about. In life, the other guy doesn't always agree—not, at least, without some struggle on your part.

Gradually your rehearsal will take on the form of the finished scene. Some actors feel comfortable only when every gesture, every inflection, and every pause is rehearsed to repeatable perfection. Others like to keep the scene much more fluid and improvisational—particularly insofar as the movement, timing, and emotional levels are concerned. For a fully produced play, repeatability is a crucial factor, since lighting cues, scenery shifts, and special effects must be timed precisely to your actions. In a classroom presentation, on the other hand, it is almost always best to keep the scene fairly fluid, concentrating on the vitality and intensity of the character-to-character interaction rather than the fine points of performance finesse.

How much rehearsal do you need? The professional rule of thumb is one hour per minute: that is, an hour of rehearsal for each minute of stage time. A standard two-hour play, therefore, would normally be given three weeks (120 hours) of rehearsal at a professional theatre. Consequently, you should expect to schedule, for your five-minute acting scene, about five hours of rehearsal. But a produced play requires attention to many technical details that are rarely encountered in the classroom scene. It is not unreasonable, therefore, to plan a rehearsal schedule of three one-hour periods for a five-minute scene, provided that the actors do their individual study beforehand and are off book at least midway through the *first* rehearsal.

You should be aware that a great deal of professional film and television acting, some of the highest quality, is performed with virtually *no* formal rehearsal. Indeed, in many cases, actors in film/television media are hired for one day only, making any real rehearsal simply impossible. Even in live theatre, understudies frequently perform publicly without any rehearsal. Rehearsal can be most useful to an actor, but there is no absolute minimum length of rehearsal time that must precede performance. Rather, the rehearsals should be used to build the basis for strongly pursued stage interactions and to create the basic structure of a staged acting scene.

Rehearsal Alternatives

Repetitive rehearsals are not, of course, the only means of preparing for your performance.

Improvisation—where you and your partner enact your parts, inventing lines and movement rather than relying on the memorized text—is a time-honored way of immersing yourself in the scene's situation and developing the intensity of the relationship without regard to the precise plotting or character development of the script. You may choose to improvise the situations that precede your scene or follow it. Improvisation takes its own direction and gives you the opportunity to explore the characters in the fullest possible range. Often, particularly in a scene set in a remote period, improvisation unlocks the deepest meaning of a scene's emotional conflict and makes you aware of the depth of feeling your character experiences.

Massage provides an opportunity to get close to your partner physically and lose your natural inhibitions about touching and being touched—inhibitions that can stand in the way of developing a strong relationship onstage. With your partner lying down, gently "stretching" his or her head, limbs, muscle mass, fingers, and toes is an excellent actor massage that helps to align the spine and promote a more relaxed intimacy that can lead to emotionally vivid acting (see Exercise 1–2). Mutual massage can also break down tension and establish trust in its place. Trust is a valuable ingredient in any scene.

Partying, believe it or not, is also a good preparation for acting. Acting is serious business, of course, but it is not necessarily a businesslike business, and establishing personal rapport and sympathy is often critical to a scene's success. Partying cannot replace rehearsals, but getting together just for the fun of it can supplement more serious work perfectly. Sensing your partner's joys and excitements helps you share in his or her idealism and expectations; it helps you to know your partner as a whole person and interact with him or her more effectively and with deeper feeling. Actors, of course, are not necessarily any more gregarious than the rest of the population, but long-lasting professional friendships seem to be particularly characteristic of the acting society.

◆ E X E R C I S E   10–1

The Gentleman Caller II

Before beginning this exercise, you should have read *The Glass Menagerie* and memorized the Gentleman Caller scene in Exercise 9–1.

Now select a partner and study and rehearse the scene for class presentation. Between rehearsals, revise your GOTEsheet and make notes on how you feel the scene is developing. Experiment with the concept of shaping the scene from within—that is, try to get the most out of your acting partner while rehearsing, not by telling her or him how to act the other role. After three to five hour-long rehearsals, and one or more "alternative" rehearsals, present the scene. How was it different from the unrehearsed first-time presentation? Was it better in rehearsals than in the class presentation? (The usual answer is yes. But you will learn to overcome self-consciousness as you become accustomed to acting in front of an audience.) More important, were you able to use the rehearsals to improve your understanding—and hence your acting—of your role?

Summary

Rehearsal, the public part of scene preparation, comes from a word implying repetition and digging; rehearsals are opportunities to go over your part several times, exploring and experimenting as you go. Rehearsals should enable you to slide into your role rather than jumping into a fully theatrical performance, and your rehearsals should encourage improvisational exploration of your character-to-character relationship. You should make no attempt to direct your partner in rehearsals, but should try to shape the scene by acting it. There is no rule governing the number of rehearsals that are necessary, but three to five hours for a five-minute scene is a good starting point. Alternative methods of rehearsing include open improvisation and other person-to-person interactions tangent to the actual material.

L E S S O N

11

Staging the Scene

Stage Directions

In a produced play, the staging is generally initiated by the director, and the setting is fixed before rehearsals begin.

In a scene for class, *you* will determine where the scene is set, what sort of furniture and props will come into play, where the doors will be, and what the movement will be like. You will also create the behavior of the action: the laughing, drinking, smoking, walking, standing, and sitting that may or may not be particularly specified by the text.

You should know that the published acting editions of most plays contain stage directions added by the original stage manager, which do not carry the authority of the playwright. You need not follow them; in fact, you should feel free to disregard *all* stage directions except those that are explicitly required to further the plot. You are certainly not going to have the Broadway set for your scene, and the original stage directions were chosen for their effectiveness in the context of the original production's scenery, lighting, and overall stylization. In your classroom presentation, the staging should simply liberate and enhance your acting. You should cross out the written stage directions (and stage descriptions), therefore, and start afresh.

Creating the Locale

The tendency among beginners is to have two characters sitting or standing somewhere talking to each other. There may be scenes where this arrangement is the best one possible, but they are rare. In the first place, "somewhere" is just too abstract for the actor's necessary sense of specificity. Where is this somewhere? What's there?

An interior scene can provide a host of locales that provide opportunities and obstacles that will shape your acting. Where are the doors? Where do they lead? Who might be coming in from each? What objects are there? A scene set in a kitchen can, for example, be played at the sink, at a table, by the refrigerator door, at the silverware drawer, on the floor, against the wall, or in various combinations of these locations. Which one or ones make the scene's interaction more intense? More believable? More confrontational? Look at this kitchen scene from Arthur Miller's *Death of a Salesman:*

WILLY: I hope we didn't get stuck on that machine.

LINDA: They got the biggest ads of any of them!

WILLY: I know, it's a fine machine. What else?

LINDA: Well, there's nine-sixty for the washing machine. And for the vacuum cleaner there's three and a half due on the fifteenth. Then the roof, you got twenty-one dollars remaining.

WILLY: It don't leak, does it?

LINDA: No, they did a wonderful job. Then you owe Frank for the carburetor.

WILLY: I'm not going to pay that man! That goddam Chevrolet, they ought to prohibit the manufacture of that car!

LINDA: Well, you owe him three and a half. And odds and ends, comes to around a hundred and twenty dollars by the fifteenth.

WILLY: A hundred and twenty dollars! My God, if business don't pick up I don't know what I'm gonna do!

LINDA: Well, next week you'll do better.

WILLY: Oh, I'll knock 'em dead next week. I'll go to Hartford. I'm very well liked in Hartford. You know, the trouble is, Linda, people don't seem to take to me.

This lovely scene—seemingly innocuous dialog culminating in a shocking revelation and reversal—can take on many different colors depending on where in the kitchen the actors choose to play it. Suppose Willy is fixing himself a cup of coffee, or Linda is polishing the knives, or Willy drinking a glass of milk, or Linda sitting at the table going over the bills. Suppose there is a drawer to be slammed shut, a drink to be put down a bit too sharply, a knife to be handled a bit too longingly. What happens if Willy is sitting and Linda standing—or the other way around? Suppose Willy kicks the refrigerator (the "machine" he mentions in his first line), hurts his toe, and sits— what response will that stimulate in Linda? If Linda walks out of the room while saying "next week you'll do better," what response will that stimulate in Willy? There are no right or wrong answers to these questions, no right or wrong ways to stage the scene. But there are self-stagings that will encourage stronger acting from both partners.

You should understand, of course, that the architecture and furniture involved in this scene need not be remotely realistic in appearance. The refrigerator can be a wood block or the back of a chair, but Willy can still kick at it and hurt his toe, providing the obstacle that will make his scene vivid and his acting more fully fleshed. Just let the class know, in advance, that "the back of this chair is a refrigerator," and then act as though it were: That's part of acting, too.

Movement and Stage Business

Movement is not essential in any scene, and movement inserted in a scene merely to liven things up does more harm than good. But natural movement that comes out of the scene's situation, and out of the interplay of the characters, can evoke stronger, fuller, and deeper acting from both partners. Movement, because it involves the whole body—muscles, skeleton, internal organs—makes the actor organically active and involves the actor bodily in acting a role—and embodying a character.

Moreover, movement creates a general context for the acting of a play's transitions, discoveries, climaxes, and reversals. Learn Willy's last line in the above scene, for example, and give it while jogging. Inevitably, you will stop jogging—or at least change the rhythm of your jogging—as you start to say, "You know, the trouble is, Linda . . ." Jogging would (probably) be inappropriate behavior for Willy in this scene, of course, but drying dishes, playing solitaire, or flipping a coin wouldn't be.

Movement also creates opportunities for physical contact and interaction that would not occur if the actors simply decided to sit down and play the scene "in place." Willy jogging with Linda would have to reach out and stop her if he decided to stop himself. If Willy were playing solitaire, Linda could help him make a move ("Well, next week you'll do better") and Willy could grab her arm ("Oh, I'll knock 'em dead next week") and then let go of it ("You know, the trouble is . . ."). The physical interaction will stimulate emotional interaction and give contour to the evolving relationship between the characters.

The importance of finding good stage business has long been recognized by directors; it can prove immensely helpful to actors as well. Stage business —the seemingly minor and unconscious physical actions of the character— provides a pattern of behavior that becomes the baseline of a scene, and usually a baseline that is more interesting than two actors facing each other and talking. Well-chosen stage business has several beneficial functions: It relaxes you because it starts you "doing something"; it tones you up because it keeps you busy; it keeps you mentally alert because it doubles your focus; and it intensifies your responses, which are reflected unconsciously in your stage business activity. If Linda is adding up figures in an account book in the *Death of a Salesman* scene, the way she fingers her pencil will reflect her growing anxiety. If Willy is nursing a cup of coffee, his divided interest between drinking his coffee (something good) and paying his bills (something bad) will keep his feelings jumbled, and his reactions will be far more volatile (and interesting) than if he simply listens to Linda in a stupor.

One of the best things about stage business is that it makes stillness, when it occurs, pay off. When Willy stops jogging, or stops drying dishes, or when Linda puts her pencil down and quietly looks at him, both actors and audience will feel the depth of the moment far more than if both actors were static to begin with. So try to find appropriate and dramatically stimulating stage business possibilities for your scene. How will your acting develop if you play the scene at the piano? At the bar? At the barber shop? In the men's room? At the basketball court? While walking? While exercising? While playing solitaire? While getting dressed?

Interesting Positions

In the earliest days of Greek sculpture—the era art historians call archaic or preclassical—statues of humans showed the figure erect, facing forward, one foot about six inches ahead of the other. As sculpture developed, the human form was shown in more and more dynamic positions, until by the late Renaissance it was depicted in all its writhing, twisted possibilities. The same sort of development happens in acting. The beginning actor is usually stiff and adopts rigid, symmetrical, square-shouldered positions, often sitting or standing primly, facing his or her partner head-on. You must learn to break down this stiffness. Even positions fixed by the situation (a witness in a witness chair, a family at the dinner table, Prometheus chained to his rock) can be explored with an eye to the possible dynamics of your physical positioning.

In an acting class, you are usually limited to the furniture on hand for the staging of your scenes. A sofa is a wonderful luxury for that purpose, for it permits thousands of positions: lying, sitting, sitting on the sofa's arms or back, and innumerable combinations of these. An armchair also offers a great many possibilities. But even without these, you should be able to use furniture, props, and arrangements of your scene locale to create opportunities for positions that are physically interesting and challenging. What happens if your partner's head is in your lap? Or you are sitting on a chair while your partner lies on the floor (beneath you) and then rises to stand (above you)?

It is almost always effective, in staging a two-person scene, to have the principal targets of your attention on opposite sides of you, at least at key moments; this is so that you can turn from one to the other. Such turning is an action in itself, both a turn *away* from someone or something and a turn *toward* someone or something else. And, as turning also shows the audience more of your face, it also displays your feeling: whether you are turning sadly, happily, angrily, fearfully, or in a state of shock. Having two or more targets of attention, and having them widely spaced around you, leads your acting toward bold physical moves and stimulates an active movement contour for your performance. If your acting partner, the ringing phone, and door offering you escape are all bunched together on your left, you'll be quite limited in choosing where to turn or what to do.

During a class break, if you have one, or after an exercise when your classmates have not yet returned to their seats, look at the positions people take when just talking or lolling around. Aren't they interesting? Generally, their positions are very interesting and much more dynamic (even in repose) than the positions these same people take in their first acting scenes. Our bodies are *naturally* dynamic and interesting, but we naturally stiffen into "sit up straight" positions when we find ourselves on public display. You should learn to transcend this tendency in your own work.

Reaching the Audience

One of the major responsibilities of the stage director is to block (stage) the play in order to make the lines and the plot very clear to the audience. This means taking into account the size of the auditorium, the orientation of the stage to the house, the vocal projection of the actors, the lighting, and myriad other factors. In an acting class, this responsibility is yours. Certainly the class audience must be able to see and hear your scene adequately if they and the instructor are to give you a valuable critique. Your job in staging your scene is to make it reach the audience.

Try to ascertain, first of all, what the instructor expects for the physical orientation of the scene. Some instructors like to have scenes performed in the round, others on a proscenium stage or in a proscenium format; still others will permit you to place the audience as you wish. In any event, this factor is your primary consideration. How far away is the audience going to be? In the scene exercise, how important is full projection? If there is a chance that, at this stage of your work, full projection can be achieved only with a loss of honesty and realism, which should you go for? Ask your instructor for guidance.

In a proscenium format—that is, with the audience on one side of you— your staging pattern should keep your face more on the downstage (audience-facing) side than on the upstage side. There are many ways of doing this without being blatant about it. You can enter the scene diagonally from the rear. You can seat yourselves at the upstage sides of a square table placed diagonally to the audience. You can loll about on a sofa placed diagonally toward the audience with your head on the upstage side and your partner sitting on the upstage part of the sofa back and facing you (and then falling into your lap). You can look out an imaginary window facing into the audience. Your partner can come to you, put his or her arms around you as you both look out, first facing straight ahead and then turning to each other. These are all standard directorial techniques that you can adopt to get your scene out to the audience while you are playing very intensely and honestly with each other; they are usually preferable, from an acting point of view, to simply standing face to face with your partner throughout the scene.

◆ E X E R C I S E   11–1

Setting the Stage

Memorize and rehearse either the Gentleman Caller scene from *The Glass Menagerie* or the Willy–Linda scene from *Death of a Salesman*. Arrange your set with an eye to the discussions in this chapter, and prepare the scene accordingly.

Now restage the same scene in a completely different setting—for example:

1. At a piano

2. On beach towels at a beach

3. At an outdoor café

4. At a ballet barre

5. On a living room couch

Begin the staging with Willy or Laura actively doing something with regard to the "set" environment—playing the piano, applying suntan oil, doing exercises at the barre, writing a diary entry—and Linda or Jim doing something quite different and unrelated. Then stage the scene by exploring all possibilities for movement, business, physical positions and dynamics, and projection. Have a friend watch and comment.

Then return to the author's setting and restage the scene in its "proper" environment. Have you learned anything from going outside the standard set that can help you upon your return? Probably so.

Ask yourself: What positions give you the greatest sense of involvement? Of freedom? Of power? Of rapport with your partner? These are the positions you will want to find in your acting scenes. What positions make you feel inhibited? Self-conscious? Tense? Isolated? Stiff? These are positions to avoid.

Summary

Your self-staging should not be an attempt to give a final staging patina to your scene. Rather, it should create a movement pattern that brings out the best acting from you: the most vigorous struggle to achieve your victory, the most provocative tactics, the most enthusiastic pursuit of your character's goals. Staging for your scene should be chosen mainly because it stimulates *you*: It makes you work harder—it requires that you be more forceful, more seductive, more amusing, or more inspirational—to get what your character wants.

Choices

The Need for Choices

The exciting actor differs from the unexciting actor chiefly because of the quality of her or his acting choices: the choices of goals to pursue and tactics to employ. For these are choices, not givens, and they demand the actor's own imagination as much as they require script analysis and research.

The actor's choices are not always apparent in the lines of a play. In fact, sometimes the choices are not even mentioned in the lines. For example:

VERSHININ: If they are not giving us any tea, let's at least philosophize.

TUSENBACH: Yes, let's. What about?

VERSHININ: What about? Let's dream . . . for example, of the life that will come after us in two or three hundred years.

TUSENBACH: Well? After us they will fly in balloons, styles of coats will change, they will discover the sixth sense, perhaps, and develop it; but life will remain quite the same, a difficult life, mysterious and happy. And after a thousand years, man will be sighing the same: "Ah, how hard it is to live!" and meanwhile, exactly the same as now, he will be afraid of death and not want to die.

VERSHININ: How shall I put it? It seems to me everything on earth must change little by little and is already changing before our eyes. In two or three hundred, eventually a thousand years—it's not a matter of time—

95

a happy life will come. We won't share in that life, of course, but we are living for it now, working, well—suffering; we are creating it—and in that alone lies the purpose of our being and, if you like, our happiness.

(Anton Chekhov, *Three Sisters*)

This conversation between two young military officers seems straightforward enough, but if actors simply played the superficial philosophizing, they would miss the point of the scene entirely—which is that both officers are performing for the women they love, who are listening in the background! Tusenbach is trying to persuade Irina (who is playing cards elsewhere in the room) that his life is terribly hard without her; Vershinin is suggesting to Masha—without saying it in words—that she could find happiness with him. This is, then, not a scene of philosophizing at all, but of romance—even though the romantic partners don't speak to each other.

This understanding should dictate Vershinin's and Tusenbach's tone of voice, deportment, gestures, smiles, enthusiasm, wittiness, bravura, sensitivity, and stage business. And yet none of this appears in Chekhov's stage directions! Thus the actors must choose whether to be sitting, standing, dancing, moving, laughing, singing, joking, moralizing, parodying, pontificating, balancing on one foot, smoking a cigar, looking around the room, or whatever combination of those and other choices will provide the basic *inner and outer* action of the scene, for which the spoken lines are merely a convenient vehicle.

Good Choices

Good choices are bold, scary, and exciting. They are choices you can pursue vigorously and with enthusiasm. They involve other characters as well as yourself. They are both psychological and physical: They involve your mind and body and your partner's mind and body. Good choices stimulate your own emotions when you play them with your partner.

Bad choices are safe, sane, and ordinary. They do not tax your feelings; they provoke in you no joy; they neither frighten nor absorb you. Purely intellectual choices involve neither your feelings nor your body. They are easy and pedestrian. They are self-contained, involving no one but you.

Good choices might be:

I want her to love me.

I want him to cry.

I want him to wet his pants.

She might kill me.

She might kill herself.

I want her to kill herself.

These are not exaggerations. Plays are about moments of crisis, not casual conversations about ordinary day-to-day events. In the theatre, even seemingly casual conversations, such as Vershinin and Tusenbach's above, will lead in to life-changing decisions. (Because of what happens in that scene, Vershinin will have an affair with Masha, and Tusenbach will die before the play is over.)

Bad choices might be:

I want to express myself.

I want her to understand my position.

I want to persuade him to agree with me.

I worry that he won't agree with me.

I am afraid of losing.

I want to win.

I want him to admire me.

These are bad choices not because they are wrong, but because they are not very provocative—to you, the actor, or to the audience. They are general rather than specific, intellectual rather than psychological or physical, and self-contained rather than interactive.

As you can see, sex and violence predominate in the good choices; rational decision-making predominates in the bad choices. Because of the perennial furor over sex and violence in the cinema and on television, it might seem ironic to focus on them as good choices for the actor. But the furor has obscured the obvious: *All* great plays involve sex or violence—or, more likely yet, sex *and* violence. This means not only the great tragedies— *Prometheus Bound, Medea, King Lear,* and so forth—but also great comedies, farces, and melodramas; or, for that matter, bad comedies, farces, and melodramas. Indeed, the theatre was created to help humankind come to terms with life's big mysteries: the ecstasy of sex, the terror of violence— and sometimes the terror of sex, the ecstasy of violence—and for an actor to avoid these mysteries is to miss not only the opportunity of acting but the whole point of the theatre.

In making your acting choices, therefore, *always look for a sexual interest,* and *always look for a potential terror.* Sexual interest includes romance, success, dominance, and even wealth, all of which can have sexual components. Terror includes embarrassment, confusion, humiliation, and pain, all of which have a terrifying component. Make choices that inspire your feelings, that get under your (and your acting partner's) skin. Choices that are merely rational—no matter how rational—will not lead to an exciting performance.

Choose to find your partner interesting. Your partner is an interesting person. Did you know that? Often we don't even notice. We think "He (she) is 'just' my acting partner." But that acting partner is a caring, feeling, fearing, loving person—sometimes frustrated, sometimes beautiful, sometimes explosive. Your partner is capable of violence, brilliance, panic, and schizophrenia; your partner *could* become your lifelong lover or your bitterest enemy or both.

These statements are facts. It is up to you not to dispute them but to work them into your acting relationship. Finding your partner fascinating, or scary, or adorable, or exhilarating is a *choice,* and a choice you must learn to make.

You must choose, therefore, to find your partner interesting: to make him or her a worthy opponent if the scene involves opposition, or an alluring sex object if the scene involves sexual attraction, or a frightening menace if the scene involves terror. Only if you give your acting partner the potential for love, for violence, for brilliance, and for explosive surprise will you truly get involved with him or her on a personal level.

There are many ways to discover how interesting/fascinating/scary your partner really is. Conversation is the most obvious, particularly personal conversation about growing up, about one's plans for the future, that sort of thing. It is important to see your acting partner as an evolving person like yourself, not as a fixed stereotype. Your acting partner has a past and a future, she or he is in flux, is changing, is still an *unfinished* human being. The more you realize this, the easier it will be to play dynamically with your partner, to try to work your magic on him or her and allow his or her magic to work on you.

Study your partner while you rehearse your scene. How does she or he react to your threats in the scene? To your smiles? To your touch on her or his neck? You don't need to come up with answers to these questions. Indeed, they are fundamentally unanswerable in a real relationship. You need only to search them out and to recognize the mystery, complexity, and fascinating profundity of your acting partner. Even in a seemingly commonplace scene, this awareness will prove beneficial.

Choose goals that excite you personally and physically. The audience will never be excited for you if you aren't excited for yourself. Remember, you are not telling or describing a story, you are *embodying* it; and your

> HITLER AND JESUS
>
> *What actors can do without lecturing is show that in each of us there is Hitler and Jesus, and if you are a truly gifted actor you can find that in you, and bring it out, and say, "See, we share this."*
>
> RICHARD DREYFUSS

body must share in the enthusiasm of your pursuit. Imagine winning your goal in the scene: Would winning make you want to jump up and down? No? Then you have made a poor choice.

Choose fears that frighten you personally and physically. Does it upset you to think that your partner might turn his back on you? How much? Does it upset you to think that your partner might stick pins under your fingernails? How much?

Which imagined event stimulates the most revulsion in you? The most physical nausea? That is the most powerful image to choose. Using each of these images, play the following line to your partner: "I don't want to see you again." Which image made your voice quiver? Which choice most successfully embodies a touch of fear in the line?

Choose to use everything you've got. In going for your goals, and in challenging your fears, show us every usable thing inside yourself: your capacity for both total love and extreme cruelty, your spiritual hunger, your reckless craziness. Don't hide behind shallow politeness or tentative efforts. Let us see the demon in you, and the child.

Choose to touch your partner. It is equally logical to touch or not to touch your partner; both choices can be defended in a theoretical analysis. But the best acting choice usually is to touch, out of either anger or affection, or, even better, a mixture of both.

Touching your partner is both physical business and personal contact; it usually intensifies the rapport between actors and deepens the concentration of both partners. More important, it makes *you* feel more involved in the scene. Therefore, in rehearsing a scene, try to find a reason to

rub your partner's shoulders or back;

stroke or tousle your partner's hair;

playfully poke your partner with your toe;

take your partner's hand;

grab your partner's wrist;

embrace (hug) your partner;

cuddle your partner from behind;

slap your partner on the shoulder;

reach for your partner's neck.

All of these touching actions should be noninvasive; you mustn't construe your acting assignment as a blanket permission to take sexual liberties with anyone or to engage in unrehearsed roughhousing. Still, actors must be prepared to be touched, to hug, to kiss, and to engage in staged physical combat (with appropriate training) as part of their artistic work. Your instructor will help you set appropriate boundaries for this touching if you so require.

Touching your partner need not be overtly sexual, and in most scenes not directly connected with sexual overtures (a brother-to-brother scene, for example), touching is obviously a matter of sharing friendship rather than soliciting romance. But touching is so fundamental to intense human relationships that it is invariably useful in acting; there are few acting scenes that cannot be improved simply by directing the actors to touch each other in some way during the crucial exchange. Touching the neck, which is both an erogenous zone and a point of extreme physical vulnerability, can by itself triple the emotional involvement of both actors in a scene representing, for example, a lover's quarrel. Try it.

Choose to make contact. Beginning actors often tend to look away, move away, stare at the floor or ceiling, or turn their backs on their partners at a scene's crucial moments. This behavior comes partly from a mistaken sense of what "looks theatrical" and partly from shyness and uneasiness. It is partly a holdover from adolescence, when major confrontations were avoided by running to your room and slamming the door. In acting, you should never "slam the door."

When someone shouts at you face to face, your blood pumps faster, even if you know it's only a scene in acting class. That moment when your blood surges forth is a great acting moment; you mustn't waste it in a meaningless pause while you turn your back and compose your response. Beginning actors continually overrate the effectiveness of long pauses, even-tempered responses, and deeply furrowed brows.

Similarly, when someone smiles engagingly at you, making you feel suffused by human warmth of a sort mere stage directions cannot create, you are in a particularly wonderful emotional state for acting.

It is precisely at these moments—when you are a bit flustered, a bit moved, not entirely sure of yourself—that you should maintain eye contact with your partner and say your line. These moments are fleeting; they may last only a split second, but these moments of deep personal contact provide the human vulnerability that makes acting a lively art.

If you retreat from your partner at that moment, by closing your eyes, staring at the floor, or turning your back in heroic defiance (which usually reads as adolescent pique), you have retreated from the most unique and exciting part of acting: your raw feelings and your own particular sensitivity. Please don't slam the door on yourself in this way. When someone shouts in your face, shout back, or try to laugh, or cry, or hug the so-and-so, or all of the above! Don't turn your back; to do so is to turn your back on acting itself.

Choose to try to smile. Most people in most person-to-person situations want to be there, want to be liked by the person they are talking with, want to encourage the other person to be friendly. Consequently, most people smile much of the time. Lovers breaking up smile—or try to—as do quarreling siblings, labor negotiators, and conspiring executives. To smile while quarreling gives the quarrel a hidden dimension and suggests the possibility that, at the deepest level, both partners seek a reconciliation. This suggestion is both realistic and dramatically effective because it creates sympathy for the characters. Then, when the smile can no longer be maintained—when it struggles against the tears—your scene develops a powerful poignancy. "I want to smile" is one of life's most universal intentions, since it means "I want to be in a situation that pleases me." Everybody wants that, and therefore it should be one of your goal choices.

Choose to hurry your partner. A good pace usually means a rapid pace; when reviewers dislike a play, they usually say that it was "slow" or that it "dragged." But good pace doesn't mean that you have to speak rapidly. What it does mean is that you must be driving hard toward your goal, and that drive means you not only want it but you want it *now.*

"Pacing up a scene" means that you should try to hurry your partner along somewhat, that you should need to win and win quickly. Taking a pause before your speeches—trying to build up feeling before you speak—not only wastes time, but shows that you're "only acting." In real life, people don't try to build up their emotions before they speak. They speak and then find that they have built up emotion!

Thus, in your preparation, choose to find time's winged chariot at your back. Your scene must have a sense of urgency. Sweep your partner off his or her feet; leave your partner speechless with your dazzling argument; but don't plod along with the facts, or indulge in your feelings, or pose nobly and thoughtfully in the glow of your own magnificence.

Choose to be loud. Nothing infuriates the audience like not hearing, and you certainly know that it is unwise to infuriate the audience, even for the best of reasons.

There are reasons to be loud and reasons to be soft. If you are clever enough, you can always find both. Choose reasons to be loud—at least loud to the point that you can be heard clearly from anywhere in the room.

In scenes where you must be quiet so as not to be overheard by the people upstairs, choose to make the ceiling four feet thick.

In scenes where you tell someone that you love him or her, say it in a way that suggests you don't care if the whole world hears—indeed, say it so that the whole world *does* hear.

In scenes when your anger can be expressed either coolly or explosively, choose to express it explosively.

Remember, you can justify the opposite choice perfectly well. But in most cases, that would justify bad acting; you would win the battle and lose the war. In addition to being heard by the audience, the "loud" choices stimulate more feeling from your acting partner, which will return more stimulation to you. The cool, quiet, logical choice, eminently justifiable, leads to uninteresting theatre most of the time, yet it is a seductively safe way to play a scene, particularly for the beginning actor. Try the bolder, louder, explosive choices first. They are harder to get out but more liberating. Later, perhaps with a friend acting as a director to guide you, they may be pruned back. Bold choices taken in rehearsal can prove wonderfully enlightening even if toned down by the time of performance.

Choose to do something stupid. This is not facetious advice. Often when I (as a coach) feel a scene is plodding lamely along, I suddenly order the actor to jump up and down, or do a dance step, or sing a song. Or I holler, "Do something stupid!" Though this command seems to have no immediate relevance to the dialog, and though it always makes the actor acutely uncomfortable, it more often than not stimulates a deeper level of involvement and creativity. Perhaps it's because it reminds the actor that intense human interaction (which is what the scene is about) is always uncomfortable and awkward, though acting may not be, and this instruction brings the awkwardness to the fore—and with it, a level of unplanned reality. Perhaps it's also because "doing something stupid" surprises your acting partner and makes the ensuing interaction more nervy, open-ended, and unpredictable. And, finally, perhaps it's because all great theatre involves an element of the absurd, the awkward, the final chaos of life itself. Probably all three factors come into play, and you can make them come into play in your own scenes if, from time to time, you make the exciting choice to "do something stupid."

◆ E X E R C I S E   12–1

Bold Choices

Study your GOTEsheet for the Laura–Jim scene, or the Willy–Linda scene, or any other scene you have prepared. Do your listed goals really stimulate you psychologically and physically? Do your fears make you cringe? Are your tactics boldly chosen? Are your expectations vivid and exciting? Did you, in playing those scenes, work to find your partner fascinating? Did you touch your partner? Was the quest for victory an urgent one? Were you able to smile? Were you able to shout?

BOLD CHOICES

I'm a reasonably calm and quiet-spoken person, until I'm onstage, at which point—to the moon!

JOHN LITHGOW

Go back to one of those scenes and rewrite your GOTEsheet with bolder choices. Then play the scene with your partner, implementing those choices. Find points in the scene—mere moments—when you can be explosive or desperate, or where you can reach out and touch someone. Making bold choices is something that you will learn to do a small step at a time, but those steps can be very important in your development as an actor.

After playing the scene, ask your partner whether she or he was more stimulated, more frightened, more attracted, more emotionally *involved* with you than before. Chances are the answer will be yes. And if your partner was more involved, chances are you were also.

Summary

The quality of your acting is determined by the choices you make, what you choose to play. Good choices, which are bold and interpersonal, stimulate the emotions of both you and your partner. Bad choices may be logical, but they are unstimulating emotionally and psychologically. Good choices usually involve implied sex and violence, which invoke humankind's most urgent lusts and terrors. Choose to find your partner fascinating. Choose goals and terrors that affect you personally. Choose to touch your partner, to quicken the pace of your scene, to confront your partner face to face, and to find reasons to be loud rather than quiet or "cool" and, on occasion, to do something downright stupid.

L E S S O N

13

Performing

Stage Fright

The time comes when the study is complete, the rehearsals are over, the choices are made: Now you perform your scene publicly.

For most actors, tension, nervousness, and stage fright threaten to cancel out the careful preparation. Even veteran actors experience stress in performance, sometimes extreme stress. Fear of the audience, fear of criticism, fear of rejection, fear of forgetting your lines, and fear of looking foolish are the inhibiting factors that may not even surface until the moment of performance, when their appearance can become immediately debilitating.

How can you avoid this fear? First of all, you should recognize that a certain amount of tension is inevitable and may even be desirable. Many actors reach the fullest level of performance only with the added "danger" of a public audience. Even without consciously holding back in rehearsal, many actors find that the presence of a live audience stimulates them to let go. The audience can spur an actor's power and belief, much as the cheering crowd can intensify an athlete's performance or a speechmaker's eloquence. There is nothing wrong with making use of the added edge of excitement that an audience provides.

But stage fright—the numbing fear of evaluation by others—can just as easily dampen your enthusiasm, inhibit your movement, constrict your voice, and paralyze your reflexes. Scenes rehearsed with great passion and fervor can dry up in performance and become mere shadows of their former selves. It is useless to complain that "it was better in rehearsal." Your job is to learn how to make it better in performance.

Classroom Performance

A good classroom performance requires preparation. First, take the time to set your scene properly: Put the furniture in the proper place, decide where the (imaginary) door is, where the stove is, and what real properties are represented by substitute items. Insofar as necessary, the audience also should be informed of these requirements of the scene. Then your scene should be announced, quite briefly, with any essential details not obvious from the scene itself explained.

Then you and your partner should go to your opening positions and *prepare.*

The duration of that preparation varies according to your instructor's guidelines. Some actors like to take a very long time—a minute or more. It is to your advantage, however, to learn to make your preparation in as brief a period as possible—for example, five to ten seconds. Though brief, your preparation should be comprehensive. It should include

- A moment of sheer physical release, perhaps by shaking out your arms, kicking your legs, doing a full body bend, or pounding your fist into your hand.

- A quick study of your partner, bringing up what you find most fascinating/scary about him or her.

- A flash on what *excites* you in the situation of the scene. What's the *best* that can happen to your character?

- A flash on what *terrifies* you in the situation of the scene. What's the *worst* that can happen to your character?

- A final GOTEcheck, perhaps in this order: "I'm gonna (EXPECTATION!) win this (GOAL!) by doing this and this (TACTICS) to him/her (OTHER). And I'm gonna win it now!"

Running through this little litany will hurtle you out of your own person (as an acting student) and into the persona of the scene. During this quick run-through, you will enter the play, realize the excitement the situation holds for you, see the potential for joy and pain your character faces, and see your acting partner not as a fellow student but as a character for or with whom you have a deep need or quest.

Concentration on the other character, and what you (your character) want that other character to do or to believe, is the best cure for stage fright. That concentration focuses your energy, liberates your resources, organizes your choices. It will help you to forget the audience and to shape the scene from within, not from without. It will help to eliminate your

> ### WHAT MY MIND'S ON
>
> *I'm never thinking about motivation, or family history, or any of that stuff when I'm working. I'm thinking about, "Why is he looking at me like that? Why is his eyebrow standing up? Is he lying to me?" Whatever it is that I'm going through with that character, with that other actor, that's what my mind's on, not style or background or anything else.*
>
> MARY STEENBURGEN

"director's eye" that continually stands outside your role, an eye that can only confuse you and dissipate your character's energy.

Things to ask yourself during the performance are not "How am I doing?" or "What is my next line?" but:

- ◆ Is my partner's face flushed?

- ◆ Is my partner (my partner's character) telling the truth?

- ◆ Does he love me?

- ◆ Will she succumb?

- ◆ Must I press harder? Softer? Do I have him on the run?

- ◆ Can I make her listen better? Understand better? Understand *me* better? Care more? Like me better?

The more you concentrate on your partner's character, the less you will be aware of the audience. The more you ask yourself real questions about your partner's character, the more you will be involved in the scene and the more you will create a real situation.

Play for Results— In the Other Character!

Actors often ask whether, in class work, they should concentrate on results or on the process of acting. The answer might be confusing unless we realize that there are two interpretations of the word *results* in this context.

One is the result as seen by the audience: in other words, theatrical effectiveness. It is almost certainly a mistake for a beginning actor to directly attempt to deliver a sophisticated theatrical result in this sense of the word —that is, to deliver a full-fledged and crisply polished professional performance. Among other reasons, it just can't be done—not without sets, lights, a

THE GIVE AND TAKE

Put all your attention on the other person, which frees you from any self-consciousness. If you can see the experience they're *having —What's their face doing? What are they feeling?—that's truly listening and responding. That's the give and take, and the aliveness, that I value.*

CHRISTINE LAHTI

director, a supporting professional cast, several weeks of rehearsal, and, perhaps most of all, a "real" (and demanding) theatre audience. Better, in class, to concentrate on the process of developing a role through making good choices and through your active involvement with the goals, tactics, and expectations of your character.

But some elements of process include going for certain results: results as seen not in the audience but in the other actor or actors.

In your scene, if your goal is to make the other character love you, try during the scene to make the other actor love you. If you are trying to scare the other character, scare the actor. Try to create real, physical results. Try to make the other actor sweat, relax, smile, laugh, cry, or vomit. Try to make his or her heart palpitate or knees weaken, either in fear or in adoration. *Look for results from the other actor, not from the audience.* If you generate a response from your acting partner, you will also create an impact on the audience watching you.

Actors legitimately differ on how much on-the-spot spontaneity should enter into actual performance. Certainly any physical action that is potentially violent—such as slapping or pushing—should be well rehearsed and performed exactly as rehearsed. Sexual advances should be similarly prepared so that both partners agree on what will and won't be done—and that agreement must be honored in the performance. And, certainly, actions in a directed play should be performed as rehearsed, subject to the director's instructions (which may or may not allow for on-the-spot improvisation). But an acting class offers considerable leeway for in-performance improvisation. Frequently, actions taken on impulse will be preferable to those carefully rehearsed. Acting class should be a place for experimentation, and you should give yourself ample room for experimenting in the performance mode itself.

You should end your scene by saying "Scene" or "Curtain" when you finish—allowing a momentary pause after the last line or stage action—and then returning to your seat unless instructed otherwise. This is not the time for grimacing, scowling at your partner, or shrugging as if to say "I guess that wasn't very good, was it?" Learn to respect your work and the work of your partner. Do not offer lame excuses or blame your partner or skulk into the background. If something went horribly wrong in performance, you should certainly be able to ask to repeat the scene. If you are asked whether anything went wrong, you should tell the truth without accusing anyone: It is appropriate to say "We skipped a section of the text" but unwise to say "Joe dropped his lines." Publicly accusing your partner of ruining the scene will make it more difficult to rework the scene effectively and sensitively.

After performing your scene, you should do a quick review in your mind: Were you concentrating? Were you pursuing a goal? Did you move your partner? Surprise him or her? Were you as concentrated, as intense, as free, and as relaxed as you were in your best rehearsal? If not, why not?

Most important, be prepared to learn from your performance. Acting class is a place to learn, not to show off your wares. You have worked hard on your part, memorized your text, developed and studied your GOTEsheet, rehearsed your scene, performed with eloquence and vigor, and still you are going to receive criticism. Your classmates may be grudging in their approval. Your instructor may talk darkly about your "problems." Your acting partner may stonewall you from across the room. Where did you go wrong?

You didn't. In acting class, you are learning, but you still have a long way to go.

Summary

Stage fright can affect all actors and can destroy the result you thought you had achieved in studying, staging, and rehearsing your scene. Proper preparation and intense concentration will help to lessen the effects of stage fright; so will going for physical results in your stage interactions and keeping your scene improvisational in nonessential matters of blocking and inflection. After a scene, you should leave the stage without apology and should review your work in terms of your preparation and choices.

L E S S O N

14

Evaluation
and Improvement

Helpful Criticism

It is often said of writing that the best writing is rewriting. So it is with acting. A scene is not "finished" the first time you act it in front of others. A
professionally produced play does not reach its finest form until weeks or
months into its run; it takes a long time for acting to ripen and mature. As
an actor, you will need a chance to prune your excesses, probe your
strengths, and polish your rough edges.

Most scenes will improve markedly following judicious critique and
reworking if you respond to the criticism positively and engage yourself in
the acting process more fully than before.

The first thing to realize after a critique of your scene—particularly after
a harsh critique—is that you weren't really *terrible*. Most of us overreact to
negative remarks; rare indeed is the actor who has not quit the profession a
hundred times (momentarily, at least) after a waspish review, or a sneering
criticism, or even after the damnation of faint praise.

The second thing to realize, however, is that you probably weren't *wonderful* either. Sure, it would have been better with lights and costumes, or
with the right props, or if what's-his-name hadn't forgotten his line and
blown your first cue; still, there is work to be done—*your* work—and by
doing it you can take giant steps.

111

The first step is merely listening carefully to the critique, regardless of its source. Certainly there are going to be friends or teachers whose opinions you particularly trust, but the fact is that audiences consist of more strangers than friends and more nonactors than actors or acting teachers. If *anybody* thinks your scene can be improved, then it probably can be, even if that anybody hasn't a notion as to how to go about improving it. Accept the validity of criticism, even if you don't accept the suggested diagnosis or cure.

As you listen to the criticism, try to answer these questions: What didn't they like? Did they understand the story? The relationship? Could they hear? Most important, did they care? That, of course, is the sine qua non of theatre: Remember, nobody pays an audience to care about the characters. Making them care is your job. If they didn't care, you haven't succeeded, no matter how "correct" you were.

Many things get said in a critique, some wise, some foolish, but you can learn from them all. Here are some of the most common criticisms with suggestions for your future improvement.

Indicating and indulging are among the most common problems of beginning actors. Although they are not identical problems, both involve the playing of emotions, rather than actions.

Indicating means that you are trying to show the emotions of the character, rather than playing the intentions of the character, or the GOTE of the scene. For example, if in reading the scene you decide the character should be sad and then you play "being sad," you are simply indicating a feeling to the audience, not experiencing it yourself. If, on the other hand, you play "I want him to marry me," and the other character says, "Leave me alone," you will *be* sad, and you don't have to indicate it. Moreover, you might find yourself smiling at that moment (that is, smiling to make him change his mind) rather than "looking sad." Indicating your character's presumed feelings, therefore, is wrong for two separate reasons: because it creates only a simulated emotion that the audience sees through, and because it leads you to make unrealistic and often undramatic choices.*

Indulging means playing an emotion for all it's worth, mainly to show off your ability to emote. In the example above, the indicating actor would try to look sad; the indulging actor would whoop out great sobs of anguish and despair. Indulging may make you feel good—or at least feel like you're acting up a storm—but it is rarely if ever effective, inasmuch as it calls attention to your acting rather than to the character's plight and feelings.

---

* While indicating emotions is usually considered an acting fault, indicating *objects* (or people or places) by pointing, nodding, or gesturing toward them is, within limits, perfectly acceptable and, in many cases, desirable. See "Pointing" in Lesson 19.

In the theatre, emotion must always be seen to come out of a character's working through a situation and working through his or her relationships. The best way to generate emotion is to play your GOTEsheet boldly and sensitively—that is, to stimulate your feelings by directly pursuing real goals, with and through real people (your scene partners), by using real tactics. The worst way to generate emotion is to decide which emotion to portray and then try to manufacture it on your own.

To rework a scene critiqued as indicated or indulged, restudy the GOTEsheet with an eye particularly to your goal and your interaction with the other actor. For a scene labeled indulgent, you should also rethink the expectation and figure out how you can play the scene more positively. In a scene criticized for indulgence, also consider the time factor. Are you hurrying your partner adequately? Do you want what you want *now*—instead of after having a good cry about it? Remember, the business of the scene is getting what your character wants, not shedding lots of unnecessary tears in the process.

The scene was boring! Chances are no one will ever say directly that your scene was boring, but if the audience was inattentive and the response unduly faint, you can certainly tell that you have failed to stimulate the imagination.

Scenes are boring for a variety of reasons—usually because the choices are timid and impersonal and the underlying relationship is too intellectual, too rational, too expository, too polite. No one gets bored at a sexy scene or a violent one, no matter how clumsily played. Rethink your choices, and re-examine the scene for underlying sexual or threatening potential. Get personal with your partner. Strengthen your tactics. Choose to make the scene mean something very vivid to you—something you can get your body into as well as your mind. Intensify your images of victory and your fantasies of defeat.

I couldn't hear! This common criticism should be met in two ways. First, restage your scene so that you open out more to the audience. If it's an intimate scene, put more space between you and your partner so that you aren't tempted to whisper. Then find *reasons* to pick up the scene's volume. If your line is "I love you" and your inclination is to whisper it, change your inclination: Say the line so that the whole world hears!

Every actor has the obligation to make herself or himself heard at all times. In Part Five of this book, the technique section, there are some specific suggestions that will help you. But at any point in your learning process, you must know that being heard is *your* responsibility—sometimes your first responsibility—as an actor.

When an actor is inaudible to the audience, he or she is often inaudible to the other actors onstage. In other words, the actor is speaking more quietly than he or she would be in the same situation in life (when we are almost never inaudible to the people we're talking to). Stage fright, in any of its many varieties, is the culprit here. Don't ever excuse inaudibility because you were simply "being real." Chances are you were not only being nontheatrical, you were being unreal as well.

That was great! The most devastating criticism of your scene, sometimes, is unmitigated praise. How do you rework a scene that's been praised to the skies? You must take the praise as a challenge to do even better—and to show yourself that you can do even better.

You must remember that in acting, "really great" is not enough, that no amount of praise should stop you from working to get deeper and deeper into the actor's art. The actors who are really "really great" are one in a million, perhaps one in a generation. Acting is one of those rare professions that truly achieve the rank of art—which means that those practitioners at the very summit of their craft are true immortals who will be remembered centuries beyond their times. Are you there yet? Of course not. Don't ever let praise, no matter how well intended or sincere, stand in the way of reaching your highest potential.

Reworking

When you have brought together the criticisms that can help shape your work and have evaluated your preliminary presentation with your partner, your scene can be rehearsed with an eye to focusing on the specific problems you were able to isolate. You should experience a sense of freedom at this point: You have already done your scene once; your "first-night" jitters are over, and you can now get on with the work of working on *yourself*. This stage separates the serious student from the casual one, because this is where the hard work begins—work that is not always immediately gratifying, work that does not have the immediate thrill of first-time performance.

Choose a fellow student whom you and your partner trust and ask him or her to observe the reworking rehearsals and judge whether the problems seem to be improving. Sometimes the use of a tape recorder or a videotape recorder (if you are fortunate enough to have such equipment) can be most helpful in spotting what the critics saw and correcting it.

Your work will not always improve; occasionally, in fact, it may go downhill. Sometimes the scene just isn't right for you, or you're not ready for it, or the chemistry between you and your partner is off. Don't fall back on excuses, however, and don't be quick to blame. It is your challenge to make every scene your most fantastic, every partner your best one, and every role your favorite. No one is going to do this for you, either now or in the future. Reworking should be approached with enthusiasm and dedication, which will not always be rewarded by quickly won success but must be relentless nonetheless.

Often you will have a chance to re-present a reworked scene. If you have a choice in the matter, you should do so only when you have made a serious effort to rethink your approach and have made serious changes in your performance. Don't simply hope for a better mood or a sudden inspiration. Reworking is *working,* and without understanding that, you will have little improvement to show.

◆ E X E R C I S E   **14–1**

Scene Presentation

Select a partner and a scene. Following all the lessons in Part Three, memorize, study, rehearse, stage, and present the scene. Then, guided by a class critique, restudy, restage, re-rehearse, and re-present the same scene in a subsequent class meeting.

Summary

The education of an actor does not end with the first performance; performances are just steps in the learning process. Even good acting can be critiqued, restudied, re-rehearsed, and re-presented to advantage. It is up to you to learn how to take criticism (indeed, how to solicit criticism), how to learn from it, and how to grow by it. Growth is not always continuous and not always easy; the best results involve hard work and little glamor, but the finest acting is always accomplished through relentless diligence.

The Actor's Instrument

PARTS TWO AND THREE ARE CONCERNED WITH PROCESSES OF acting: approaching and preparing dramatic roles. Anyone who has mastered those twelve lessons might be said to have learned "how to act." But becoming an actor means a lot more than learning how to act; it also means becoming a trained and capable acting *instrument*.

The instrument consists of the actor's personal attributes and abilities: appearance, speech and movement capabilities, emotional depths, intelligence, mind–body coordination, sense of timing, sense of drama, and presentational skills. For the actor is both a player and the instrument played; the actor, in other words, plays upon herself or himself in much the same way that a violinist plays upon a violin. Carrying that metaphor one step further, we can say that an actor, like the violinist, can be no better than the instrument—no matter how brilliant his or her approach or dedication to fulfilling tasks. Thus the actor will be rewarded by having a versatile and splendid instrument; or be held back by possessing an instrument that is unresponsive or undisciplined, making her or him unable to execute commands with passion, subtlety, excitement, or vivacity.

A fundamental goal for every would-be actor is to develop an instrument that can be employed in a wide range of tactics and can bring to life a wide variety of roles. Certainly raw acting talent is a probable factor in an actor's subsequent career, but, now more than ever, a trained acting instrument is every bit as necessary—if not more so. Most often today, the theatre looks for actors who have completed substantial training in actor-training programs. Don't underestimate the amount of training most young American stage actors have as they enter the profession. Typically, a beginning actor at an American regional professional theatre might be expected to have an undergraduate drama degree, a graduate (M.F.A.) or Professional Actor Training Program degree, and two or three years of nonprofessional apprentice work or experience with a semiprofessional theatre company. And this is *intensive* training, not casual classes at odd times. Most professional actor-training programs involve students in thirty to seventy hours a week of classes and rehearsals for about three years.

You will not have a professional actor's instrument, then, in a matter of a few weeks or months; nor will Part Four provide you with more than an outline of what you will be working on if you want to pursue acting beyond the beginning level. But the time to start developing your instrument is now. For as you learn how to "play" your instrument, you will want to own a better one.

15

The Actor's Voice

Breathing

Most people think of the voice as the most important element of the actor's instrument. Asked to name the three most important aspects of acting, Tommaso Salvini, the great nineteenth-century star (and favorite of Stanislavsky), said, "Voice, voice, and more voice." We have moved away from the oratorical style of Salvini's era, to be sure, but a supple, commanding, and engaging voice is as important as ever.

Voice is not taught in a day; most successful vocal-training programs last at least two years, usually three. That's three years of weekly or biweekly classes and *daily* drills, lasting about an hour each. Because we have all been using our voices for years, much that must be learned requires unlearning deep-rooted habits. Moreover, we tend to resist that unlearning —deep down, we like the way we speak—and one of the actor's hardest tasks is simply learning to believe in the steps necessary to vocal improvement, beginning with learning to breathe.

Breathing is the basis of voice, as it is the basis for life. To *inspire* means to breathe in—as well as to nourish the *spirit* (from the Latin *spiritus*, meaning breath). Breathing is as natural as sleeping—except that you cannot do either unselfconsciously when being stared at by an audience. The actor's goal is simply to breathe naturally while under the pressure of performance—and to provide sufficient lung power to support a voice that may be challenged in acting more than in any other activity.

The *yawn* is the ideal breath because it comes from a relaxed body and because it takes in a substantial quantity of air in an unforced manner. But

119

the actor cannot yawn continuously during a play—except perhaps in Chekhov. When you yawn, chances are, you breathe not from your chest but from your abdomen. And that's where the actor's support breathing must originate. The shallow chest breaths that characterize many beginning actors are the result of tension and self-consciousness—the same sort of tension that would cause shallow breathing if we were to come upon a mugger in a dark alley. Deep body breathing, as deep as possible, gives the voice its fullest support and the body its fullest relaxation.

◆ E X E R C I S E   15–1

Breathing from the Abdomen

Breathe deeply from the abdomen. Yawn, stretch your arms, and breathe again. Lie down, knees raised, feet and back on the floor. As you breathe, mark the movement of your abdomen and try to minimize the movement of your chest. Now stand and walk about the room, swinging your arms freely and tasting the air as you breathe it in.

Phonation: Making Sounds

Oddly, nobody knows for certain how sound is made by the human voice. We do know that the sound is caused by air passing through vibrating vocal folds (also called vocal cords), but whether the air vibrates the folds, like a clarinet reed, or whether the folds, like a violin string, vibrate the air, is a subject of great debate among laryngologists (vocal specialists). However it happens, making sounds with your voice (phonation) is a spontaneously learned phenomenon that the actor must cultivate beyond its everyday function.

The easiest sound to make is the vowel *ah,* and the best way to make it is with the most open-throated and relaxed voice possible. *Ah* is the vowel on which singers and actors routinely warm up their voices, practice scales, and learn to develop resonation and vocal power.

◆ E X E R C I S E   15–2

Sounding

Breathing from the abdomen, say *ah* with each exhalation in any of the following ways:

1. ah hah hah hah hah hah hah

2. pah pah pah pah pah pah pah

3. ahhhhhhhhhhhhhhhhhh (sliding down the scale)

Now, turning the body from side to side, walk around the room and make the same series of sounds, gradually increasing the volume toward the end of each breath:

4. ah hah hah Hah Hah HAH HAH HAHH HAHH! *HAHHH!*

5. pah pah Pah Pah PAH PAH PAHH PAHH! *PAHHH!!*

6. ahhhhhhhhhhHHHHHHHHHHHHH*HHHH!* (sliding down the scale)

What happens when you increase your volume? Do the vocal folds vibrate faster? No, for faster vibrations would simply raise the *pitch* of your voice (make the sounds go higher on the scale). Volume is primarily a function not of phonation, but of *resonance.*

Resonance

Resonance is the re-sounding of vocal fold sounds. Re-sounding is a simple phenomenon. Vibration, as of a tuning fork, creates sound, but it also creates other (sympathetic) vibrations, which themselves create sound. Often these secondary sounds, caused by sympathetic vibrations, are louder and fuller than the original tuning-fork sound itself. A tuning fork struck and placed against an empty cigar box, for example, can create an amplified sound far greater than the original because of the resonation of the air within the cigar box.

In the human voice, most of the actual sound is provided by the resonation of three "cigar boxes" inside the vocal apparatus: the pharyngeal (throat), oral (mouth), and nasal (nose) cavities that lie above the vocal folds. Air that is first vibrated by the vocal folds then passes through these three empty cavities and creates sympathetic vibrations in both the tissues and the air within them; what emerges is the rich, full-voiced sound that is characteristic of the peculiar shapes and sizes of each individual's resonating capacities. Much of our resonation is biologically determined; indeed, "voiceprints" identify individuals as clearly as fingerprints do. But we also have a certain degree of control over the amount of resonation we can produce. If properly exercised, this control can favorably alter the power, timbre, tone, and character of our voices.

Virtually *all* acting students need to improve resonance, simply because the resonance required of the actor is far greater than that required of most other professionals. The actor must be prepared to be full-voiced continuously for several hours at a stretch on a daily basis, must project with authority, and must be able to "play upon" an instrument with many subtle gradations of resonation—which itself demands a "resonance reserve" that can be called on at an instant. Resonation is one way an actor can increase his or her volume and vocal power without straining the voice. Resonation is a way of making your cavities work for you rather than against you—and is therefore a vocal asset that must be carefully cultivated.

But how do you improve your resonance? *Relaxation* is the first principle. A relaxed throat is an open throat, and an open throat provides deep, mellow resonance. Thus, rolling the head easily about, "floating" it atop the spine, is a standard actor's exercise for relaxing the neck and opening up the pharyngeal cavity.

Posture is the second principle. You would need a movement or vocal coach to work with you to get the best results, but you can get a good start just by developing a comfortably erect posture, with your weight centered, your spine lengthening easily upward, and your head "floating" freely atop your spine. With your muscles then relaxed—particularly in your neck, your jaw, and your face—you will be more generally resonant than before.

Speaking itself is the third principle. An open-jawed, open-mouthed articulation provides greater resonance than a close-lipped, tight-jawed, constricted speech. The vowel *ah* is the standard warm-up vowel for actors and singers because it is made with the jaw fully dropped, providing the greatest oral resonance and thereby the least demand on the vocal folds themselves. *Ee* and the French *uu* are, by contrast, the least resonant vowels because they require a tightening of the jaw, in the first instance, and a closing of the lips in the second—both practices necessarily reducing the amplitude of resonation.

The placement of vowels—that is, the place in the mouth where they are actually formed—determines to some extent how they are resonated. *Ah,* for example, can be fully resonated in the pharynx—or, by widening the lips, tilting the head backward, and raising the larynx, can be shunted more into the nasal cavity, where it will prove more penetrating but also more strident. Nasal resonance creates a harsher sound than pharyngeal resonance, but there are many occasions when a harsh sound is desirable, for reasons of either characterization or projection. The actor should learn how to vary resonance by shifts in the placement of vowels.

◆ E X E R C I S E   15–3

Exploring Resonance

1. Stand with your feet slightly spread and your arms held loosely at your sides. Say "pah pah pah pah pah" while twisting your arms and torso lightly side to side. Say it again while tilting your head slowly forward, then back. Say it again while yawning and relaxing your throat completely, "letting go" so that your Adam's apple seems to "fall" down into your chest. Form the sound as deep in your throat as you can. Say it again while shunting the air out through your nose. Where do you seem to feel the greatest resonance? The mellowest resonance? The most penetrating?

2. Place one hand on the top of your head and say "pee pah pee pah pee." On which syllable do you feel the most vibration? You should feel it on *pee,* which is formed high in the front of the mouth and thus generates more head and bone (skull) resonance.

3. Place one hand on the bridge of your nose and say "pah pin pah pin pah pin." Which syllable causes the most vibration? *Pin* will, of course, because it has a nasal vowel and thus creates more nasal resonance than *pah*.

4. Put your hands on your cheeks and say "oo ee oo ee oo" or "oo ah oo ah oo ah." Which vowel creates the most cheek vibration? *Oo* will, because *oo* is formed high in the back of the mouth, making the cheeks a strong resonator for *oo*.

5. Pair with a partner and place your hands on his or her head, nose bridge, and cheeks, by turns, testing his or her resonance as your partner tests yours.

Exercise 15–3 merely shows you what parts of your body are resonating most strongly on particular vowels. Using different vowels, you can also feel resonating vibrations on the collarbone, shoulder blades, forehead, and other parts of the upper body.

Pitch

Pitch is the highness or lowness of a musical tone. Technically, as we have seen, it is a function of the frequency of the vocal fold vibrations: the faster the vibrations, the higher the pitch. Most everyday adult speaking takes place within a fairly restricted tonal pitch scale, which we sometimes call "monotoned" (or, more figuratively, "monotonous," meaning, literally, "on one note"). When we are excited (and less inhibited), however, our pitch range is expanded: Listen, for an example, to children's hollering on a playground. One of your goals in acting will be to allow yourself the uninhibited excitement that will naturally call into play a broader tonal scale—a larger pitch range.

Your voice is more resonant at different pitches because the resonating tissues are themselves "tuned" to vibrate, sympathetically, with specific notes on the scale. Ordinarily, lower notes develop more pharyngeal (throat) resonance, while higher notes resonate more in the nasal passages. But every voice is different in this respect—which is why you can identify most of the people you know simply by the sound of their voices.

◆ E X E R C I S E   15–4

Exploring Your Pitch Range

- ◆ Repeat Exercise 15–2, using first high notes, then low notes, then a sliding scale of high notes to low notes.

- ◆ Repeat, using a sliding scale of low notes to high notes.

- ◆ Repeat, letting your pitch rise and fall within the same phrase, then fall and rise within the same phrase.

A Stageworthy Voice

Speaking is a natural ability, but the actor's voice is cultivated because it must meet certain demands rarely present in everyday life. Stage speaking is to daily conversation what Olympic high hurdling is to the morning jog; it demands training and conditioning as well as above-average gifts. The training is normally carried out under the eye of an accomplished vocal coach, but the conditioning is up to the actor. An hour a day of vocal workout is to the actor what the daily playing of scales is to the concert pianist and daily calisthenics are to the professional athlete. During that conditioning practice, however, the actor can certainly explore his or her own vocal capacities. Sometimes a tape recorder is helpful in developing stageworthy sound. Exercise 15–5 will prove a good starting point for a daily warm-up and exploration.

◆ E X E R C I S E   15–5

Speaking with Resonance

Warm up by repeating Exercises 15–2, 15–3, and 15–4. Then, by memorizing the phrases in the list below, one at a time, recite each phrase twenty times while exploring your own speaking mechanism by taking different postures, deepening your breathing, playing with several "up and down" pitch variations, and seeing how you can develop new areas of resonance. Try to communicate some meaning with your text, but don't worry too much about "interpretation" at this point; the words should mainly serve as a vocalizing exercise. Do this exercise with a tape recorder or ask a friend to check your results.

   Recite these phrases in the shower if you like. The bathroom will enlarge your resonance, as if you were speaking inside a violin box, and the steam from the shower will keep your vocal folds moist and fresh.

1. "Roll on, thou deep and dark blue ocean—roll!"

2. "Is this a dagger which I see before me,
   The handle toward my hand? Come, let me clutch thee."

3. "Was this the face that launch'd a thousand ships,
   And burnt the topless towers of Ilium?"

4. "Four score and seven years ago our fathers brought forth on this continent a new nation, conceived in liberty, and dedicated to the proposition that all men are created equal."

5. "O Romeo, Romeo! wherefore art thou Romeo?
   Deny thy father, and refuse thy name;
   Or, if thou wilt not, be but sworn my love,
   And I'll no longer be a Capulet."

6. "Is anybody home?"

7. "Pickle him in pickle sauce!"

8. "You think I'll weep;
   No, I'll not weep.
   I have full cause of weeping; but this heart
   Shall break into a hundred thousand flaws
   Or ere I'll weep. O fool, I shall go mad!"
9. "In the beginning God created the heaven and the earth."

10. "Blasts and fogs upon thee!"

Summary

The actor's voice is primary to her or his acting instrument and must be trained and conditioned to meet the demands of the theatre. Breathing, the making of sounds, resonation, and pitch flexibility and control—the primary tools of the voice—can be cultivated through instruction and exercise.

16

Stage Speech

Good Diction

Voice produces sound; speech produces language.

The process by which raw vocal sound is transformed into speech begins with *articulation:* the shaping of vocal noise into independent and recognizable units of spoken language, or *phonemes.* There are about forty phonemes in spoken English, plus various phonemic combinations, and the fine actor can speak all of them clearly and distinctly.

Good *diction* has long been considered essential to acting, primarily so that the actor can be clearly heard and understood in all parts of the theatre, and so that the actor can make the most of the author's words and the character's verbal tactics, wit, and persuasive authority. Good diction also means adhering to a standard way of pronouncing words—so that the actors will seem to be "all in the same play" and a sense of shared ensemble will be created through the play's words.

In some cultures the standard stage pronunciation requires a lofty tone not ordinarily heard in daily life. The British theatre, for example, favors "Received Pronunciation" (you can hear it on the BBC), which has been "received" from schooled elocution rather than from normal social conversation. The German theatre, similarly, uses what is called *Hochdeutsch* (high German) for most classical and modern plays. The standard American stage speech, however, is simply a refinement of middle American pronunciation, emphasizing naturalness rather than elevated elocution. Learning standard American, as it is called, requires overcoming speech impediments, such as lisping, and eliminating unwanted regional dialects. Learning standard American, then, requires learning the standard speech sounds of the American English language: how to make them and how to use them.*

Speech Sounds

Formal speech training begins with identifying the forty basic speech sounds and practicing them in various combinations until complete mastery is achieved. This process takes years. It cannot simply be covered as a single part of a beginning acting class; but an elemental understanding of the basic speech sounds can be achieved quickly, and improvement in speech clarity, power, and precision can be developed after short periods of practice.

The *vowel* sounds of English are divided among those that are formed in the front of the mouth, in the back, and in the middle.

Front Vowels

ee as in *beet, heat, feel, see, seize*

ih as in *hit, tin, rift, pill, skit*

ay as in *bake, cane, staple, cradle, straight*

eh as in *bet, sled, when, threat, kept*

aa as in *cad, bat, stab, pal, add*

Back Vowels

ah as in *father, Charles, hard, party*

a as in *wants, pot, God, pollen, bottom*

aw as in *all, bought, cough, walk, trawler*

o as in *old, coat, stoke, protest, folk*

---

* I should note here that there are, of course, many plays written to be spoken in *nonstandard* British, German, and American, as well as in other languages, and that there are now an increasing number of directors in this and other countries who do not insist on any standard way of speaking even in plays that represent characters of a single social class. These directors—some of whom use the designations "post-Brechtian " or "postmodern"—prefer to hear each actor's natural dialect, "deconstructing " the theatrical illusion by retaining an emphasis on the theatrical machinery, the acting process itself.

ooh as in *foot, look, tootsie, put, good*

oo as in *boot, cool, rude, too, food, true*

Mid Vowels

uh (stressed) as in *cup, rubble, ton, up, none*

uh (unstressed) as in *above, sofa, pencil, amount, unwrap*

ur as in *further, cur, stir, purple, murder*

Diphthongs are glides between vowels—two vowels that are sounded in sequence and seem at first hearing to be one.

Diphthongs

ay-ee as in *hay, say, feign, weigh, play*

eye (ah-ee) as in *I, fly, high, sky, mai tai*

oy (aw-ee) as in *boy, coy, royal, poi, alloy*

you (ee-oo) as in *ewe, few, putrid, puerile, cue*

ow (ah-oo) as in *how, now, brown, cow*

oh (o-oo) as in *slow, throw, go, crow, toe*

Learning to speak vowels clearly and cleanly, and to hear the difference between vowels in similar-sounding words (such as *offal* and *awful*), is particularly important to the actor because the vowel sounds of stage speech carry the tone of the dialog and convey the nuances of a character's tactical pursuits. Also, the vowel sounds of a person's speech often characterize his or her regional background: A trained ear has no trouble identifying the Virginian, the Wisconsinite, the Texan, and the New Englander simply by hearing their *ahs* and *ows*. Actors practice vowel drills in order to develop clarity and strength in their vowels and also to approximate the norm of standard American rather than their native local dialect.

◆ E X E R C I S E   16–1

Vowels

Singly or in a group, practice the vowel sounds by reciting the words listed after each vowel on pages 128–129. Notice how the vowel is formed in the mouth. Then speak the diphthongs slowly and see if you can identify which two vowels each diphthong consists of.

◆ EXERCISE   16–2

Repeating Syllables

Pair with a partner, and turn back to back. One person will recite as clearly as possible, *in any sequence,* any three of the following syllables. The partner will then try to repeat the syllables exactly. Then reverse roles and repeat the exercise.

poh	pooh
pih	poo
pay	puh
peh	pur
paa	pie
pah	poi
paw	pyu
po	pow

Do the exercise two or three times; then increase the number of syllables recited to five. As you continue the exercise, increase the speed. You may also try using other initial consonants, such as *k* or *d,* which involve other articulators.

The twenty-five *consonants* of English speech are divided into the *plosives* (made by holding the air momentarily before exploding it outward); the *fricatives* (made by blowing air between the articulators—the tongue, teeth, lips, and hard and soft palates); the *nasals* (made by passing air through the nose); the *glides* (made by moving the tongue); and the *blends* (made by combining other consonants).

Plosive Consonants

t as in *tickle, touch, ten*

d as in *dance, delve, dead*

p as in *potato, pill, purpose*

b as in *bombshell, baseball, bed*

k as in *kick, kindred, collection*

g as in *giggle, get, go*

Fricative Consonants

f as in *football, fill, from*
v as in *voter, veil, vigor*
th (unvoiced) as in *think, theatre, thrill*
th (voiced) as in *there, then, they*
s as in *settle, send, century*
z as in *zeal, zoo, zebra*
sh as in *shipshape, shell, sure*
zh as in *leisure, seizure, azure*
h as in *hail, high, hiccup*

Nasal Consonants

m as in *mystery, men, meal*
n as in *needle, nil, nothing*
ng as in *sing, song, kingship*

Glide Consonants

l as in *leader, listen, look*
r as in *real, rotate, roughhouse*
y as in *yellow, yesterday, yolk*
w as in *willow, won't, warrant*
wh as in *which, whippoorwill, where*

Blended Consonants

ch as in *chipmunk, choke, child*
j as in *jump, jail, gentry*

Developing crisp, clean consonants helps the actor convey precise meaning and gives the actor's speech a commanding authority. Consonants punctuate speech sound and are crucial in developing the sharpness of an intellectual argument, a witty retort, or a persuasive demand. Consonants are not as susceptible to regional variation as vowels are (an exception is the Cockney *fing* for *thing*) but are, on the other hand, more prone to impediments. The formation of consonants requires rapid and accurate movement of hundreds of muscle systems in the mouth and perfect placement (at the rate of about ten per second) of tongue, teeth, lips, jaw, glottis, gums, and palates (together, these are called the *articulators*). No actor can afford to have flabby, unresponsive, or lazy articulators. Consonant drills, therefore, aim to make an actor's consonants razor sharp.

◆ E X E R C I S E   16–3

Consonants

Repeat the following consonant drills until you can do them comfortably, rapidly, and, if possible, wittily.

1. Tip it, pippet; tip it, pippet; tip it, pippet.
2. Dab a gak, dab a gak, dab a gak, dab a gak.
3. Azure zoo, azure zoo, azure zoo, azure zoo.
4. Think this fink, think this fink, think this fink.
5. The vase is shaded, the vase is shaded, the vase is shaded.
6. No ming no mong, no ming no mong, no ming no mong.
7. Yell when wending, yell when wending, yell when wending.
8. Jump Chuck, jump Chuck, jump Chuck, jump Chuck.
9. Tapocketa pocketa pocketa pocketa pocketa.
10. Libid ibid libid ibid libid ibid.
11. Rilly billy dilly killy, rilly billy dilly killy.
12. Potato pit, potato pit, potato pit, potato pit.
13. This is it, this is it, this is it, this is it.
14. Calumny, mercantile, exaggerate, elevate, anglophile.
15. Big a pig gig, big a pig gig, big a pig gig.

◆ E X E R C I S E   16–4

Speeches

When you feel comfortable with the simple drills in Exercise 16–3, try reading the following lines from Shakespeare's *Macbeth*.

Reading aloud, repeat the lines until you can read them clearly and accurately. Note the importance of clear articulation in these speeches.

MACBETH: If it were done when 'tis done, then 'twere well
  It were done quickly. If th' assassination
  Could trammel up the consequence, and catch
  With his surcease, success; that but this blow
  Might be the be-all and the end-all—here,
  But here, upon this bank and shoal of time,
  We'd jump the life to come.

LADY MACBETH: Glamis thou art, and Cawdor, and shalt be
  What thou art promised. Yet I do fear thy nature;
  It is too full o' th' milk of human kindness
  To catch the nearest way. Thou wouldst be great;
  Art not without ambition, but without
  The illness should attend it. What thou wouldst highly,
  That wouldst thou holily; wouldst not play false,
  And yet wouldst wrongly win.

No one can say that the speeches in Exercise 16–4 are easy, even for the veteran classical scholar or performer, but you can certainly see that clear articulation is absolutely crucial if any interpretation is to make sense. Only careful speech can distinguish "surcease, success," and "highly . . . holily," and yet these are the sorts of verbal problems with which the actor must deal moment by moment in an articulate play.

For more advanced work in speech and diction, you will want to take special classes or individualized training. But running the vowels and consonants, as in the previous exercises, can help you to understand your own manufacture of phonemes, and to learn how to speak them with clarity and distinction. Speech drills also exercise the articulators and the muscles that move them, giving you a greater capacity to be sharp and subtle with your language, and therefore more powerful in your playing of tactics toward a stage victory. Drilling phonemes also helps give you a confidence toward stage speaking and an ear toward correcting your own impediments or regionalisms—particularly if you can work under the guidance of an interested and qualified teacher.

Summary

Each actor must cultivate the ability to articulate the forty-odd English-language phonemes (speech sounds), for this ability underlies powerful, fluid, subtle, and confident stage speaking and therefore tactical interplay. Mastering the phonemes also is the key to eliminating speech impediments, regional mispronunciations, and speaking timidity. Dramatic improvement in your speaking will come about only with concentrated study under a qualified instructor or coach. Speech drills, however, exercise the articulators and help you gain control of your speaking mechanism.

17

Using the Voice

Liberation

In pursuing your character's goals, getting your character's GOTE, your voice and speech are the primary tools at your disposal. The voice must be free to coax, to bully, to soothe, to inspire, and to explode. The speech must allow you to articulate, persuade, harangue, dazzle, enchant, and entertain. But voice and speech cannot reach these heights if they are inhibited.

The liberated voice is free from socially bred inhibitions: excessive politeness, timidity, deference, or propriety. The actor's liberation is both psychological and technical. The actor needs confidence that absolutely anything can be said onstage so that breathing and speaking mechanisms will be relaxed and supple enough to make speech vibrant and precise.

Self-consciousness is the inhibitor of speaking. The voices of childhood —yelps, squeals, shouts, silliness, and all—are necessarily channeled during long years of social conditioning into acceptable communicative mechanisms—but at what cost! The average adult voice, perhaps still varied and pungent in the privacy of the shower or the fraternity/sorority drinking party, becomes a timid and wary instrument under the close public scrutiny of a gathering of academic peers. *Politeness* (the word has the same root as *politics*) is the necessary lubricant for social interaction, but it stands in the way of vocal and speech development; excessive politeness is the enemy of exciting acting.

The social conditioning we have all passed through (and continue to pass through) produces a fascinating variety of misshapen voices. (Psychiatrists often make their initial evaluation of a patient's problem by noting the specific strains in the patient's voice during their first interview.) Some young women use the classic "little girl voice," a half octave too high, maintained from childhood in an unconscious attempt to remain "Daddy's little girl," or perhaps to avoid competing too directly with a roughhousing older brother. Some young men have a nasal whine left over from those days when direct confrontation of the parent or teacher was impossible and wheedling was the only way to make an impact.

Sometimes the voices of both sexes suggest that terror underlies every public statement: that even to say "here" in answer to a roll call may result in a crack on the knuckles for some reason or other. If any of these descriptions seems to fit you, don't worry: Everybody experiences, to one degree or another, these vocal shortcomings. There is almost no one whose voice does not "go dead" at one time or another: when you suddenly see that everybody is looking at you, or when someone asks you a question you cannot answer, or when you suddenly feel that you're inappropriately dressed. The actor's problem is not worrying about a dead or timid voice but, rather, finding the way to counteract it, to bring life and energy to the art of speaking.

◆ EXERCISE 17–1

Rude Chants

Chant, as a group:

1. Kill, kill, kill, kill, kill!

2. Barf, barf, barf, barf, barf!

3. Penis, penis, penis, penis, penis!

4. Urine, urine, urine, urine, urine!

In this impolite exercise, the point is not to giggle or pretend you're saying something else but, rather, to allow your voice the freedom to say, at full volume and with clear speech, the sort of words you don't usually say in public. Try these also:

5. Testicle, testicle, testicle, testicle, testicle!

6. Copulate, copulate, copulate, copulate, copulate!

7. Intercourse, intercourse, intercourse, intercourse, intercourse!

8. Masturbate, masturbate, masturbate, masturbate, masturbate!

As an actor, you should be able to say *anything* boldly on stage. No words, no matter how personally odious to you, should simply stick in your throat.

◆ E X E R C I S E   **17–2**

Rude Cheering

1. Repeat the chants in Exercise 17-1, exploring your pitch range and resonance possibilities.

2. Chant a "cheer" of "Kill, barf, penis, urine!" Make the cheer *purposeful*: This is the team you are rooting for. Make them win! Make them hear you and know you are cheering them on! Make up gestures and movements for the cheer.

3. Do the same with "Testicle, copulate, intercourse, masturbate!"

This exercise is easy to expand with other words, but keep the doors closed. Your class is a large enough public for this exercise!

Inhibition takes many forms. Another common form is a fear of mispronouncing or misusing large words. In their daily lives, many young people retreat behind a vocabulary of simple language, fad words, and common clichés simply to avoid the possibility of making a mistake. (And how terrified we were, as adolescents, of making a mistake!) Therefore the language they bring to acting is essentially slovenly, immature, and bland. In the theatre, of course, language is created by playwrights, but most young actors have initial (and sometimes continuing) difficulties in rising to the language of the play. Often they consciously or unconsciously rewrite the script into their own words; more often they stumble over or swallow any four-syllable words they find in the text. You can lick this problem. An actor must love words and wordplay. While it is true that many dramatic characters are inarticulate (particularly in plays from the 1950s), a great many more are not; each actor must rise to the level of verbal dexterity that the character has achieved—and often the characters are verbal dynamos.

◆ E X E R C I S E   17–3

Fancy Talk

Separately, and after checking the meaning and pronunciation of words unfamiliar to you, say to someone (real or imaginary) with a good deal of *fun:*

1. Throckmorton's in an anomalous predicament!
2. I detest John's egregious braggadocio!
3. What a stentorian denunciation!
4. Her perfidious egalitarianism is obnoxious!
5. Thwart Ellen's obstinacy!
6. Could you correlate the data mellifluously?
7. Long live ubiquitous serendipity!
8. Disambiguate your metaphor!
9. Come to the Christmas colloquium.
10. Restrain your ribald riposting!
11. Cease your antediluvian antics!
12. Your libidinous delusions are tantalizing!
13. I adore elocutionary magnificence!
14. Startling complexities abound!
15. Beware the inevitable consequences!
16. Facilitate copulation!
17. Barf before pontificating!

The last two sentences combine Exercises 17–1 and 17–2. Make up additional combinations of long words and "rude" words, and speak them freely in all ranges of your voice. Examples of speeches to say to a (real or imaginary) partner:

1. "I fart at thee!" (Ben Jonson, *The Alchemist*)

2. "The bawdy hand of time is on the prick of noon." (Shakespeare, *Romeo and Juliet*)

3. "Extraordinary how potent cheap music is." (Noel Coward, *Private Lives*)

4. "WEE! WAA! WONDERFUL! I'm stiff! Stiff in the wind! My mane, stiff in the wind! My flanks! My hooves! Mane on my legs, on my flanks, like whips! Raw! Raw! *I'm raw! Raw* " (Peter Shaffer, *Equus*)

5. "Come down outa dere, yuh yellow, brass-buttoned, Belfast bum, yuh! Come down and I'll knock yer brains out! Yuh lousy, stinkin' yellow mutt of a Catholic-moiderin' bastard!" (Eugene O'Neill, *The Hairy Ape*)

6. "Oh, I should think I was poor and had nothing to bestow if I were reduced to an inglorious ease and freed from the agreeable fatigues of solicitation." (William Congreve, *The Way of the World*)

7. "You see, you piss better when I'm not there." (Samuel Beckett, *Waiting for Godot*)

8. "Detested kite! Thou liest." (Shakespeare, *King Lear*)

9. "I'm a bad publisher because I hate books. Or to be more precise, prose. Or to be even more precise, modern prose, I mean modern novels, first novels and second novels, all that promise and sensibility it falls upon me to judge, to put the firm's money on, and then to push for the third novel, see it done, see the dust jacket done, see the dinner for the national literary editors done, see the signing in Hatchards done, see the lucky author cook himself to death, all in the name of literature. You know what you and Emma have in common? You love literature. I mean you love modern prose literature, I mean you love the new novel by the new Casey or Spinks. It gives you both a thrill." (Harold Pinter, *Betrayal*)

10. "Reaganite heartless macho asshole lawyers." (Tony Kushner, *Millennium Approaches*)

11. "Move your nigger cunt spade faggot lackey ass out of my room." (Tony Kushner, *Perestroika*)

◆ EXERCISE   17–4

Address a Group

Thus far you have spoken your lines to a single (real or imaginary) partner. Now address an imaginary group. Using the fanciful sentences, rude chants, and dramatic texts in the previous exercises, deliver them to:

1. A college class

2. A kindergarten class

3. A bar full of people

4. An army battalion

5. A sorority luncheon

6. Your family

Enlarging the audience to your remarks draws forth more vocal power and articulation and makes you use "more voice" than you need when you are simply addressing an intimate friend. Addressing people who are noisy, deaf, deranged, hostile, or unintelligent can add verbal force and articulate distinction to your speech. Practice enlarging your audience for larger speeches, perhaps by assuming that your character wants to be overheard by others in an adjacent room. This technique can bring your voice and speech to necessary stage levels without sacrificing the directness or honesty of your delivery.

Purposefulness

Purposefulness is what ties the liberated voice to the actor's approach. For the actor's voice and speech are not developed as ends in themselves; an instrument, after all, is useful only while you use it. Basically, the actor's speaking mechanism is the prime weapon of the character's tactical pursuits —the prime implement for getting your character's GOTE.

In the theatre, as in life, people should speak not because they have to but because they *want* to. Every word you speak onstage must be (and seem to be) directed toward your goal; every word must have some tactical service to your cause. As a character, you should not appear to speak simply because the author put words in your mouth but, rather, because you have desires, plans, objectives—and because speaking out is the way you expect to get them! Every word spoken onstage, therefore, must be spoken with purposefulness. Words must come from human desire, not mechanical necessity. This purpose, above all else, brings compelling power to your vocal instrument.

Some examples illustrate how purposefulness affects the way you use your voice:

You are at a football game as the guest of a friend. The people around you cheer. You do not care who wins the game, but you cheer because you're supposed to.

You are at a football game rooting for your team, for people with whom you identify. You cheer. Your cheers are more vigorous; your voice is fuller and more intense. Why? Because you care. Because you are using your voice to try to help your team. You have a purpose.

You are instructed to say, as distinctly as possible, "Pull up on the door handle." You do so.

Your two-year-old sister is crying in a locked car; nearby a building is on fire. You tell her, "Pull up on the door handle!" You are more distinct, your speech is clearer, more demanding, more penetrating. Why?

Good stage speech results from allying purpose with a liberated and versatile vocal mechanism. It is not sufficient to have a good voice; the actor must *want* to vocalize and must want to demand, cajole, attract, or compel others with the voice as a primary instrument. Even the simplest and most technical vocal exercise—"bah bah bah bah bah," for example—can be enhanced by giving the exercise an interpersonal purpose (to calm someone's nerves, to amuse someone, to solicit someone's sympathy). When your purpose is strong enough, it will override any shyness or timidity or inhibitions you might have. Utterly mild and noncommunicative persons can break through giant psychological sound barriers when they see someone stealing their car, or kissing their sweetheart, or running the wrong way with the football. Create, in your mind, a sufficient goal, and energize your voice and speech in its pursuit.

◆ E X E R C I S E   17–5

Adding Purpose

Go back to Exercise 15–5. Using the same speeches, create a strong situational goal for each speech and speak the words purposefully to a (real or imaginary) partner.

Summary

The actor's voice and stage speech are to be *used*, not merely exhibited. To this end they must be free from inhibiting factors, particularly shyness, excessive politeness, and fear of making verbal mistakes. The actor should develop confidence in his or her verbal dexterity, should become comfortable with both rude language and intricate linguistic construction. *Purpose*, finally, is the motive force of good stage speaking; the actor must ally his or her voice and speaking mechanism with a will to achieve goals in a dramatic situation.

L E S S O N

18

The Actor's Body

Agility

Body training for the actor follows many separate paths. Perhaps surprisingly, *developing strength and stamina* is first on the list. One doesn't always associate athletic functions with artistic endeavors, but the sheer physical work of the actor is often grueling. After all, the demands of the role may involve several hours of onstage time, running up and down stairs, fighting, dueling, changing costume, *with maximum physical control*. Mere enthusiasm will not accomplish this control. Such famous actors as Jane Fonda and the late Laurence Olivier have been well known for their demanding physical regimens, developed as a result of their acting careers. Bodybuilding, aerobic exercise, and competitive athletics are now routine activities for actors of all ages.

Develop dexterity and coordination. "Learn the lines and don't bump into the furniture" is the traditional "first lesson" of acting. Physical dexterity means more than merely not bumping into the scenery, however, and more than being able to speak and move at the same time. The actor who is physically coordinated—who can move *with precision and passion at the same time*—can convey meaningful behavior with far more complexity than the actor who merely speaks the words trippingly on the tongue.

Develop physical dynamics. Dynamics means physical force in action. The actor is always either in action or potentially in action, always moving or on the verge of moving. An actor who seems just about to hit out, kiss someone, explode, throw something, or bolt away is an exciting, dynamic actor. The body can be trained toward this dynamic, supple, physical readiness.

Develop specific movement skills. Finally, actor training involves the learning of specific physical patterns, such as ballet, ballroom dancing, period dancing, fencing, hand-to-hand combat, mime, gesture, martial arts, period movement, and circus technique. These skills are often useful in themselves, and they increase the actor's physical versatility, confidence, and poise. Additionally, they aid an actor's sense of timing and physical aesthetics. Indeed, the relationship between acting and dance has been intimate since the dramas of ancient Greece. Many actor-training programs begin with dance, mime, and stage movement.

Exercise 18–1 gets the blood moving, loosens and stretches the ligaments, flexes several hundred muscles, and makes you feel good. It is only a warm-up, however. After fifteen minutes of sitting in a classroom chair, you're back where you started. Therefore actors need to know how to warm up fast and effectively, for they will do it often.

◆ E X E R C I S E   **18–1**

Fast Warm-Up

Go back to Exercise 1–1, and repeat that warm-up briskly, adding the following exercises before running in place:

Standing erect, swivel your hips—five times to the left and five to the right.

Drop your chin to your chest, and let the weight of your head slowly bend you over, vertebra by vertebra, until your fingers touch the floor. Bend your knees as necessary.

Tap the floor with your fingers. Make a rhythm of tapping on the floor. Add the fingernails to the tapping. Add the palms.

Rise up slowly, uncurling the spine vertebra by vertebra.

Extend the head upward without straining, allowing it to "float" freely atop the spinal column.

Rotate the head in leftward and rightward spirals, each time spiraling it into a relaxed "floating" position atop the spine.

Bounce ten times, arms at your sides.

Bounce ten times, arms akimbo—going in all directions.

Run in place or jump an imaginary rope while clapping your hands—for fifteen breaths.

TENSION AND ENERGY

To relax does not mean that you should become a bag of bones. A cat or dog at rest are completely relaxed, yet they are still capable of making sudden and definite movements. The purpose of [Alexander] technique is not to get rid of tensions, but to reorganize them into a source of energy and satisfaction.

MATTHIAS ALEXANDER, AS PARAPHRASED BY EDWARD MAISEL

Alignment

The proper alignment of the body—all vital organs poised in a balanced relationship to maximize their healthy functioning—was the primary goal of Australian-born actor/educator F. Matthias Alexander (1869–1955), whose Alexander Technique is the best-known and most effective alignment system for actors. The basic Alexander alignment is a standing position with

1. The head "floating" easily atop the spine

2. The neck free and relaxed

3. The shoulders spread out (not back)

4. The torso lengthened and widened; the rib cage expanded; the vertebrae separated, not crunched together

5. The pelvis freely rotating, the hip joints free and rolling

The Alexander technique produces not a specific posture but an inner alignment of bodily organs. It promotes good posture, but it also promotes relaxed breathing, deep resonance, clear speech, and coordinated whole-body movement. Alexander adherents also add health, longevity, improved appearance, and enhanced self-image to this list.

The Alexander alignment works because it gives the lungs room to function; it reduces constriction in the throat and mouth; and it gives the diaphragm enough pelvic support to provide a basis of sustained full breathing. The body is poised so that movement springs quite naturally from every limb or digit, or from the trunk itself. Compare this with the hunched-over position of most adults at work or watching television.

The following exercises are necessarily introductory. Enthusiasts of the physical training methods described below devote lifetimes to the study of the various potentials of the human mechanism. But all the exercises suggest ways in which the actor can begin physical self-exploration and self-training to develop greater strength, stamina, dexterity, coordination, and physical dynamics.

◆ E X E R C I S E   18–2

Improving Alignment

Stand on the floor, legs comfortably apart. Hunch your shoulders down, squeeze your head down onto your neck, lock your knees, clench your fists, and say, "Hah hah hah hah hah." The sound will be *terrible*. Now try the following.

Relax your arms, open your fists, swing your arms lightly, and let your head "float" upward, keeping your chin level.

Rotate your head one or two times each way, ending in a spiral and "floating" your head as high as you can without straining.

Flex your knees slightly and rotate your hips, coming to rest in a balanced position.

Broaden your shoulders straight out, left and right, and open your rib cage, raising and expanding your ribs outward, forward, and upward. (Imagine a gentle tug from two wires attached to your ribs three inches below your nipples, each pulling upward at a 45-degree angle forward and outward.)

Lengthen your spine without locking it. Say, "Hah hah hah hah hah."

Twist your torso freely; walk and turn and reach while maintaining this alignment. Say, "Hah hah hah hah hah."

Exercise 18–2 will have an immediate short-term result: You will notice greater resonance and freer breathing right away. It is not a simple matter to make this improved alignment a part of your unconscious daily movements, however, nor is it a simple thing to sustain the alignment—at first—without feeling stiff and awkward. Good internal alignment takes a great deal of practice and concentration: You are changing habits of a lifetime, and you cannot expect to do that easily or quickly. But the end result will be greater physical and vocal presence and ability.

Walking

"Cross left," says the director, and the actor knows to walk to her or his left. But how to walk? Fast? Slow? Plodding? Shuffling? Slovenly? Assured?

It's surprising, but you can often tell inexperienced actors simply by the way they walk on the stage: What they have been doing since they were a year old suddenly seems tentative, even clumsy. Maybe this has happened to you. Part of it is self-consciousness, of course; there's nothing like fifty

WALKING AND TALKING

What is acting? It's walking and talking. But it isn't. It's about seeing the possibility or significance of those moments.

FIONA SHAW

bright lights in your face, and the knowledge that you're wearing splashy makeup for the first time, to make the butterflies dance in your belly. But part of it is not realizing that walking is part of the action of the play—and vitally connected to the goal, or GOTE, of your character.

For every move on stage must be *purposeful;* it must serve your character's quest to achieve a goal with someone else. And every move is tactical as well; like speech, walking is tactical: You may walk quickly to accomplish something in a hurry, slowly to sneak up on someone, casually to put someone at their ease, or boldly to command authority. And there are many different verbs we can use to convey different ways of walking: We can stride, slink, stroll, march, pace, promenade, saunter, tramp, stalk, parade, stomp, skip, tiptoe, run, jog, and sidle, among others. Any of these sixteen verbs can replace "cross" in the director's request to "cross left." But few directors think to use them. (Nor should they. That's up to you.)

But whatever you do, don't just "cross." What you see, above all, in inexperienced actors is that they are walking because they were told to, not because they *want* to. Remember: The actors may be told what to do, but the *characters they play* must be seen as *wanting* to do it. Choose an *active,* not passive, means of moving, and using one of the sixteen verbs will guarantee that you will do so.

◆ E X E R C I S E   18–3

Sixteen Walks

Explore all of these "sixteen verb" walks. Start by walking in a circle; then, as the instructor or group leader calls out, stride, slink, stroll, march, pace, promenade, saunter, tramp, stalk, parade, stomp, skip, tiptoe, run, jog, and sidle. Make these be *your* walks, not stylized "character walks," but for each one invent on-the-spot your own inner story and inner GOTE; for example, "I'll stomp over to my teacher and demand a grade change" or "I'll sidle over to Ashley and ask him/her to join me for lunch." After a while, continue the exercise but lose the circle and walk in spontaneously chosen directions with each change of verb. Walk toward and away from people designated in your "inner story"—while knowing that they may be walking toward or away from you.

◆ E X E R C I S E   18–4

Walk and Talk

Pair with a partner. Face each other from across the room. Pair one of the below lines with one of the above walks and "cross left" (or right) to your partner while "walking and talking" *and while maintaining eye contact with your partner at all times.*

1. "How would you like to be my running mate?"
2. "Why don't you want to go to the Ping-Pong match?"
3. "Your roommate's been arrested!"
4. "We've got only five hours before the exam."
5. "I just scored two tickets to the concert. Wanna go?"
6. "Well, I guess I just have to say it wouldn't be fair."
7. "Listen, I think you're terrific; it's just that, well, you know, the other students . . ."
8. "So. You think you're going to win today? Right?"
9. "What's the matter with you today?"
10. "Hey, I got the part!"
11. (sing) "There's a bright golden haze on the meadow . . ."
12. (sing) "Happy birthday to you, happy birthday to you, happy birthday . . ."

Maintaining the eye contact will concentrate your focus on your goal, and your GOTE, and keep you from "checking out your walk."

What sort of shoes are you wearing? A walk is not only a move, it is also a sound. Depending on the actor's shoes, the composition of the stage floor, and the degree of silence during the cross, an actor's footsteps can be a crucial part of the play's sound design. Actors who seem to "own their own feet" can make a powerful contribution to the play by the assured sound and bearing of their approach. And as Tadashi Suzuki, the well-known

Japanese director and acting teacher, reminds his students (and readers), the feet are primary to the actor's instrument because they are the only parts of the body to touch the ground.*

Sitting and Standing

Sitting and standing are also movements we use every day in our life, yet they too can look awkward and timid onstage. Obviously the same rules apply: *All* movements, not just stage crosses, must be seen to come from the character's pursuit of a goal—and active rather than passive movement is crucial in these cases as well. Sitting can also mean perching or flopping or easing down to a chair; standing can be anything from gently rising to leaping to one's feet.

◆ E X E R C I S E   18–5

Walk, Talk, Sit

Pairing with a partner, and using the same lines as in Exercise 18–4, "cross" to your partner, who is seated, and, while maintaining eye contact all the time, sit in a chair or a couch next to him or her with the last word of the line. (Ideally, the room where this exercise takes place has two chairs and a couch and the partner is seated in a chair between a second chair and a couch.)

Maintaining eye contact while sitting may be difficult at first, but *keep looking at your partner, not at the chair!* If you are unsure of where the chair is, you can touch it, but don't look at it. While it is true that, in real life, we may look at a chair when sitting in it (to make sure we don't miss the seat!), this is hardly a bold choice (see Lesson 12). The goal you are trying to achieve with your partner must be seen as a more important goal than not missing the seat! If you appear only as a person anxious not to embarrass yourself by the way you sit, you will appear as a very uninteresting character: no playwright has ever written a play about a person who was afraid of missing the seat when he or she sat!

Vary the exercise by your footwear—from hard-sole shoes (including high heels where appropriate) to athletic shoes to flip-flops to barefoot.

---

* Suzuki, Tadashi. *The Way of Acting*. Translated by J. Thomas Rimer. New York: Theatre Communications Group, 1986.

There should be a marked difference with many of these variations: What can you learn from them? And how can you apply it?

Velocity: Accelerating, Decelerating, and Constant

The ability to control acceleration and deceleration is crucial in developing physical dexterity and in creating the dynamics of movement. Accelerating and decelerating movements make clear that you are thinking while moving, that your mind is generating the movements you make. Constant velocity movements, on the other hand, indicate that you are simply executing movements generated by someone else—the director, for example.

Constant velocity movements figure in the portrayal of characters "trying to get a grip on themselves," such as a recovering drug addict putting down the bottle of pills. But for beginning actors, constant velocity movements usually show that the actors are moving only because they have to—or are supposed to—and not because they want to. This is invariably a serious flaw.

◆ E X E R C I S E   18–6

Acceleration/Deceleration

1. Stand, extend your arms outward, palms front, elbows slightly flexed.

2. Now bring your palms together in a clap, moving your arms at a constant rate of speed.

3. Now clap at a constantly accelerating rate of speed.

4. Now clap at a constantly decelerating rate of speed.

Notice the characteristics of the three claps. The first (constant rate of speed) is like perfunctory applause. The second is a gesture of victory— "Eureka!" The third is like bringing the hands together in prayer.

Practice constant, accelerating, and decelerating motions while repeating each of these actions five times:

1. Putting your hand down on a table

2. Moving your hand toward—and seizing—a prop revolver your partner is holding

3. Turning to look at someone behind you

4. Punching a pillow

5. Getting out of a chair

6. Walking to a predetermined spot on the floor

7. Sitting down

8. Lifting a drink (shot-glass size) to your lips and drinking it

9. Touching your partner's neck

10. Touching your partner's hair

11. Taking off your sweater

12. Putting a bottle of pills on a table

13. Lying down on a sofa

14. Pointing your finger at someone; pointing at some *part* of someone

---

Accelerating motions tend to be exciting and enthusiastic. Decelerating motions tend to be graceful and gentle. Constant motions tend to be bored and dutiful. Guess which kinds are most useful in acting. And guess which kinds you most often see with beginning actors!

Counterpoise

Contraposto is an Italian word, used mainly in the analysis of paintings and sculptures, describing counterpoised physical positions in which the body is twisted so that the shoulders and the hips, the arms and the legs, are in different planes. Michelangelo's paintings and sculptures, which are known for their contraposto, are especially illuminating for actors.

The counterpoised body is both dynamic and balanced; it can be coiled for action even though it seems to be at rest. By contrast, the standing-at-attention, squared-off body—a product of "stand-up-straight" discipline rather than actor training—is static and uninteresting on stage and is impossible to mobilize emotionally or physically.

◆ E X E R C I S E   18–7

Contraposto

1. Feet planted comfortably on the floor, the body aligned as in Exercise 18–2, turn the hips ninety degrees to the left.

2. Extend the right arm up and away. Turn the head another ninety degrees left. Flex the knees.

3. Spring to the reverse position.

4. Relax.

5. Walk, with a decelerating velocity, to a point ten yards away, turning as you come to a halt.

6. Walk, with a decelerating velocity, to a chair ten yards away; turn and coil as you sit.

7. Toss your head one way, then another.

8. Look one way and point another. Reverse.

9. Get a good sturdy sofa away from a wall. Using the sofa's seat, arms, and back, find ten physically dynamic contraposto positions for yourself, moving from one to the other in a fluid acceleration/deceleration movement. Play a scene or improvisation with someone, moving around the sofa in this fashion.

The body contracts on itself for protection. It extends outward for expression and sometimes for attack. The magnitude of contractions and extensions is one signification of an actor's physical freedom: Children, for example, are usually quite uninhibited in extensions; adults are far more often restrained.

◆ E X E R C I S E   18–8

Contraction/Extension

1. To the sounds of a drumbeat, or a command, CONTRACT! . . . CONTRACT! . . CONTRACT! . . CONTRACT!

2. To the sounds of a drumbeat, or a command, EXTEND! . . . EXTEND! . . . EXTEND! . . . EXTEND! . . . LEAP UP! . . . LEAP UP! . . . CONTRACT!

3. Walk with a decelerating speed and roll into a tight spiral, knotting yourself up into a little ball. Hold for ten seconds, compressing and compressing, and then EXPLODE!

4. Respond to an imaginary:

   Punch in the stomach

   Fire in the seat of your pants

   Heart attack

   Shout to surrender

   Cry for help

The Dynamics of Effort

A system of movement analysis invented in the 1940s by Hungarian-born Rudolf Laban (who also invented the world's first system of dance notation) is immeasurably helpful in defining, isolating, and developing movement skills in actors. Laban's movement system is laid out in a short (85-page) book, titled *Effort*.* In it, Laban ingeniously charts all human movement according to three factors: exertion (light or strong moves), space (curving or straight moves), and time (steady or pulsing moves).

Putting these together, Laban came up with these eight basic movement types: slashing, pressing, wringing, punching, gliding, flicking, dabbing, and floating.

	Exertion	Space	Time
Slashing	Strong	Curving	Pulsing
Pressing	Strong	Straight	Steady
Wringing	Strong	Curving	Steady
Punching	Strong	Straight	Pulsing
Gliding	Light	Straight	Steady
Flicking	Light	Curving	Pulsing
Dabbing	Light	Straight	Pulsing
Floating	Light	Curving	Steady

* Laban, Rudolf, and F. C. Lawrence. *Effort*. London: MacDonald & Evans, 1947.

A slashing move, for example, requires strong exertion, it curves in space, and it starts and stops suddenly (pulses). A gliding move, by contrast, requires only light exertion, it tends to be straight through space, and it is continuous rather than sudden.

The table shows merely Laban's eight major movement categories; he subsequently subdivides these eight into twenty-four, depending on which of the three factors dominates, and then to forty-eight, depending on whether the movements are loosely or tightly controlled by the mover. But Laban's eight basic categories are useful ways of isolating the major types of movement, each of which can be practiced in isolation so as to become distinct—that is, distinguished from more generalized moves.

◆ E X E R C I S E   18–9

Distinct Movements*

Miming all of the props mentioned:

1. Hit a nail with a hammer, throw coal with a shovel, whip an egg with a whisk. (slashing)

2. Crush peppercorns with a mortar and pestle, cut leather with a knife, squeeze a spring between your hands. (pressing)

3. Pull a cork with a corkscrew, pluck feathers from a chicken, stretch an elastic band. (wringing)

4. Pat dough with your hands, type on a keyboard, shake seeds through a sieve. (dabbing)

5. Smooth clay by hand, smear cement with a trowel, smudge putty with a putty knife. (gliding)

6. Snap a towel, count the pages of a book by flipping them, break a string with your hand. (flicking)

7. Scatter seeds by hand, stir oil paint with a stick, polish a tabletop. (floating)

8. Thrust a pitchfork into a hay pile, thrust a shovel into dry sand, pierce a thin tabletop with an awl. (punching)

---

* This exercise is adapted, almost directly, from *Effort* (pp. 28–31).

In each exercise, the effort level, or the spatial aspect (curving or straight), or the tempo will be the dominant one. Can you tell which by doing the action?

◆ E X E R C I S E   18–10

To Be or Not to Be

Repeat Exercise 18–9. With every distinct move, say the first line of Hamlet's great soliloquy: "To be or not to be, that is the question." Imagine on each occasion that you are talking to a group of people who know you, and making it clear to them that you are trying to decide whether you should keep on living or embark on a course that may lead you to death or even suicide. See if you can get a response from them. How does your speaking the line vary when you're slashing, or punching, or flicking? How does the imagined response vary? It is easy to picture different Hamlets playing the line while engaging in each of Laban's movement types.

◆ E X E R C I S E   18–11

Walking and Kicking

Walk around a room in a floating manner. A gliding manner. A pressing manner. A slashing manner. What sort of circumstances could lead you, in real life, to do this?

Kick or stamp or push with your foot an imaginary object in each of the eight basic Laban movements. What sort of circumstances could lead you, in real life, to do this?

Move your pelvis in each of the eight basic Laban dynamic patterns. Circumstances?

Distinguishing and isolating movements, Laban-style, is like learning to play the individual notes of a piano. Few sonatas allow you to play a single note at a time, at least for any appreciable length of time, and stage movement, like piano music, is a living complex of its various elements. But learning to isolate the dynamics of the body, like learning to play upon the keys of a piano, gives you a vast palette of strategies to employ in seeking the goals of your character on the stage.

Summary

The actor's body must be trained into a supple, strong, energetic, dexterous, and dynamic instrument. Physical training programs, which may take years, involve the learning of precise movement skills, such as mime and formal dance, but some simple exercises can start you immediately on the road to establishing good physical alignment, integration of onstage speech and movement, control over the movement direction and velocity (acceleration and deceleration), dynamic counterpoise and balance, and the potential for bold (explosive) physicalization.

L E S S O N

19

Voice and Body Integration

Coordination

The integration of body and voice—"being able to walk and talk at the same time"—is the acid test of the actor's instrument. Master this and you will progress accordingly. Fail and you must go back and try again.

In life we speak and move at the same time without thinking; in the theatre, however, we are required to think: to learn lines written by an author and movements initiated by a director. To reproduce these unselfconsciously isn't easy. Concentrating on our lines, we may stiffen physically; concentrating on our movement, we may let our dialog come out stilted and mechanical. The fluidity of speech and motion, common enough in our everyday existence, is easily lost through the divided consciousness of acting.

Concentration on the character's goal, and on the tactics of expectations necessary to gain that goal, through or with the other persons in the play, will integrate the actor's mind. Thus, pursuing the GOTE principles will pull together the liberated instrument and make it compelling.

Once developed, the actor's instrument can be used only when it is forgotten. While playing a concerto, the violinist is not thinking about strings and bows and frets; the violinist is thinking about making music. Likewise, in playing the role, the actor is not thinking of phonemes or decelerations; she or he is thinking of goals and how to achieve them quickly. Finally, the actor *becomes* an instrument.

Developing good voice–body integration, or coordination, demands that you are quite clear about what you want in a scene and that you are entirely free to put your whole body (voice and movement) into achieving your goal. If this concentration on victory is your mainspring, both voice and body will serve that concentration: They will be integrated by the strength of your commitment to get what you want.

The following exercise should be a useful first step in integrating voice and body.

◆ EXERCISE 19–1

Commands

These exercises begin where Exercise 18–5 (Walk, Talk, Sit) left off.

1. Try to make a (real or imaginary) partner come to a specific spot by walking five steps to the spot while saying, "Come right here!" As you reach the spot, pivot around and point to the floor. The movement and speaking should be simultaneous, and you should pivot and point while you are still speaking. Experiment with various timings of this.

2. Do this exercise with these alternate lines:

   a. "I want you to come right here, please."

   b. "Listen, George, I think it's very important that you come right here before I get any angrier than I already am."

   c. "Come, friend." (Or "Come, my darling.")

3. Do this exercise while walking to a sofa, or to one of two adjacent chairs, turning and sitting during your last line. Choose lines from 1 and 2 above, or write new lines. (But write, don't improvise.)

You should be able to marry short lines with long moves, and long lines with short moves, and, in fact, to time out any combination of movement and speech in an effective, relaxed, confident manner. Work also on completing your movements with a decelerating turn or sit synchronized with your last word.

◆ E X E R C I S E   19–2

Speeches with Business

Study and memorize one of the following speeches—all of which are taken
from the opening scenes of plays. Or memorize a short speech from the first
few pages of any play of your choice. From the context, imagine whom you
are speaking to and use your imagination to create a GOTE approach to
the speech. Rehearse the speech privately until you feel confident of the
lines.

1. "Since the Professor and his wife came to live here, life is off the
   track. . . . I sleep at odd hours, for lunch and dinner I eat a lot of highly
   spiced dishes, drink wine . . . all that is not good for your health. We
   never used to have a free minute. Sonia and I worked—I can tell you that
   —and now it's only Sonia who works, and I sleep, eat, drink. . . . There's
   no good in it." (Anton Chekhov, *Uncle Vanya*)

2. "We've been in rehearsal four days. Due to a technical fluke with the
   contract—not your fault, of course—Mr. Billy Hertz, our leading man, is
   on his way to Hollywood and a flowery two-picture deal. As of today,
   here and now, we are minus a leading man. Since we are booked into
   Boston on the 28th, we are in trouble!" (Clifford Odets, *The Country
   Girl*)

3. "Honey, don't *push* with your *fingers*. If you have to push with something, the thing to push with is a crust of bread. And chew—chew! Animals have sections in their stomachs which enable them to digest food
   without mastication, but human beings are supposed to chew their food
   before they swallow it down. Eat food leisurely, son, and really enjoy it.
   A well-cooked meal has lots of delicate flavors that have to be held in the
   mouth for appreciation. So chew your food and give your salivary glands
   a chance to function!" (Tennessee Williams, *The Glass Menagerie*)

4. "The street is lined with cars. There's not a breath of fresh air in the
   neighborhood. The grass don't grow any more, you can't raise a carrot
   in the back yard. They should've had a law against apartment houses.
   Remember those two beautiful elm trees out there? When I and Biff hung
   the swing between them? . . . They should've arrested the builder for cutting those down. They massacred the neighborhood." (Arthur Miller,
   Death of a Salesman)

Now, with the speech learned, practice "delivering" it to a (real or imaginary) partner, using real props—or substitute props—and performing one
of the following pieces of stage business at the same time:

1. Changing your clothing

2. Mixing and drinking a Manhattan cocktail

3. Mixing, dressing, and tasting a fruit salad

4. Shuffling a deck of cards and dealing out two hands of gin rummy

5. Peeling and eating a banana, then disposing of the peel

It is, of course, necessary to have the business well in hand. You must, for example, know how to mix a Manhattan cocktail in order to do it, and your speech, convincingly. Choose business that is progressive (not simply repetitive) and sufficiently complex so that it involves several parts of your body.

You will probably find that Exercise 19–2 requires a good deal of practice. You will quickly find that there are literally thousands of ways in which your lines and business can be coordinated. How does the behavior affect the speech? How do the speech and the feelings that come with it affect the behavior? Don't try to "interpret" the speech according to the context of the play; treat the speech simply as an isolated exercise, and let the speech create behavior that supports your delivery. Can you combine certain behaviors with the language so as to charm your partner? To threaten him or her? To beg for pity? To subvert? To frighten? To overwhelm?

◆ E X E R C I S E   19–3

Physical Punctuation

Select any speech that you have memorized, possibly one from the preceding exercise, and deliver it to a (real or imaginary) partner while doing a repetitive physical action, such as

1. Jogging in place

2. Skipping rope

3. Beating egg yolks

4. Doing sit-ups

5. Combing your hair

6. Playing the piano

7. Dribbling a (pretend) basketball

8. Shaving

Talk "over" the physical action; make yourself understood—and your intentions felt—over and above the distraction of your movement.

Now "punctuate" the speech by stopping your movement at a certain point in the text. Experiment with several possible moments. Experiment with stopping one movement—and later in the speech starting another one.

You are your own best teacher of what "works" in Exercise 19–3. Much of the director's work in staging a play is finding the right physical punctuation to drive home significant emotional transitions. You can anticipate this work in your acting by finding out how a change of physical rhythm coordinates with a change in the plot or in a character's intention or understanding of a relationship.

◆ E X E R C I S E   19–4

Physical Rhythms

Memorize one or more of the one-line speeches in Exercise 17–3. Deliver each speech to a (real or imaginary) partner together with an accelerating movement of your hand, such as pointing or slamming your fist on a table.

Deliver each speech with a decelerating movement, such as sitting in a chair, crossing the room and turning, or touching your partner.

◆ E X E R C I S E   19–5

Verbal Rhythms

Give each of the following commands with an accelerating tempo, then with a decelerating tempo.

1. "Get out of this room."

2. "Give me that!"

3. "Go out there and win!"

4. "Kiss me before I explode."

5. "To be or not to be, that is the question."

Combine the accelerating tempo with an accelerating arm/hand movement. Combine the decelerating tempo with a decelerating physical movement.

Pointing

While indicating emotions is usually considered an acting fault (see Lesson 14), indicating *objects* (or places or people) by physically pointing, nodding, or gesturing toward them is often instrumental in acting performance. In the case of demonstrative pronouns ("that," "those," "these," "this"), some sort of physical indication is often absolutely required, as in "Bring me that book" (when there are several books on the table) or "I'll take one of those" (when there are several groupings of objects in the room). Without a gesture of some sort, it is often impossible to determine the antecedent (referent) of such a pronoun.

More generally, pointing or gesturing, when not overdone, creates a basic and credible opportunity for expressive movement, engaging the body in the actions of the mind and voice. To say "I'm going with her," while turning and pointing to the woman in question, not only clarifies which woman you're referring to but also establishes a physical and spatial bond between you and the actor playing that role, almost always augmented with a deeper psychological connection which makes the relationship between you and "her" more vivid—certainly to the audience, but usually to yourself as well. It also gets you moving, and sharing more of your face and body with the audience on several sides.

Pointing, gesturing, or looking at what you speak of also helps you establish the seeming reality of dramatized places, including divine realms in which your characters believe. To give a toss of your head toward the stage door or window on "He's out there" makes the idea of an "outside" more real, both to an audience and to yourself, though the indicated area is actually nothing but backstage clutter. Looking heavenward when calling upon God's name in Hamlet's "O God! God! How weary, stale, flat and unprofitable seem to me all the uses of this world!" will engage your Hamlet in a dialog with, or a searching for, this "God," rather than a mere statement or expletive. And if as St. Joan (in Shakespeare's *I Henry VI*) you glance up on the word *above* when declaring yourself as "chosen from above," the gesture will make you more intimidating to the church officers who are persecuting you and will also intensify your feeling—or imagination—that you are indeed communicating directly with a divine presence.

In short, selected and discreet pointing—with your finger, thumb, open hand, both hands, head, eyes, or raised eyebrow—can make your acting clearer, more specific, more physical, more active, and more authentic: spatially and emotionally connected with other actors, surroundings, and the (fictional) places represented in the play.

◆ E X E R C I S E   19–6

Pointing

With a partner, and imagining a simple situation provoking such a line, play each of these sentences first without gesturing, then again with a turn and a pointing gesture on the italicized word—using your finger, thumb, open hand, both hands, head, eyes, or raised eyebrow—and evaluate the difference in your reading. Then try it once more but with a different look or gesture.

1. I want *you* to have this.

2. And what am I supposed to do with *this* one?

3. Quick, go over *there*.

4. Shhhh. Sneak over *there*.

5. Your thoughts come from the devil, but mine come from *God*.

6. She came up from the *train station*.

7. John's *upstairs*.

8. No, you rat, I accuse *you*.

The following is too complicated to be used in an exercise, but try to figure out how Shakespeare may have wanted the italicized words in this speech—of a "Stranger" in *Timon of Athens*—to be performed:

> Who can call him
> His friend that dips in the same dish? for, in
> My knowing, Timon has been *this* lord's father,
> And kept *his* credit with *his* purse,
> Supported *his* estate; nay, Timon's money
> Has paid *his* men their wages: *he* ne'er drinks,
> But Timon's silver treads upon his lip;
> And yet—O, see the monstrousness of man

When he looks out in an ungrateful shape!—
He does deny *him,* in respect of *his,*
What charitable men afford to beggars.

So support your meaning with visual indications; as Shakespeare said, suit the action to the word.

Tempo

The ability to experiment with tempos—both physical and verbal—is an acting asset. There are no intrinsically "right" or "wrong" tempos in the theatre, and rarely do tempos simply accelerate or decelerate in straight-line fashion; but a rhythmic variety is characteristic both of fine acting and of life itself. The beginning actor is often stuck in a repetitive, plodding rhythm, which is neither dramatic nor lifelike but, rather, a product of stage fright and dutiful "line reading."

How do the varying rhythms in Exercise 19–5 affect your feelings? Your interaction with your partner? Ask your partner—if you have one—what impact your accelerated deliveries, or your decelerated deliveries, had on him or her. Get comfortable with this exercise by repeating it several times, varying your text, intention, rhythm, and acting partner.

◆ E X E R C I S E   19–7

Speech/Movement Timing

Select a one-minute speech from any play—such as the speeches in Exercise 19–2. Analyze the GOTE for the character in that speech. Plot out a series of actions that coordinate with the speech, such as crossing the stage, walking around a sofa, picking up a book and tossing it aside, sitting down, smiling, tossing your head, and crossing your legs. Define where the other characters are located. Rehearse the speech very carefully so that you can time the actions to specific words. Create a pattern of accelerating and decelerating movements and verbal tempos. Create two or three punctuations. Let the speech climax at the end so that the crossing of the legs becomes a significant action concluding your line of thought.

When you can do this unconsciously, you will have taken a very long stride toward becoming an actor.

Actors with Disabilities

The emphasis on voice and movement in actor training should not obscure the fact that some actors are disabled in one way or another. There are very fine actors who cannot hear or speak: Witness the Theatre of the Deaf. And there are excellent actors who are paraplegics and amputees. There is certainly nothing superhuman about most actors' instruments, and some indeed transcend serious limitations. Acting is a portrayal of human life and the human condition, and anyone who has a sense of that and can portray a goodly fraction of it will find the opportunity to do so. But voice–body integration—the integration of such capacities as the actor has and can nourish—is a critical step in every actor's development, for only through such integration can an actor maximize his or her potential.

Summary

Concentration on goals and on the GOTE of the character integrates the voice and body components of the actor's instrument. Moving and speaking simultaneously and unselfconsciously is difficult for actors to master, but it must be learned if acting is to be fluid, rhythmically dynamic, energetic, lifelike, and properly punctuated. Each actor may have limitations or disabilities, but developing the acting instrument means integrating, as much as possible, all your capacities for dramatically effective speech and movement.

20

Imagination and Discipline

Fantasy

Imagination (fantasy, creativity, inspiration) is the wellspring of the acting impulse. Discipline (responsibility, punctuality, preparedness) shapes actors into an ensemble of collaborative creation. Without either, fine acting cannot exist; therefore both imagination and discipline must be developed and integrated in the actor's personality.

Imagination is the source of the actor's goal, the source of victory and intention. Romeo wants to marry Juliet, and that is the goal the actor pursues. But how does the actor pursue it? Not simply through clinical observation or rational depiction. "I want to marry Juliet" is a lively, compelling, intense fantasy. It obviously has deeply sexual origins. It may also engage fantasies of worship, adventure, social acceptance, class revenge, and fetishism, as well as fantasies of annihilation, damnation, gluttony, domination, and isolation. The most exciting Romeo is clearly the one whose fantasies are the liveliest, most provocative, most insistent, and most enchanting. The actor who is simply pursuing a marriage certificate will be a pedestrian Romeo, no matter how brilliantly he reads Romeo's lines.

When approaching a part, the actor quickly comes to grips with the character's major goals and intentions. Research into the part, into the period of the play, and into the psychology of the character can further

IN DIALOG WITH YOUR IMAGINATION

Actors have to have a fundamental ability to be in permanent dia-logue with their own imaginations, so that when they utter forth something, people hear them.

FIONA SHAW

define the character's goals. But defining goals is only the first step in play-ing them. One still must bring them to life; and here *your* life—the life of your mind—plays a crucial role.

The imagination is a rich, unfettered world where anything can happen, where lust, torture, bestiality, suicide, and apocalyptic experiences of inde-scribable dimensions all have their place. These private places are rarely shared even in the most intimate relationships. Some private places are securely locked away: At times we refuse to admit, even to ourselves, that we have such thoughts. (Such locking away, called *repression,* is often the cause of serious neurotic disorders.) Often our secret fantasies are so unset-tling in our conscious contemplation of them that they come to the fore only in our dreams and nightmares. Certainly the theatre has been one of society's great inventions for dealing with this private world of the imagina-tion: The continuing uproar over the predominance of sex and violence on television does not obscure the fact that the theatre, at its deepest level, is about little else.

As an actor must be uninhibited vocally and physically, so he or she must be uninhibited in the imaginative life. We not only want to see Romeo "want to marry" Juliet, we want to see him *tremble* at the sight of her. We want to see her struggle to catch her breath when she sees him for the first time. We want to see the blood rush up in their cheeks; we want to see their lips quiver. We also want to see their absolute *terror* of saying the wrong thing. In short, we (in the audience) want to see the actors experience all the rapture, confusion, and anxiety of the profoundest first love there ever was! This occurs in the voice and body—but in the mind as well. Indeed, the mind is confronting the body, and the fantasies of the mind are straining against the limitations of the physical being.

Self-Exploration

The actor's imagination—the actor's fantasies and fears—are often well submerged, frequently all but inaccessible. Imagination exercises can help the actor probe his or her own unconscious, inducing a "daydream" state where the emotions, memories, and longings commingle just below the sur-

face. These exercises in self-exploration are akin to hypnosis and meditation—both of which are often used by actors to attain what Stanislavsky
called the "creative mood."

♦ E X E R C I S E   20–1

Cold/Hot

For this exercise you need a group leader or instructor and a room whose
lighting is controlled by a dimmer.

Lie or sit on the floor. As the light brightens, imagine that the temperature gets warmer, then hotter, then uncomfortably hot, then *painfully* hot.

Imagine that by chanting "ohhhhhhhhhhh," you and the others can
appease the gods that control the temperature.

As the light fades, imagine that the temperature cools, that it gets cold
and then freezing.

Imagine that you are dying.

Imagine that by chanting "eeeeeeeeeeee," the group can appease the
gods and restore warmth to the world. Imagine that rhythmic stamping
reinforces the chant.

The group leader may improvise additional variants for you to imagine.

♦ E X E R C I S E   20–2

Age Regression/Advancement

Look at a partner; study him or her well. Feel your partner's face with your
hand. Imagine your partner at half his or her age. At half again that age.
Imagine your partner as four years old. As two years old. As a naked infant.
As a naked adolescent. Realize that your partner *was* a naked adolescent.

Imagine your partner at double his or her age. At age eighty-five. Look
beneath your partner's skin at the skull. Feel your partner's skull. Imagine
your partner dead, lying in a shallow grave. Imagine your partner as a skeleton. REALIZE THAT YOUR PARTNER *WILL* BECOME A SKELETON.

Back away from your partner so that several yards separate you. Envi-
sion your partner's birth-to-death cycle. Imagine, in fantasy, relationships
between your partner and persons in your family, or persons close to you,
or you yourself at different ages.

On signal, approach and hug your partner.

The group leader may improvise additional variants for your imagination.

Fantasy is most effective as an individual exercise, not a class exercise. Fantasizing sexual or violent relationships, for example, may be embarrassing when "performed" at an instructor's command; if given free play within an acting scene, however, such fantasizing can give life to the most pedestrian stage relationship. You are always the master of your own imagination. When you are freed from inhibition and from worry over remembering your lines, the creative use of your imagination can give your stage character as much sensitivity and liveliness as you experience in your own dream/nightmare world.

◆ E X E R C I S E   20–3

Facing an Imagined Death

Memorize these lines of Lear's from *King Lear*:

> "[. . .] No, no, no life!
> Why should a dog, a horse, a rat, have life,
> And thou no breath at all? Thou't come no more.
> Never, never, never, never, never!"

In this moment in the play, King Lear grieves over the body of his youngest daughter, Cordelia, who was just hanged. As Lear, you have cut her down, killed the person who hanged her, and carried her dead body onstage.

Make a circle with other members of your group. An object (it could be a person) is placed in the center, on the floor, representing the body of Cordelia. One at a time, deliver the speech. Do not try to imitate the character of King Lear as you might know it; let the line come from you, just the way you are, but try to make yourself confront the fact of this death that lies in front of you. Try to inquire of the gods—or your God—why this object, your daughter, should lie dead here instead of some dog or rat.

Try again, with the last words of the speech, to come to terms with your daughter's very real death. Try one more time.

As you do the exercise a second and third time, "imagine" the object in the center of the circle is something very specific in your life. A favored pet, perhaps, or younger sibling, or even an image of yourself. After the exercise (but not during), reflect as to how the object you imagined affected your feelings, your vocal delivery, and your general behavior while giving the speech.

◆ E x e r c i s e   20–4

Facing Love

Memorize the following lines of Juliet's from *Romeo and Juliet:*

"My bounty is as boundless as the sea,
My love as deep—the more I give to thee
The more I have, for both are infinite."

At this moment in the play, Romeo has just declared "love's faithful vow" to Juliet for the first time, asking for hers in return.

Deliver this line to an imaginary Romeo—and then another and another, without regard to your or your Romeo's gender. Don't try to imitate what you think Juliet might be like, but deliver the line as you yourself would to a real person you actually love, or would like to love, or someone you would like to love you. On a subsequent occasion, imagine the object of your love to be a god, or spirit, or animal.

These last two exercises are very powerful if you imagine them—and experience them—fully. They will undoubtedly engage your deepest emotions (see Lesson 21), if you allow them to do so. Great acting always engages the emotions, and almost always through the medium of imagination. Imagination is what makes a play seem real to you, even when you rehearse and perform it night after night. Imagination is what allows you to play both the eighty-year-old man (King Lear) and the thirteen-year-old girl (Juliet). Imagination also gives you the confidence to speak with conviction and emotional honesty lines written four hundred years ago.

For there's nothing remote or "literary" about facing death or facing love. It's entirely real: Shakespeare did it, we will do it, and our audiences will do it too. And no matter how often we may face death, or face love, we never really understand it fully, we never master it, we are always awed by it. The same might be said about acting, and about great theatre. It always

DISCIPLINE

To be an actor in the theatre is to teach yourself and keep yourself disciplined and honorable. And if you do that, you get a chance to fly in this kind of emotional paradise that acting can be. Acting is just as hard as ditch digging. And if you do all the yeoman work, inspiration will come.

FRANK LANGELLA

transcends what we know. Acting is an art that spans the known and the imaginary universes.

Discipline

Discipline is the flip side of imagination. It is the final element in an actor's instrument and the one that should be taken for granted by the time an actor begins serious study.

Unlike most of the creative arts, acting is a team enterprise; an actor is, by necessity, a team player. Rehearsals, although frequently improvisational, freewheeling, and fun, are serious artistic collaborations. Absolutely faithful attendance and punctuality are universally required.

The discipline of the actor is what permits the shared trust of the ensemble. If the imagination is to be free and the fantasy uninhibited, then each actor must feel the support of the whole and must know that the trust will not be misplaced, the fantasy not misread, and the emotions not ridiculed. An atmosphere of trust permits the wildest leaps of imagination and the most daring personal choices.

The theatre is always greater than the sum of its parts. Acting excels only inasmuch as *interacting* excels. To be on time, to learn your lines on time, to commit to the reality of the situation and style, to treat the work seriously and with spirit—these are the marks of the disciplined actor and the joys of the disciplined acting company. *There is no better place to learn discipline than acting class.* People do not work one way in school and another in the professional world; discipline is an artistic habit, and it has its own artistic rewards. It is not merely something you have to accept; if you are a serious actor, you accept it because you *want* to.

There are, obviously, no "discipline exercises." Show up on time, lines learned, ready to go, and commit yourself. Do your homework. Experiment. Share with your co-workers. And do it every day of your life. That's discipline—starting now.

Summary

Imagination and discipline are the intangible aspects of an actor's instrument—intangible because they are attitudes rather than skills. The actor's imagination must be liberal, provocative, and lively; the actor's self-discipline must be firm, unambiguous, and freely given. Imagination and discipline can be practiced, perhaps even taught, but they are intrinsic aspects of every committed artist in the theatre. They should come into play *now,* not at some vague future in your studies or career.

21

Emotion—
and Acting Theory

Many Americans—even those unconnected with the theatre or theatre arts —have heard about something called "Method acting" or simply "the Method." What does this mean?

The method referred to is that of the late Lee Strasberg, who developed it at the Actors Studio in New York during the 1940s and '50s. It, in turn, derives from the acting system developed some forty years previously by the Russian actor and director Konstantin Stanislavsky at his Moscow Art Theatre. The essence of Method acting is that the actors draw deeply on their own emotions and experiences while playing their roles. In Stanislavsky's version of it, the actors "live the life" of their character during the performance. The opposite of this approach is sometimes called "technical acting" or "presentational acting," where the actors are seen as objectively and technically creating their characters, and then presenting (rather than representing) those characters to the audience, miming but not necessarily feeling the characters' emotions.

These two contrary notions of acting have, over the years, created a worldwide debate in acting circles, with American actors tending to favor the more representational (and Russian) methods, and British actors (as well as French and German) thought to favor a more presentational approach.

But the debate is hardly this simple. Most American actors are clearly aware of the necessity of a disciplined and controllable stage technique.

And British actors are deeply influenced by the teachings of Stanislavsky, which form, by way of example, the core first-year acting curriculum of the Royal Academy of Dramatic Arts in London.

Nor is the debate strictly a modern one. Indeed, the extent to which actors might be said to feel or not feel the emotions of their characters, and believe or not believe they "are" the characters they play, constitutes what Professor Joseph Roach, in his book *The Player's Passion: Studies in the Science of Acting,** has called "the historic, continuing, and apparently inexhaustible combat between technique and inspiration in performance theory." It is useful to probe at least briefly into this fascinating and important issue.

More than two thousand years before Stanislavsky and Strasberg considered the matter, the Greek philosopher Socrates queried Ion, a rhapsodist (reciter of poems), as to the role of real emotion in performance:

SOCRATES: Tell me, Ion, when you produce the greatest effect upon the audience . . . are you in your right mind? Or are you not carried out of yourself? Does not your soul, in ecstasy, seem to be among the persons or the places of which you are speaking?

ION: That strikes home, Socrates. I must frankly confess that at the tale of pity my eyes are filled with tears, and when I speak of horrors, my hair stands on end and my heart throbs.

Obviously, Ion "lived the life" of his characters, feeling the emotions of his roles, and feeling himself to be in the presence of the characters in his tales. But, as Socrates' inquiry soon reveals, Ion was also aware of the powerful effects his acting had on his audience:

SOCRATES: . . . and are you aware that you produce similar effects on most of the spectators?

ION: Only too well; for I look down upon them from the stage, and behold the various emotions of pity, wonder, sternness, stamped upon their countenances when I am speaking.†

And so we see that Ion considered his acting both representational (he felt himself among the characters of his story) and presentational (he was checking out the audience all the while). It is a paradox, Socrates realized: Ion was both "in" the fiction of his recitation and, at the same time, outside of it.

---

* Newark: University of Delaware Press, 1985
† Quoted in *Actors on Acting,* rev. ed., ed. Toby Cole and Helen Kritch Chinoy (New York: Crown, 1970), pp. 7–8.

Horace, the Roman poet (65–8 B.C.), turned Ion's paradox into a famous maxim of the ancient world: "In order to move the audience, you must first be moved yourself." And this Greco-Roman "Method" belief held near-absolute sway in the theatre for at least the next fifteen hundred years. We are fortunate to have some examples of its use in classical times. The Greek actor Aesop, we are told, became so overwrought during a performance of Euripides' *Orestes* that he ran his sword through a stagehand who had chanced to stray into his line of sight. Polus, another ancient Greek actor, placed the ashes of his own dead son onstage in order to inspire himself while giving Electra's speech of lamentation in the Sophocles play. Quintilian, the first-century Roman orator, describes envisioning his wife's and children's imaginary death "with such extreme vividness" that he was "so moved while speaking that I have not merely been wrought upon to tears, but have turned pale and shown all the symptoms of genuine grief."

And yet these same actors also sought to present their characters according to the stage conventions of their times. Quintilian, for all his tears and passion, urged his fellow actors to achieve the "regularity and discipline promised by calculation"; and cautioned, for example, that "it is never correct to employ the left hand alone in gesture" and "the hand [may not] be raised above the level of the eyes."

So again we have the paradox: The actor performs with true emotion but also follows a calculated discipline of gestures, phrasings, and deportment. These ideas held sway up to and through the Renaissance, affecting Shakespeare, Molière, and virtually all playwrights and actors until the late eighteenth century. In many of these periods, natural emotion seemed to be favored by commentators; in others, conscious technique, but normally both were considered relatively equal in an alliance of seeming opposites.

In 1773, however, Denis Diderot, the famous French encyclopedist, tackled this issue head-on, in a startling book titled *The Paradox of Acting*. Though not published until forty-six years after Diderot's death, this book was widely circulated in Europe from its time of writing. Diderot begins with the radical thesis that "a great actor . . . must [be] an unmoved and disinterested onlooker." He continues: "They say an actor is all the better for being excited, for being angry. I deny it. He is best when he imitates anger. Actors impress the public not when they are furious, but when they play fury well." By contrast, Diderot explained, "Actors who play from the heart . . . are alternately strong and feeble, fiery and cold. . . . Tomorrow they will miss the point they have excelled in today." Thus, Diderot maintains, "The actor who plays from thought . . . will be always at his best; he has considered, combined, learned and arranged the whole thing in his head."

Even those performances that move us deeply, Diderot insisted,

are all planned, . . . they have [all] been practiced a hundred times. . . .
At the moment when [the great actor] touches your heart he is listening

to his own voice; his talent depends not . . . upon feeling, but upon rendering so exactly the outward signs of feeling that you fall into the trap. He has rehearsed . . . every note of his passion. . . . You will see him weep at the word, at the syllable, he has chosen, not a second sooner or later. The broken voice, the half-uttered words, the stifled or prolonged notes [are all just] . . . a magnificent apery.

The actor, Diderot concludes, "is not the person he represents; he plays it, and plays it so well that you think he is the person; the deception is all on your side; he knows well enough he is not the person."*

Diderot's view was rooted in his confidence that all knowledge, including art, was rational and could be categorized, analyzed, alphabetized, and (given his profession) encyclopedized. Diderot's work typifies the Enlightenment era in which he lived, with its demystification of both medieval superstition and Renaissance idealism. The subsequent ages of romanticism and realism, however—particularly in the theatre—brought a strong rebellion against the "objective" rationalism of Enlightenment thinking.

"Put life into all the imagined circumstances and actions," Stanislavsky wrote in *An Actor Prepares*, "until you have completely satisfied your sense of truth, and until you have awakened a sense of faith in the reality of your sensations." By "life" Stanislavsky meant the ambiguity of emotion, the mystery of love and death, and the confusion of experience. To create this life on stage, Stanislavsky sought to identify the separate steps of the actor's preparation. Absolutely primary to his vision was that the actor seek, in the act of performance, to resolve his or her *character's* problem (in Russian: *zadacha*), as opposed to his or her mere *actor's* problem. Thus the actor playing Juliet concentrates on winning Romeo's love (or her father's respect, or her nurse's complicity), rather than showing the audience how romantic (or poetic, or young, or pretty) she is. By this means, according to Stanislavsky (and to the author of this book you are reading), the actor represents Juliet as a real and whole person, rather than simply presenting Juliet as a fictional character of the Shakespearean tragic stage. The character's *zadacha* is Stanislavsky's key.

Zadacha was translated as "objective" by Elizabeth Hapgood in the English-language version of *An Actor Prepares*,† and that word, along with "goal" and "intention," are used more than "problem" to refer to this concept today. But regardless of the term used (and "goal" is used in this book), Stanislavsky's basic understanding—that the actor plays a character

---

* In Cole and Chinoy, pp. 162, 170.

† *An Actor Prepares*, Constantin Stanislavski translated by Elizabeth Reynolds Hapgood (New York: Theatre Arts Books, 1936), but see *Stanislavsky in Focus*, Sharon Marie Carnicke (Amsterdam: Harwood Academic Publishers, 1998), for a fuller description of Stanislavsky's Russian terminology.

by actively seeking to solve the character's problems, and by pursuing the character's goals—has become fundamental to basic actor instruction almost everywhere in theatre today. It is by pursuing the character's goals, rather than by simply trying to please or entertain the audience, that the actor enters into the full dramatic and emotional life of the character. And while this method is particularly obvious in modern realistic dramas, Stanislavsky and his followers have applied it in historical and more stylized plays as well.

Stanislavsky was one of the first theatre artists to systematically investigate the notion of motivation in acting and to advance the concept that every move onstage must be seen to correspond to what the character (and not just the playwright or director) is striving to achieve. He created the notion of "public solitude" to indicate the way in which an actor must focus his or her attention on the events of the play rather than simply on the play's impact on the audience. He established the notion that the play's text was accompanied by a "subtext" of meanings (chiefly unspoken and undescribed character goals) hidden beneath the lines. He hated all forms of empty theatricality, where the actor simply relied on established gimmicks or conceits. He insisted that an "artistic communion" must exist among the actors, in which actors must invest themselves deeply, drawing heavily, therefore, upon their own personal feelings in establishing a rapport with their characters, their fellow actors, and the fictional events of the play.

And Stanislavsky was profoundly, almost obsessively, concerned with the actor's emotion. Discovering in the writings of the nineteenth-century French psychologist Théodule Armand Ribot that memories of past experiences are recorded by the nervous system and can be stirred by the right stimulus, Stanislavsky began to experiment with recalling his own past emotional states, eventually developing an acting technique known as "emotion memory" (or "emotional recall" or "affective memory"), whereby an actor mentally substitutes these remembered situations from his or her own life into the action of the play so as to reach the emotional levels dramatically required. By this substitution of remembered feelings, Stanislavsky sought to make acting natural, truthful, and emotionally vivid for the performer and audience alike.

But Stanislavsky was also quite well versed in external theatrical technique. Born to an affluent, aristocratic family, he had performed in plays, operettas, and operas from the age of six, often in the large, fully equipped theatres in both his family's Moscow home and country estate. A promising singer, he had studied with a major Bolshoi Opera star; Tchaikovsky had proposed writing an opera for him. Like Quintilian, Stanislavsky fully recognized the necessity for rational control in performance. "Feeling . . . does not replace an immense amount of work on the part of our intellects," he said. And so he studied elocution, dance, and phrasing as passionately as emotion. At some point in the middle of his career, Stanislavsky even discarded emotional memory in favor of a more physical approach and

DOING, NOT SHOWING

You have got to start doing things and not showing them. Don't have any preconceived ideas about how the scene is going to play. Just go on a moment to moment reality level and don't presuppose anything.

JAMES DEAN, ADVISING THE 18-YEAR-OLD DENNIS HOPPER
ON THE SET OF *REBEL WITHOUT A CAUSE* (1955)

devoted most of his later work to the exploration of physical actions as the key to stimulating truthful acting. He began to reproach his actors for excessive wallowing in private emotions. "What's false here? You're playing feelings, your own suffering, that's what's false. I need to see the event and how you react to that event, how you fight people—how you react, not suffer. . . . To take that line . . . is to be passive and sentimental. See everything in terms of action!" he said.* Stanislavsky, too, believed in a paradox of acting.

No country—not even Russia—has been as influenced by Stanislavsky's teaching as the United States. By 1920 two of Stanislavsky's disciples, Richard Boleslavsky and Maria Ouspenskaya, moved to New York and founded the American Laboratory Theatre, bringing Stanislavsky's new "System" to the attention of American actors. Among their converts was an Austrian immigrant, Lee Strasberg, who headed the Actors Studio in New York from 1951 until his death in 1982. Strasberg's ensuing "Method," derived from the early version of Stanislavsky's System, and including emotional recall as a principal technique, proved the most influential actor-training theory in America during the 1950s and '60s. Perhaps because it privileged actors over the script, making their own feelings as much the "subject" of the play as their character's actions, serious American actors and not a few celebrities, such as Marilyn Monroe, flocked to his school. Other American acting teachers, some of whom, like Stella Adler and Sonia Moore, had studied with Stanislavsky at a later point in his career, preached the Russian master's later creed of physical actions rather than emotional memory. To this day, almost all American teachers pay homage to Stanislavsky, often framing the debate on acting theory as the opposition of his early teachings with his later ones.

So what are *your* feelings on this fascinating issue? The teachings and theories of Stanislavsky and Strasberg can certainly not be ignored. They have revolutionized the modern theatre and reflect, as well, a tradition

---

* Quoted in Jean Benedetti, *Stanislavski* (London: Methuen, 1988), pp. 77, 271.

going back to Plato and Horace. But the words of Diderot cannot be simply set aside either; they contain undeniable truths, and everyone who works in the theatre knows that great performances (which must, in most cases, be delivered night after night) usually come out of tremendous discipline, planning, calculation, and contrivance. Obviously, acting is a form of Ion's paradox: It is *both* technique and inspiration, head and heart, presentation and representation, calculation and spontaneity. Real emotion is in a tension with rational control. Some exercises might help you to get more of a handle on all of this.

◆ E X E R C I S E   21–1

Playing (with) Real Emotion I

This is a modification of emotional memory, blending imaginary dramatic reconstruction with real events and characters drawn from your own life. It also taps in to Stanislavsky's notion of physical actions.

Go back to Exercise 20–3, "Facing an Imagined Death." Re-memorize the lines of King Lear and form a circle with your acting group, as in that exercise.

Now think about someone in your own life who has died. The death need not be recent, nor need it necessarily be anyone for whom you remember grieving very deeply. But let yourself think, now, about how wonderful that person (we'll call her "she") was. Think about the wonderful parts of her that you haven't thought about for years. Imagine those wonderful parts you never got to know.

And now imagine her lying eyes closed, on the verge of death, in the center of the circle. Walking around her, study her labored breathing. Try to breathe "for" her. And now, as you see her approach her dying gasps, imagine that she opens her eyes and looks at you. Imagine her trying, and failing, to reach her arm out to you. Keep trying to breathe "for" her. Now imagine God sending his messenger down to take her breath away for the last time. As this happens, as the messenger approaches her, give Lear's speech, knowing that no matter how quietly you speak, God and God's messenger—and the spirit of your imagined (real) person—are listening.

Pause but don't break out of the exercise when you come to the end of the speech. Think once more about how wonderful the person in your life was, and how much more wonderful she was than you knew at the time.

Do the speech again. This time, at the second "never," kneel by her hand. And on the last "never," close her eyelids.

Do it again.

EMOTION

The most important thing [in acting], the one thing you can't get away without, is the ability to summon an emotional state to the surface. We, as a population, are conditioned from our early childhood against that: to be strong, not to cry, not to show our feelings in public. Actors have to break through all of that conditioning and be in control of it at the same time. That's the great magic: to be able to summon the demon and then control it.

JAMES CAMERON

Discuss with your fellow students: How truthfully do you think you faced a "real death"? And how truthfully did your fellow students feel you faced such a death? In other words, how truthfully did you portray a person facing a real death? The answers might surprise you.

Self-Consciousness

Self-consciousness is, of course, the inhibitor of normal emotion; when we are concentrating on how we're coming across and how we're being perceived, we are highly aware of our appearance, our behavior, and even our feelings. And so, when burdened with self-consciousness, we don't really *have* feelings: We restrict or inhibit them. The only way to fully experience these feelings is to release these inhibitions by concentrating on something other than ourselves. Concentrating passionately on an imagined event—including a dramatic event—can free us to experience emotion profoundly and naturally. What helps in such a situation might be that the imagined event

- ♦ incorporates something deeply familiar (for example, a real person in your life)
- ♦ is inspiring (the person was wonderful)
- ♦ is tragic (a real, wonderful person is dying)
- ♦ holds the potential for hope (she is trying, with her last breath, to look at you and reach toward you)

Your breathing "for" the dying person makes you concentrate on—and empathize with—her physiological state, putting you in her place, and distracting you from yourself and your own concerns as an actor.

> EMOTION TAKES US
>
> *In our struggle to control [emotion], we are* overcome *by tears or laughter, rage or joy, etc. The emotion takes us, we do not take it.*
>
> UTA HAGEN

Your kneeling next to her and closing her eyelids gives you a strong physical action that connects you with her, and the earth she's lying on, even more strongly.

The repetition of the exercise can also reduce self-consciousness. Having performed the exercise once, you can plunge even deeper into it a second time, with the confidence that you've already proved that you can get through it (presuming that you did!). And then a third. Conversely, there may come the time that your self-consciousness will return, as you feel—by your repetitions or by others'—that you have explored and experienced the exercise as fully as humanly possible. Even the best actors have their limits, but remember that it's the work of the actor to keep emotions "fresh" and actions "alive" despite weeks, months, or years of continuous rehearsal and performance. Even film actors, who in theory create each moment of their performance only once, in fact have to re-create their performance over and over in "takes" that may have to be matched to each other in the editing studio, each with an identical action and emotional intensity.

◆ E X E R C I S E   21–2

Playing (with) Real Emotion II

Re-memorize Juliet's lines from Exercise 20–4. Now think of a person, of either sex (but we'll call this person "he"), whom you were deeply infatuated with some time ago—but never spoke seriously with.

Imagine yourself on a date with him, in a romantic setting with him, in a wildly erotic setting with him.

Play the speech to him as if he were with you in this setting.

Now play it while dancing with him. Snuggling in a hayloft with him. Rescuing him from his chains.

Now pair with a partner. Blur the lines between the real person with whom you were infatuated and your present partner. Transfer your infatuation to your partner. Play the line to your partner, convincing him of your passion for him. Play it dancing with him.

In discussing this scene, *don't* discuss the real person you were infatuated with. The emotional substitution will be all the more powerful when it is your secret, and yours alone. All the feeling and emotion must be expressed and experienced with and toward your acting partner.

Emotion is a tricky thing. In real life, we're rarely aware of it until it passes: Our knees buckle *after* the train that almost hit us goes by, not *during* the danger. And the moment we start to think "Boy, am I moved," that emotion has already started to fade away. The late French actor Jean-Louis Barrault, in a famous metaphor, compared emotion to perspiration; his idea was that emotion, like sweat, can't simply be willed into flowing, but must arrive naturally and organically when we're deeply engaged in passionate activity. As an athlete doesn't "try to sweat" to show how intensely she is competing, so an actor shouldn't "try to emote" to indicate the intensity of her performance. Rather, you, as an actor, should pursue your character's goals—get your character's GOTE—and then the emotions (as well as the sweat) will flow accordingly. Some of the substitutions and techniques described above might help it flow more fully.

Summary

Actors—and writers on acting—have argued for more than two thousand years as to whether the actor actually experiences or only technically presents genuine emotion onstage. Although Denis Diderot persuasively propounded the extreme view of "technical" or "presentational" acting, most who consider the subject consider that genuine emotion is an essential, if paradoxical, component of acting. The techniques of Konstantin Stanislavsky, sometimes transmitted through Lee Strasberg's Method, have had a powerful, if often controversial, impact on bringing emotion into American acting.

V

The Actor's Technique

YOU HAVE STUDIED YOUR GOTE, YOU HAVE WORKED ON DOZENS of exercises, you have prepared a number of scenes and, following a critique, you have improved and re-presented them to at least some general satisfaction. Are you an actor now?

Probably not. First, you will almost certainly still need work on these same basics: intensifying your pursuit of goals, expanding your tactical ranges, freeing yourself from psychological and social inhibitions (while onstage, anyway), making more exciting acting choices, and creating more inspirational expectations that will draw from you your most powerful and dramatic performing abilities.

And, second, you will need to develop expert acting *technique*. This is virtually the "Acting Two" section of this book.

Technique is a word most American actors regard with mixed feelings. On the plus side, technique is simply what distinguishes fine artists or craftspersons in any field. On the minus side, an empty technique—technical ability without feeling or person-to-person

TECHNIQUE

It should not for a moment be thought that [acting technique] is something to be coldbloodedly practiced and learned. Not even speech training, which is something that the bulk of actors badly need, can be done coldbloodedly, in a mechanical way.

BERTOLT BRECHT

interplay—is a shallow approximation of acting, bearing little resemblance to the real thing.

The actor's technique should be part of the entire acting experience, not a final gloss or "finesse" added at the last phase of rehearsal. Technique, indeed, is part of life itself; it helps us achieve our goals in life, as well as on the stage. Most of what we know as acting technique is simply effective human behavior: actions that are more economical, gestures that are more pointed, speeches that are more precise and more intense than ineffective ones. Learning to be a more technically proficient actor is also learning to be a more effective person-to-person communicator in daily life.

No element of acting technique is ever wholly artificial or solely theatrical. Even extremely non-naturalistic technique, as in the Japanese Noh or Kabuki drama, for example, is based on true feeling and effective action toward some sort of victory. Thus every "technical" instruction in Part Five must be regarded as an extension of the life and personality of your character and must be understood in terms of the human reality of your character's situation and GOTE breakdown.

22

Phrasing

Diction

Diction, emphasis, and inflection are three overlapping aspects of the actor's ability to speak the lines of the text. Together they constitute phrasing.

Diction is the clarity with which words are enunciated and put into action. Think of diction not simply as what is said, but what is *heard;* it is your words ringing in your partner's ear, and ringing with *meaning,* as they seek to encourage, persuade, or even intimidate your partner to act in ways that accomplish your goals.

You might think that in life, when you become emotionally intense, your diction becomes careless. But this is not true: When we are intense our diction actually improves. We speak more clearly, sharply, penetratingly, and with more precise and communicable meaning; we may even become eloquent and inspirational! The reason is clear: When we care more deeply about things, we try that much harder to communicate, to persuade, to *win* our intensely pursued goals. The more difficult the obstacle, the more taxing the situation, the more ferociously we fight to be heard and understood; consequently, the more powerful and precise our diction becomes. Diction is essentially a tool for pursuing our goals—whether in life or, when onstage, in getting our character's GOTE. The "mumbling" actors of a generation past were in fact quite unlifelike (as well as undramatic) when they affected a slovenly diction to indicate how "emotionally spontaneous" they were. For the most part they appeared only moody, uncaring, and incomprehensible.

So the "technique" of stage diction requires, at the beginning, a solid understanding of using tactics to achieve goals: specifically the tactics of clear, persuasive, and penetrating diction.

Good diction requires, of course, a comprehension of the meaning of your words and of the syntax that holds them together. In complex speech, good diction is essential just for comprehensibility. Hamlet's first line, "A little more than kin, and less than kind," is only the first of many in the play that would be rendered meaningless without clear and distinct diction. But even when the meaning of the speech is not in the actual words at all, diction remains crucial. Communication requires tying your words to your GOTE, specifically to the tactics that your words serve. Look, for example, at Jim's line in Exercise 9–1: "The Wrigley Building is one of the sights of Chicago—I saw it summer before last when I went up to the Century of Progress." The real meaning of this line has nothing to do with Midwestern urban architecture or the popular slogan of the era; rather, Jim is trying to impress Laura, and draw her out of her shyness, by demonstrating worldliness, intelligence, and bullish confidence. "I know my way around big cities, and I am fascinated by the future" is what he's really hoping to communicate: He's bragging and flirting, and encouraging Laura to do the same. Confident diction by the actor playing Jim will convey these inner messages; slovenly diction will convey the opposite. And when Laura says, a little while later, "I believe I *will* take a piece of gum, if you—don't mind," Laura's diction (and, consequently, the diction of the actor playing Laura) might seek to emulate the assurance of Jim's, tempered by a little of the elegant deference Laura has learned from her mother. Laura's diction should convey the notion, perhaps, that "I can live comfortably in your world—if you'll just show me how." In this way diction becomes not just a mark of actor technique, but of character goals and tactics.

So analyze what you are doing (or trying to do) with your acting partner —analyze your GOTE—and discover how you must use your words in that task. Are you asking a question? Silencing your partner? Seducing? Begging for approval? Provoking an argument? Making a distinction? Ending a quarrel? Proposing a reconciliation? The *content* of your speech may not always address these goals, but your diction and speaking tone will. Penetrating diction is one of the most potent tools the actor can lend to his or her character. Your instrument must be honed—and your approach focused —to deliver good diction at all times.

Good diction enables the audience to understand the play. If the actor cannot distinguish between "I ask you" and "I asked you," a moment in the play will surely suffer. After several such moments, the audience's attention will surely drift. While the audience puzzles over your meaning, it ceases to care about your emotional truth or about the play's situation and theme. Diction, then, is crucial to the theatre at every level.

Open-Mouthed Speaking

A common barrier to clear stage diction is a tight-lipped, tight-jawed speaking manner, often developed in childhood. This inhibits clear and effective diction, for which a more open-mouthed speaking manner is necessary. There can be many underlying causes for tight-jawed speech: vanity, a desire to look "tough," a distaste for overintellectualizing or overpronouncing words, wearing braces as a child, even prior abuse of various kinds. It's not easy to break these habits, but the following exercise can help liberate any actor.

◆ E X E R C I S E   22–1A

Act with Your Teeth

With a partner, exchange this dialog:

A: Yes.

B: No.

(Repeat four more times)

Do it again, using the actual movements of your mouth—the movement of your lips, teeth, and tongue—as part of your threatening or inductive tactics. Make your acting partner *see* you speak; exaggerate the movements of your teeth and tongue so as to encourage compliance (for the actor saying "Yes") or to threaten retaliation (for the actor saying "No"). I call this "acting with your teeth."

Reverse roles ("yes" sayers saying "no") and repeat the exercise.

◆ E X E R C I S E   22–1B

Do this short exchange in the same manner: Act it with your teeth. Overpronounce so that you are appealing to your partner or threatening your partner with your mouth movements as well as your words.

A: Come on over here!

B: You just leave me alone!

A: Come on over here!

B: You just leave me alone!

◆ E X E R C I S E   22–1C

Act the Laura–Jim scene with your teeth. Exaggerate the movements of your teeth, lips, and tongue, and overpronounce your words, using your mouth and your diction as part of your overall tactics to achieve your goals.

One can go overboard in this direction, of course. But, in general, actors should be "open-mouthed" in forming words and developing diction, just as they should be "open-throated" in developing good stage voices. In most cases, you should not only speak your words clearly, you should show the other characters that you are speaking your words clearly. Not only does this add to your comprehensibility, it enhances your confidence and consequently your stage presence.

Developing Diction

Good stage diction is not something you learn from a book. You learn it from experience, both onstage and in life. One of the best ways of learning good diction is simply communicating regularly with words—making yourself understood—in active and even hostile situations. Teaching children, addressing rallies, debating politics, and public speaking of any sort will sharpen your diction and train you, almost as a matter of course, in strengthening your capability for oral communication.

◆ E X E R C I S E   22–2

Repeated Sentences

Pair with a partner. Each partner selects a text, such as part of a play script or a narrative page from a book. The first partner begins by reading a sentence from the book. The second partner repeats it exactly, then reads a sentence from his or her book, which the first partner repeats.

Work up to longer and longer sentences. Concentrate on making your partner hear your text precisely and understand it. You have won the victory when your partner repeats the sentence perfectly and with complete comprehension.

Turn back-to-back and continue.

♦ E X E R C I S E   22–3

Shaw Speech

Few playwrights rely on diction as much as George Bernard Shaw, whose plays contain brilliant verbal arguments about a multitude of still-pertinent issues. Memorize any short speech (about five sentences) from one of Shaw's plays and deliver it to your partner. Then ask your partner to paraphrase the content of the speech. Your "success" is not how well you spoke, but how well you made your partner hear and understand the speech.

Switch partners and repeat the speech, working harder to make precise points. Act with your teeth, tongue, and lips, not just with your words! Make your partner hear the speech for the first time.

Switch back to your original partner for a final time. Did you improve? Ask your partner.

Emphasis

Emphasis is the stuff of oral interpretation, the decision to make one word or syllable more important than another. Almost any line can be read with a variety of emphases. Look, for example, at Macbeth's line to his wife, after murdering Duncan: "I have done the deed."

I have done the deed. [It was *me!*]

I *have* done the deed. [You thought I wouldn't, didn't you?]

I have *done* the deed. [It's all over now.]

I have done *the* deed. [It's the most *important* deed I've ever done.]

I have done the *deed.* [It's just a "deed," nothing more.]

All of those emphases are justifiable, but you can play only one of them. Which one fits the interpretation, stimulates the action, and best serves your production of the play? Should there be subemphases or equal emphases, such as "I have *done* the *deed*"? Emphasis, in a produced play, may be indicated by the director; more often, however, you will have to make these selections yourself.

Guiding your choice of emphasis should be the question, What do I want the other character(s) to hear and understand? Like diction, emphasis is a communication device; it should stimulate the right kinds of responses from the other person. What does Macbeth want his wife to understand from his utterance? If he worries that she is taking too much control, he may emphasize *I*. If he thinks she may want to turn back, he may emphasize *done*. If he thinks she may become hysterical, he may emphasize *deed*. Emphasis, then, is closely related to GOTE components, to the goal of your character, and the tactics you choose to implement that goal.

How do you emphasize a word? The most common way—in English—is simply raising its pitch, as (with the raised pitch noted by a preceding caret [^]): "I have ^done the deed," or "^I have done the deed." Increased volume also emphasizes a word, as does stressing the consonants a bit more precisely, thus "biting off" the syllables. But *coloring the vowels* of the word—giving them an enhanced, elongated, possibly unexpected *tone*—is often an even more effective way of providing special emphasis. Creating emphasis through stress and volume alone can result in strident, mechanical speaking (appropriate for certain characters, of course), while adding to that emphasis by carefully shaded tonal variations can create a more evocative, "poetic" speech useful in establishing more subtle relationships.

Movement and gesture are other ways of creating emphasis. Pointing to yourself on the word *I*, or making a fist on the word *done*, can determine what precise message Lady Macbeth (and, through her, the audience) will take from your speech.

◆ E X E R C I S E   22–4

Change of Emphasis

With a partner, and by turns, deliver Macbeth's line "I have done the deed" with each of the five emphases described previously, trying to capture the specific interpersonal meaning of each separate emphasis. Experiment with added *stress*, with *coloring* (elongating or enhancing) the vowels, and with *gestures*. How many of these emphases can you justify to yourself?

Select other lines that lend themselves to experimentation with different emphases, and see how many ways you can play them. Consider this exercise an experiment, however, and don't try to choose a "best" emphasis: That choice can come only from studying the play. Some possible lines, all from Shakespeare:

HAMLET: The time is out of joint. O cursed spite,
    That ever I was born to set it right!

KING LEAR: Dost thou call me fool, boy?

OTHELLO: I do not think but Desdemona's honest.

JULIET: You kiss by the book.

CLEOPATRA: O never was there Queen
So mightily betrayed!

◆ E X E R C I S E   22–5

Punctuate with Emphasis

Using stress and tone emphasis alone, make the meaning of these sentences clear by speaking them to someone:

1. Replace "don't" with "won't."

2. That that is, is; that that is not, is not.

3. She would, would she?

4. Look at "Casanova" over there!

5. What do you mean, "Do my duty"? Duty demands dying!

Act with your teeth!

Inflection

The word *inflection*, which comes from the Latin word for "turn," refers to the voice's rise or fall in pitch, from syllable to syllable. And the *end-inflection* is the pitch turn at the end of a phrase or sentence. Often pitch turns are the only difference between declarations and questions, as in the sentence, here unpunctuated: "You're going out". As a declaration

You're going out.

the speaker's pitch would ordinarily drop on the final word, but as a question

You're going out?

the pitch would normally rise.

Inflection is also how we denote sarcasm, in which a falling pitch is substituted for a rising one, unmistakably reversing the meaning of a line. For

THE ENGLISH SECRET

Ever wonder why American critics and audiences so adore British actors on U.S. stages? Such as Ralph Fiennes, Maggie Smith, Janet McTeer, Diana Rigg, Nigel Hawthorne, Derek Jacoby, Jeremy Irons, Ian McKellen, Roger Rees, Constance Cummings, Jessica Tandy, Stephen Dillane, Jennifer Ehle, and Pauline Collins, all of whom have won the coveted Antoinette Perry ("Tony") Broadway acting award in recent seasons? It may be because of "the English secret," the technique of using upward inflections to create a life-like and exhilarating forward momentum in a dramatic text. Though not always taught in American schools, the upward inflection is well recognized by the Brits:

If we take a downward inflection, we finish the journey. Keep the journey going, keep the inflection buoyantly up, until we reach the end of the trip.

MICHAEL LANGHAM, ENGLISH-BORN STAGE DIRECTOR; ARTISTIC DIRECTOR OF THE GUTHRIE THEATRE AND STRATFORD (ONTARIO) FESTIVAL; DIRECTOR OF DRAMA AT JUILLIARD SCHOOL

Where there is a break within the line . . . [usually] it is simply a poise on a word—i.e., the word holds and lifts for a fraction of a moment before it plunges into the second half of the line. This poise is necessary for the ear of the listener in that it allows a space, a still moment, for us to clock the key word in the line, and so be ready for the information in the second half of the line . . . Very often, when we do not understand a speech, it is because this shaping has not been attended to.

CICELY BERRY, ACCLAIMED VOCAL COACH, ROYAL SHAKESPEARE COMPANY; AUTHOR, DIRECTOR

Just remember, there's many an actor sleeping on the embankment tonight, with no soles to his shoes, for lack of an upward inflection.

DONALD SINDEN, ENGLISH CLASSICAL ACTOR

example: "That's great!" with a rising inflection, means what it says. But "That's great!" with a falling inflection, particularly when accompanied by a smirk or a raised eyebrow, means "That's terrible!" Needless to say, you must play these inflections with care.

If you listen to ordinary conversations, particularly involved conversations or arguments, you will hear a great variety in pitches and intonations and rapid shifts in the pacing and forcefulness of the spoken words. Similarly, varied inflections and a wide range of pitches and volume levels characterize exciting stage dialog. The beginning actor, often handicapped by a sketchily memorized text and ample levels of stage fright, frequently speaks in a monotonous tone with steady pitch (poor Johnny One-Note) and falling inflections that dwindle away before the line comes to an end. Continually falling inflections—of the sort you hear when someone is reading off a laundry list—identify the technically untrained actor and make the play die a slow death. Monotone is as unlifelike as it is untheatrical, so you need not worry about learning it—unless your part consists of reading off a laundry list.

In general, rising end-inflections *sustain* the action of a speech, and falling end-inflections *conclude* (or try to conclude) it. A rising inflection demands an answer or a response; a falling inflection suggests an attempt to close off discussion or to have the last word. Thus:

$$\text{Shall we } ^{go?} \nearrow$$

virtually demands an answer and suggests that the person so invited can accept or refuse. Conversely,

$$\overline{\text{Shall we}} _{go?} \searrow$$

while still technically an invitation, suggests that the "going" has already been decided; the person "asked" is merely requested to nod assent and leave. Falling inflections are characteristic of curtain lines:

$$\overline{\text{The play is}} _{done.} \searrow$$

and of argument-enders:

$$\overline{\text{No more ex}} _{cuses!} \searrow$$

Rising inflections are characteristic of real questions:

$$\text{Are you going} ^{out?} \nearrow$$

or:

Are you going out?

and of questions that imply, "Don't you agree with me?"

I think she's sad. ("Don't you?")

Similarly, we use rising inflections to point out *opposites* and *antitheses:*

Don't go left, go right.

Go right, not left.

Notice that the two words placed in opposition are both inflected upward, but the preferred word ("right" in this case) is inflected *further* upward, regardless of whether it comes first or second in the sentence. *Operative* or *key words,* such as words new to the current discussion, or highly *unusual* words, or usual words used in *unusual ways,* or words being *quoted* from someone else, are also normally highlighted by upward inflections, regardless of where they appear in a sentence:

His name is Howard.

Howard is his name.

Jacqueline said, "No."

"No," is what Jacqueline said.

Show me the money!

I think it's just empty persiflage!

Items in a *list* are likewise lifted in pitch until the last one, if the speaker really intends to communicate that the list is something important:

Get me some flowers, oatmeal, spinach, and cauliflower.

PETRUCHIO: She is my goods, my chattels;

she is my house, My household stuff, my field, my barn,

My horse, my ox, my ass, my anything!

(*The Taming of the Shrew*)

Notice that the normal inflection of a list rises steadily throughout the speech, until a falling inflection concludes it. In Petruchio's speech, a falling inflection on "chattels" will break up the speech (which restarts by repeating the subject and predicate—"she is"—immediately afterward) so that the actor does not have to reach impossibly high pitch levels.

Notice also that the pitch rise can be very slight in delivering this list; the *amount* of rise is not important, only that it is steady and perceptible.

Finally, rising inflections create exciting momentum in a speech and distinguish it from flat, droning, rote-memorized recitations. Rising inflections, by contrast, carry and build the basic idea, passion and *purpose* of a speech through its natural breathing and thinking pauses, as usually marked in the written text by commas. Lifted inflections radiate purposeful, aggressive speech, stimulating your fellow actors and compelling attention from both onstage and offstage audiences. In life as well as theatre, they are the benchmarks of exciting conversation, good argument, and high-spirited interchange.

◆ EXERCISE   22–6

Inflections

Study and produce the most vivid and engaging inflections in the following speeches and dialogs:

1. Let's go to the movie, not the play.

2. He's not a genius, he's an idiot.

3. I hate olives, pork, and sea urchins.

4. CLAUDIUS: These words are not mine.

   HAMLET: No, nor mine now.

   (*Hamlet*)

5. CELIA: Soft, comes he not here?

   ROSALIND: 'Tis he. Slink by and note him.

   (*As You Like It*)

6. LYSANDER: Not Hermia, but Helena I love!

   (*A Midsummer Night's Dream*)

7. Estelle is good, but I am better.

   (Note: In this case, "Estelle" and "I" are opposites.)

8. Where would you be without me?

9. (*proposing* to depart) Let's go.

   (*agreeing* to depart) Let's go.

10. HAMLET: To be or not to be, that is the question.

11. JULIET: Romeo, Romeo, wherefore art thou Romeo?

    (Possibly a trick question: "wherefore" means "why," not "where." The line asks, "Why does your name have to be Romeo, and you therefore a member of the family my family hates?")

12. TIMON: If thou wert the lion, the fox would
    beguile thee; if thou wert the lamb, the fox would
    eat thee, if thou wert the fox, the lion would
    suspect thee, when peradventure thou wert accused by
    the ass; if thou wert the ass, thy dullness would
    torment thee, and still thou livedst but as a
    breakfast to the wolf; if thou wert the wolf, thy
    greediness would afflict thee, and oft thou shouldst
    hazard thy life for thy dinner; wert thou the
    unicorn, pride and wrath would confound thee and
    make thine own self the conquest of thy fury; wert
    thou a bear, thou wouldst be killed by the horse;
    wert thou a horse, thou wouldst be seized by the
    leopard; wert thou a leopard, thou wert german° to   ° akin
    the lion and the spots of thy kindred were jurors on

thy life; What beast couldst thou be, that
were not subject to a beast?

(*Timon of Athens*)

This latter speech, of course, would be virtually incomprehensible without effective control of its speech inflections.

Inflections are not mere "acting technique." It was no less than Stanislavsky, the patron saint of organic and realistic acting, who advised actors to

give an upward twist to the sound of the last syllable of the last word before the comma . . . [and] leave the high note hanging in the air for a bit. . . . Almost like the warning lift of a hand, [this] causes listeners to wait patiently for the end of the unfinished sentence.

And again,

Intonations and pauses, in themselves, possess the power to produce a powerful emotional effect. . . . When you need real power in your speech, forget about volume, and remember your rising and falling inflections.*

Why, then, if inflections rise and fall in everyday speech, do actors need to *learn* to use rising inflections when they take to the stage? Because beginning actors, and sometimes experienced ones, normally read and start memorizing their lines before fully committing to playing their character's goals, and the result is an unconscious tendency to recite, as in (see Lesson 2) the flattened and often deadly "pledge of allegiance" as dutifully spoken in the school classroom.

Every speech you say, as a character, should be delivered as *created,* not *recited,* by you. You, not the playwright, should be perceived as the originator of your lines. Inflections are a technical manifestation of the extent to which you create rather than recite your text.

---

*Both quotations are from *Building a Character,* Constantin Stanislavski, translated by Elizabeth Reynolds Hapgood (New York: Theatre Arts Books, 1949), pp. 137, 141.

Phrasing

Considered together, diction, emphasis, and inflection result in phrasing. Phrasing can never be separated from the GOTE principles that give your speeches meaning and give your character the lifeblood to mean them and speak them. But your character's ability to phrase speeches and to pursue goals through words and rhetorical expression is something you, the actor, must supply.

As a first step, you should mark your script with underlines to indicate emphases. Add other notations pertaining to diction, based on the general principles of this lesson.

Which words should be elongated to reach the other's character's consciousness? Which words should be stressed? Are there any sarcastic inflections? Argument-enders? Questions demanding answers? Statements begging for agreement? Ideas needing precise clarification? More generally, how does the character use language, rhetorical expression, and gesture to further his or her cause? How does the character's vocabulary and syntax come into play in the character-to-character relationship? How does the character's phrasing show what kind of a thinker she or he is? What kind of tones does the character use? How much of a poet is he or she? How much of a bureaucrat? How does the character's GOTE translate into the character's phrasing?

Summary

Diction, emphasis, and inflection are ingredients of phrasing, which is the way the character uses words to influence events and other characters. Good phrasing has both a real-life similarity and theatrical effectiveness; it clarifies and focuses dialog, gives specific emphasis to the most important points of a scene or play, and sustains the excitement of the action and the enthusiasm of the characters. Varied and rising pitches are particularly useful as technical adjuncts to the GOTE-determined excitement of good acting.

L E S S O N

23

Attack

The First Word

Attack is the delivery of the first word of a speech. The principal rule of attacking a speech is that you must come in strong—with confidence, vigor, and enthusiasm, and also with substantial volume and pace. The weak attack, common in beginners, is filled with uncertainty, reflecting the beginner's characteristic uneasiness.

There are two reasons why your attack must be strong: a technical reason and a real-life reason. Technically, the actor must attack each speech vigorously in order to get the attention (focus) of the audience immediately at the outset of each speech. Remember, the audience does not know where to look from moment to moment; therefore it is up to you, the actor, to "pull" its attention every time you have something to say. The timid actor succeeds in doing this only by midsentence; the bold actor captures attention on the first syllable.

In real life a strong attack is even more important: In life, no playwright gives you the "right to speak." People don't automatically fall silent just because it's "your line." In life you must *earn* your opportunity to speak, and by the force of your speaking you must make everybody else stop talking and listen. This process is called *turn-taking* by conversation analysts, and it is as natural to life as it is (or should be) to the stage.

Thus the professional actor knows that he or she must "take stage" with both speeches and movement. You must not sink into the artificial comfort of the script with its planned alternation of "my lines and your lines." The

201

professional actor seizes the floor powerfully with the first syllable of each speech. Thus attack defines your presence and earns you the right to speak as a character and to shape the scene you are in.*

Sheer volume is normally a key ingredient of a strong attack. The uncertain actor, worried about making a mistake ("Is that my cue?" "Am I saying the right line?"), often reduces volume to minimize the magnitude of any possible error—committing a graver mistake in the process. In the theatre, it is almost always better to do something wrong boldly than to do something right timidly; so you should learn to give yourself the extra advantage of full projection on each opening syllable.

Volume alone is not the only attack device, however. Lengthening or coloring the vowel, sighing into an initial vowel, using an unusually high pitch, making a broad physical gesture or a noisy one, or overemphasizing an initial plosive consonant (the *p* in *perhaps,* perhaps) will also intensify your attack. So will opening your eyes wider, taking in a big gulp of air, rising from your chair, bouncing up on your toes, or taking a step forward. So will "acting with your teeth."

Remember, all of these "technical" actions are taken from ordinary life. Observe two people in an involved conversation or an argument and you will see most if not all of these turn-taking techniques coming into play— quite unconsciously and, more important, quite unselfconsciously. See whether you can put each of these attack devices into a patch of dialog you and your partner have already memorized.

The *pace* of your attack is a second major consideration. Normally your attack should be fast rather than slow, despite the beginner's tendency to be slow rather than fast.

Why should your attack be fast? Technically, to speed up the action of the play. In the final rehearsals, most directors admonish the actors to "pick up your cues!" Elapsed time between lines—the pauses of slow attacks—is wasted time as far as the audience is concerned; they are getting no information and they have no idea what you are thinking about during your

---

*How about Laura's "Hello" at the beginning of the Gentleman Caller scene (Exercise 9–1), which the playwright specifically indicates should be delivered "faintly"? Obviously, this line should not be spoken loudly, but actors will err if they simply "try to be faint" in attacking it. Laura is, in fact, trying to be bold— and, for her, she *is* being bold. The author's stage direction that immediately follows says "She clears her throat," indicating that Laura is trying to be bolder yet. The actor playing Laura must therefore try to be bold, as Laura does, but come somewhat short of the mark. It will do little good to whimper the line: Laura wants to make an impression with Jim right from the beginning; she just doesn't quite know how.

INTERRUPT YOUR PARTNER

In everyday life we often would have gone on talking if someone hadn't interrupted us. In your play, what would you have said if the other character hadn't interrupted you? Similarly, what launches you into interrupting the other character?

PETER BARKWORTH

pregnant pause. Indeed, they don't even know where to look, since they have no idea whose line is coming next.

In real life, people do not simply trade lines in alternation: They break into conversations and interrupt each other. They are eager to speak rather than simply obliged to say lines. To re-create that sort of high-intensity conversation, directors ask actors to pick up their cues, to portray a vivid discussion rather than a listless one.

When you attack a speech with pace, you are responding much more directly to your partner's line. Your emotions, stimulated by your partner, will be in full flush only for a split second: If you respond at that moment, your response will be filled with feeling; if you wait a second or two, that feeling will be dissipated. In acting, your most intense feelings should occur *while you're speaking,* not before or after, and you must seize the moment when you are most moved, not the moment a half-second later, to attack your speech.

Physical Attack

Speech is an action, and your attack on any single speech is physical as well as verbal. As an actor, you should learn to "move into" your speeches, not just utter them passively. This can mean a strong gesture on or right before your first word, or a stage move (standing up, sitting down, stepping forward), or just a toss of your head. It almost always means "acting with your teeth" and making it clear, from your head and mouth movements, that you *intend* to speak and intend to be *seen speaking.* Remember, you have to *work* to seize the floor and to "interrupt" your partner. Remember also, it is your *goal* (and your GOTE) that makes you speak and that it often takes physical action on your part to make that speech work toward —and not against—your character's goals. So be reasonably aggressive in "taking stage" when you begin your character's speeches.

Turn-Taking

A strong attack does not mean that you cannot pause during your speech, of course, or that you must race through your lines. Far from it. A strong attack means that you cannot pause unnecessarily *before* your speech, but that you seize the stage first—and then develop your nuances afterward. A good playwright will help you by giving you strong "turn-taking" attack words at the beginning of your speeches.

◆ EXERCISE   23–1

Turn-Taking Dialog

Read to yourself, and then aloud with a partner, this scene between two teenagers. The "she" in the first line refers to Eva's mother. Read the scene aloud several times with attention to making strong attacks.

ROBERT: Where does she think we go?

EVA: Oh, I tell her we just go walking in the woods, talking. She knows that but she thinks we do other things too.

ROBERT: Like what?

EVA: You know.

ROBERT: Like what?

EVA: You know. Dirty things.

ROBERT: What does she think that for?

EVA: I don't tell her, though.

ROBERT: What would you tell her?

EVA: About that. About when I have to pee and things.

ROBERT: Well, there's nothing dirty about that.

EVA: Well, don't you think I know!

ROBERT: She means other things.

EVA: What?

ROBERT: Never mind.

EVA: Well, don't you think I know?

(Lanford Wilson, *The Rimers of Eldritch*)

The scene in Exercise 23–1, fraught with repressed sexual curiosity and suspense (it will lead to a clumsy attempted rape and a shooting), is filled with awkwardness and hesitancy. The dialog clearly is not meant for racing through. Nonetheless, the scene develops its anxious intensity only if the attacks are continuously strong. Notice how Wilson, the playwright, has placed attack words such as *oh* and *well,* which can be attacked on cue and then followed by a pause. Each character speaks quickly in order to seize the conversation from the other—and then pauses to figure out what to say. Notice also how Eva uses "You know" as a temporizing answer to make Robert stop asking embarrassing questions and yet to answer in a noncommittal way.

Thus all characters in dialog try to control the conversation—even when they wish to cease conversing or cease answering questions—but the only way to do that is with a strong attack, not a weak one.

Study the following dialog, which is a more forceful argument. This is the scene (Act 3, scene 4) in which Hamlet stabs Polonius, who is hiding behind a curtain.

HAMLET: Now, mother, what's the matter?

QUEEN: Hamlet, thou hast thy father much offended.

HAMLET: Mother, you have my father much offended.

QUEEN: Come, come, you answer with an idle tongue.

HAMLET: Go, go, you question with a wicked tongue.

QUEEN: Why, how now, Hamlet!

HAMLET: What's the matter now?

QUEEN: Have you forgot me?

HAMLET: No, by the rood, not so;
You are the queen, your husband's brother's wife,
And—would it were not so—you are my mother.

QUEEN: Nay, then I'll set those to you that can speak.

HAMLET: Come, come, and sit you down; you shall not budge;
You go not till I set you up a glass
Where you may see the inmost part of you.

QUEEN: What wilt thou do? Thou wilt not murder me?
Help, help, ho!

POLONIUS *[Behind a curtain]*:   What, ho! help, help, help!

HAMLET *[Drawing his sword]*:   How now! A rat? *[Stabbing through the
curtain]* Dead, for a ducat, dead!

POLONIUS *[Behind]*:   O, I am slain!

QUEEN: O me, what hast thou done?

HAMLET: Nay, I know not: Is it the king?

QUEEN: O, what a rash and bloody deed is this!

HAMLET: A bloody deed! Almost as bad, good mother,
As kill a king, and marry with his brother.

QUEEN: As kill a king!

HAMLET: Ay, lady, 'twas my word.

(William Shakespeare, *Hamlet*)

Shakespeare's dialog, in general, displays masterful turn-taking. Shake-speare was an actor as well as a playwright, and consequently his verse is the most "actable" in the English language. The vast majority of Shake-spearean speeches—perhaps 90 percent or more—begin with one-syllable words, which are the easiest to attack, particularly in a verse form (iambic pentameter) that stresses the second, not the first, syllable. And in Shake-speare, polysyllabic opening words are usually commands, interjections, the names of the characters addressed, or repeated words from the previous line, all of which are easy to attack strongly.

In the scene from *Hamlet*, all possible turn-taking devices are in play: repeated attention-getters ("Come, come"), characters' names ("Hamlet," "Mother"), interjections ("O"), temporizers ("Why," "How now!"), and monosyllables, often in combination. Read that scene with a partner, find-ing how you can make strong attacks and still leave some room for pauses within several of the lines.

Preparing Strong Attacks

Understanding the dramatic need for the strong attack, how do you go about creating it onstage?

Confidence in your lines, and in your character's tactics and intentions, is paramount. Weak attacks almost never come from conscious decision but rather derive from actor trepidation. (Remember when you were in your elementary school choir and were shy about singing your first notes until you could confirm that everyone else was singing with you?)

Preparation, however, is a specific key to delivering strong attacks. Remember that the line cue is the actual word you come in after; the action cue is the word or phrase in the previous speech that prompts you to prepare your own speech. Thus:

QUEEN: Have you forgot me?

HAMLET: No, . . .

Me is the line cue; *forgot* is the action cue. When the Queen has said, "Have you forgot . . . ," Hamlet already knows what she's asking and is preparing his reply before she has finished her sentence. Thus when she completes her question, the word *no* is already on the tip of his tongue, ready to fly out.

Go through your script and underline all the action cues in your partner's lines—the words that tell you what you need to know before you really *want* to speak up. If you become aware of action cues, you will be able to understand—and portray—your character by picking up your partner's cues and delivering your lines with a strong attack, rather than merely following a technical command of the director.

◆ E X E R C I S E   23–2

Action Cues

Pair with a partner and select a short, intense, two-person scene made up of very short speeches. Underline all the action cues. Analyze all the turn-taking devices. Then read the scene aloud, emphasizing the attack points as much as possible without racing the lines.

Memorize, rehearse, and play the scene as you have studied it.

Summary

Attack, which is the delivery of the first word of your line, is a crucial technical element of the stage because it focuses attention on the speaking person and conveys the idea that your character *wants* to speak—and not that you are speaking only because the playwright has ordered you to. In the theatre, as in life, you must earn your right to speak; you must take the stage by the forcefulness of your speaking, and your vocal and physical attacks are the principal ways by which you do this. Strong attacks require substantial volume, energy, clarity, and pace, as well, many times, as an aggressive physical presence. You can prepare for strong attacks by studying your cue lines for action cues that spur your response shortly before it actually comes so that you will be fully ready to speak on your line cue. Picking up cues, via the strong attack, does not mean rushing or racing your lines. Pauses taken after a strong attack—within the body of your line rather than before your line—can be even more effective if the attacks in the scene are uniformly strong ones.

24

Follow-Through

The Hook

As it is important to pick up your cues, so it is important not to drop the end of your sentences. The last word of each speech must be audible and intelligible. So directors have urged beginning actors since time immemorial.

Beginning actors often drop the ends of their sentences or their speeches. When they come to the end of their scripted words, they sort of glide to a stop in the manner of a newly licensed driver gently pulling into a parking place.

But your character's goals must be pursued *beyond* the end of the line. The end of the speech is the moment when you are trying to compel your partner—the other character in your scene—to agree with you, or yield to you, or do your bidding in one fashion or another.

In acting, every line you speak must stimulate a reaction or a response from the other characters. Metaphorically, your line must hook the attention of your acting partner and demand that your partner react in some way or other. A weak follow-through has no hook—and consequently will catch no fish, no matter how beautifully cast.

Questions as Questions

The easiest lines to follow through are questions—simply because a question forces your partner to respond. When you ask, "Where are you going?" the question mark (which resembles a hook!) demands an answer and by so doing pulls your partner *and the audience* into your situation. When asked with real interrogative compulsion, questions create immediate drama; for that reason, they are used as the opening lines in a great number of dramatic masterpieces:

"When shall we three meet again?"—*Macbeth*

"What is it, children?"—*Oedipus the King*

"What's the matter?"—*Major Barbara*

"Now what's got into you?"—*The Misanthrope*

"Who's there?"—*Hamlet*

Because of their immediacy and their focus on the other person (the askee), questions can be played forcefully and followed through with rising—not falling—excitement.

And yet beginning actors tend to play questions as statements and with falling inflections rather than the rising inflection that is both more dramatic and more true to real-life questioning. For example, many beginning actors will tend to ask

"Where are you going?"

rather than

"Where are you going?"

or

"Where are you going?"

or

"Where are you going?"

Perhaps the falling inflection sounds sophisticated (at least it certainly sounds "superior"). More likely, carelessness results from knowing that the other actor is forced to respond anyway, because the script says so. But the falling inflection is both unlifelike and uninvolving—a flat statement rather than a demand for information. Try asking the question to a partner both ways, and notice how your partner responds to the various inflections.

The first rule of follow-through is to ask real questions. Give rising end-inflections as you look your partner—the askee—in the eye: *Demand an answer* with your inflection and your expression. Reach your hand out to your partner, encouraging a response. *Care* what that answer is. If you do this, everyone will hear the ends of your sentences, and you will create intense interaction onstage as you yield the floor—for the moment—to your acting partner.

Statements as Questions

While it is unwise, most of the time, to turn your questions into statements, it is usually quite desirable to turn your statements into questions. Most statements are, in fact, invocations if not direct questions: Most statements "ask" the other person to agree, or to praise the speaker, or to accept the speaker's wishes, plans, or definitions. "I'm going out" is a statement responding to the previous question, but it also can be inflected to ask a variety of implicit questions:

I'm going out. (Do you want to come?)

I'm going out. (Would you rather I'd stay?)

I'm going out. (Are you going to ask me where?)

I'm going out. (Do you want to make plans for my return?)

Again, the upward inflection of the last word, the gaze and expression of the actor speaking, and the intentions played between actors can make the line an effective stage communication, not just a flat statement of fact. Follow-through is crucial here. The line must *lead* somewhere, must demand a reaction or a response. If you can find the hidden question in the otherwise declarative speech, you can hook the other actor—and through him or her, the audience—with the parting word or syllable.

◆ E X E R C I S E   24–1

Making Questions

Play the following lines to hook your partner by ending them with an upward inflection. Make each line into either a question or an implicit question (a request for a favorable response or confirmation). Put pressure on your partner: Play for the goal of your partner's favorable response.

1. Are you sure you won't have some oatmeal?

2. How long have I been back? Six months? Seven?

3. May one still speak of time?

4. It's time for me to go!

5. What are you thinking of?

6. How comest thou hither, tell me, and wherefore?

7. I hope you're not going to make a nuisance of yourself.

8. I said, go answer the door. What are you, deaf?

9. Seems to me you were staring through the window at me.

10. I believe my attitude must be deemed the proper one.

These are all lines from well-known plays. Number 4 is Vershinin's attempted leave-taking from Olga at the end of Chekhov's *Three Sisters*. As he is waiting for Masha to arrive, he doesn't leave. His line is a request for Olga to say "Wait, don't go."

Find reasons to make all these lines similar requests.

Statements as Statements

Some statements are intended to close a discussion or end a relationship. "I am going out!" spoken very firmly, with a downward inflection on the last syllable and perhaps a gesture of finality (pointing to the floor, shaking the fist), conveys the message that "as far as I am concerned, there is no more to be said on this subject!" The most powerful lines, said in this fashion, can literally leave the other character speechless:

LADY BRITOMART: Charles Lomax: if you can behave yourself, behave yourself. If not, leave the room. . . . *[Lomax sits on the settee . . . quite overcome.]*

(George Bernard Shaw, *Major Barbara*)

TOM: You'll go up, up on a broomstick, over Blue Mountain with seventeen gentlemen callers! You ugly—babbling old—*witch! [Amanda is . . . stunned and stupefied . . .]*

(Tennessee Williams, *The Glass Menagerie*)

LINDA: You're a pair of animals! Not one, not another living soul would have had the cruelty to walk out on that man in a restaurant!

BIFF *[Not looking at her]:*   Is that what he said?

LINDA: He didn't have to say anything. He was so humiliated he nearly limped when he came in.

HAPPY: But, Mom, he had a great time with us—

BIFF [Cutting him off violently]:   Shut up! [Without another word, Happy goes upstairs.]

(Arthur Miller, Death of a Salesman)

These strong declarations provoke momentary speechlessness, as the original stage directions make clear. But you can use many such lines to attempt to "win going away." One of the differences between a scripted argument and a real one is that, in life, you are not trying to sustain dialog; you are trying to end the argument, with yourself as the victor, each time you speak. You are always trying to create "the last word." Strong follow-through attempts to create that lifelike situation; in an argument, the last word of your speech is played as what you hope will be the last word on the subject. Notice that Linda's "Shut up!" in the Death of a Salesman scene has both a strong attack and a strong follow-through, as mandated by the author's stage directions. It is a particularly powerful climactic moment of theatre for that reason.

Invocations to "shut up"—that is, speeches intended to leave the others speechless—generally conclude with a highly stressed and downwardly inflected terminal syllable, usually integrated with an authoritative physical action. The speeches need not be shouted (notice Lady Britomart's elegant tone). And they need not be successful. (Tom's denunciation of his mother actually fails, as he exits the room clumsily, breaking some of his sister's glass figurines as he goes.) Nevertheless, these lines should be played as your character's attempt to achieve a victory: to make the disagreeing characters be quiet, recognize your character's correctness (or authority), and yield to your character's point of view or leadership. The hook of the last word should be intense, accompanied by continued eye contact (are they obeying?) and physical assurance.

◆ EXERCISE   24–2

Argument-Enders

Give the following speeches to a partner, foreclosing all discussion. Use downward inflections to close each speech. Try to make any reply virtually impossible.

1. Get out!

2. The matter is closed!

3. I'll see you in court.

4. We shall never surrender.

5. Honor thy father and thy mother.

6. I may vomit.

Trail-Offs

Not all speeches have a hook at the end. Some speeches just trail off. Tennessee Williams wrote a play (*In the Bar of a Tokyo Hotel*) in which more than three-quarters of the speeches end in midsentence. Sometimes characters realize they've said all they really mean before they've completed their sentence. Sometimes they forget what they were saying while speaking; sometimes they just lapse into dreamland. Sometimes characters trail off in their speeches simply because they understand only too well that they needn't complete their words in order to communicate their thoughts.

Playing trail-offs is dangerous for the beginner because the communication must be sustained on deeper and subtler levels, without the support of the follow-through hook. But the actor should be prepared for the occasional speech that winds into one's own reflections rather than hooking into the partner for a response.

Summary

Effective follow-through on the last words of your speech is a hook demanding a reaction from the other character. Questions hook your partner when they are asked with a rising inflection and direct eye contact. Statements can be used like questions to provoke a response. Statements calculated to provoke silence from the partner can be used as attempts to end arguments and force agreement. Expression, gaze, inflection (generally upward for questions, downward for statements), and appropriate physical actions or gestures are the ingredients of the successful hook.

Line Linkage

Analyzing Dialog

Attack and follow-through are not just isolated parts of your speeches; they are integrated elements of free-flowing dialog. The link between lines of dialog—between your partner's follow-through and your attack and vice versa—is a primary technical key to building a scene's intensity.

Study the following dialog between Tom and his mother in *The Glass Menagerie*. (This is the Tennessee Williams play you may remember from Exercise 9–1. Tom is Laura's brother, and Amanda is their mother.)

AMANDA: . . . What are you looking at?

TOM: The moon.

AMANDA: Is there a moon this evening?

TOM: It's rising over Garfinkel's Delicatessen.

AMANDA: So it is! A little silver slipper of a moon. Have you made a wish on it yet?

TOM: Um-hum.

AMANDA: What did you wish for?

TOM: That's a secret.

AMANDA: A secret, huh? Well, I won't tell mine either. I will be just as mysterious as you.

TOM: I bet I can guess what yours is.

AMANDA: Is my head so transparent?

TOM: You're not a sphinx.

AMANDA: No, I don't have secrets. I'll tell you what I wished for on the moon. Success and happiness for my precious children! I wish for that whenever there's a moon, and when there isn't a moon, I wish for it, too.

TOM: I thought perhaps you wished for a gentleman caller.

AMANDA: Why do you say that?

TOM: Don't you remember asking me to fetch one?

AMANDA: I remember suggesting that it would be nice for your sister if you brought home some nice young man from the warehouse. I think that I've made that suggestion more than once.

TOM: Yes, you have made it repeatedly.

AMANDA: Well?

TOM: We are going to have one.

AMANDA: *What?*

TOM: A gentleman caller!

AMANDA: You mean you have asked some nice young man to come over?

TOM: Yep. I've asked him to dinner.

AMANDA: You really did?

TOM: I did!

AMANDA: You did, and did he—*accept?*

TOM: He did!

AMANDA: Well, well—well, well! That's—lovely!

TOM: I thought that you would be pleased.

AMANDA: It's definite, then?

TOM: Very definite.

AMANDA: Soon?

TOM: Very soon.

AMANDA: For heaven's sake, stop putting on and tell me some things, will you?

TOM: What things do you want me to tell you?

AMANDA: *Naturally* I would like to know when he's *coming!*

TOM: He's coming tomorrow.

AMANDA: *Tomorrow?*

TOM: Yep. Tomorrow.

AMANDA: But, Tom!

TOM: Yes, Mother?

AMANDA: Tomorrow gives me no time!

TOM: Time for what?

AMANDA: Preparations!

What actually transpires here? Very little, if you are looking only for plot or for strictly narrative information. You could write the events of this scene in one or two sentences. But Williams has written forty-six speeches. Why? To build a relationship, of course. What transpires is an exchange of feelings between a son and a mother; it is a carefully arranged interchange of strokings, put-downs, requests for attention, attempts to charm, attempts to outwit, attempts to achieve dominance, attempts to surprise. The goals and tactics are more subtle than in many of the previous exercises, but they are nonetheless evident to the sensitive reader–actor. These speeches demonstrate the artistry of superbly crafted *dramatic* dialog, as contrasted to narrative storytelling: The relationships are expressed through verbal interaction, not by description. Through GOTE.

You can analyze this interchange of dialog for line-linkage characteristics. First, study the particular attack and follow-through techniques. Notice that the writing is peppered with questions (twenty of them), even questions that answer questions: ". . . tell me some things, will you?" "What things do you want me to tell you?" Words repeated from line to line develop the impact of a musical refrain: "You really did?" "I did!" "You did, and did he—*accept?*" "He did!" Notice how Williams stresses attack and follow-through words in "*Naturally* I would like to know when he's *coming!*" Finally, notice how Williams uses pauses within the dialog without interfering with the attacks or follow-throughs:

AMANDA: . . . and did he—*accept?*

TOM: He did!

AMANDA: Well, well—well, well! That's—lovely!

The three pauses, marked by dashes in the original, give Amanda time to reflect, to relish her victory, and to formulate her considered opinion of Tom's act, without slowing the attacks or trailing off the follow-throughs.

Rising End-Inflections

The key to linkage is that the follow-through of one speech sets up the attack of the next speech, much like a springboard sets up a dive. Attacking from a weak cue is like diving from a broken springboard.

Look at the first four lines of Williams's dialog quoted at the beginning of this lesson: two questions and two answers. If the questions are posed and inflected as questions, the following speeches will be dramatically easy to attack. If they are simply stated with falling inflections, however, the following lines will be off to a deadly start. Witness

AMANDA: What are you looking at?

TOM: The moon.

AMANDA: Is there a moon this evening?

TOM: It's rising over Garfinkel's Delicatessen.

This is laundry-list acting. The speeches are simply read off as lines on a list; the inflections create no pressure on Tom, no interaction between him and his mother at the emotional level, and no compulsion for the audience to care. Compare with

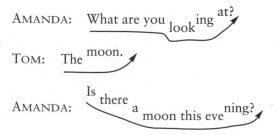

AMANDA: What are you looking at?

TOM: The moon.

AMANDA: Is there a moon this evening?

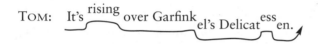

Tom: It's ^{rising} over Garfinkel's Delicatessen.

No attempt should be made to specify the "best" inflection of these speeches. Both ways of playing those lines are valid, in the sense that people can and do talk that way some of the time. The second way, however, is brighter, more energetic, more interactive, and builds more momentum. The rising inflections give a lift to the interchange and a life to the feelings that pass between the actors. The goals are clearer, the tactics more compelling, and the character's expectations are more lively (and lifelike).

In general, rising end-inflections are the technical key to keeping a scene alive and to developing the momentum of line linkage. They are crucial in *building* a scene because they lead somewhere. Rising inflections are lifelike as well as dramatic: In real life, if you are asking questions, arguing points, responding playfully, teasing, challenging, demanding, amusing, or persuading, you are probably using a preponderance of rising inflections in your speech. Conversely, if you are dutifully rote-reciting, you are probably using mostly falling (and weakly falling) inflections. Actors have a term for weak downwardly inflected cues: "He handed me a dead fish." Better to give your fellow actor a springboard: It is more lifelike, more stimulating, and more dramatic all at the same time.

Falling End-Inflections

Falling end-inflections can be used to create transitions: to end an argument, to change the subject or the mood, all without creating an unneeded pause.

Amanda: So on?

Tom: Very so on.

Amanda: For heaven's sake, stop .

Tom's falling end-inflection on *soon* makes clear to Amanda that she'll get no further with him in that line of questioning, so she has to try another tack. Her "for heaven's sake" is a temporizing phrase, one that she can attack strongly and right on cue—but one that's noncommittal enough to suggest she doesn't know exactly what she's going to say next. Noncommital phrases, such as interjections, give the character (and the actor) thinking time; they permit a rapid superficial attack while you are simultaneously summoning up your reserves for the stronger attack that immediately follows.

Attack Inflections

Attack inflections, or "front inflections," are the dive you make off the end-inflection springboard. The most exciting attack inflections come in at a *higher pitch* than the preceding end-inflection. Study this linkage:

Compare with this reading, common among beginning actors:

AMANDA: What did you wish for?   TOM: That's a secret.

An answer that "comes in on top of" (at a higher pitch than) an upward-inflected question shows a character seizing control of a scene rather than dutifully responding to an investigation. Attacks that come in low (in pitch, not in energy) can show something else. For example:

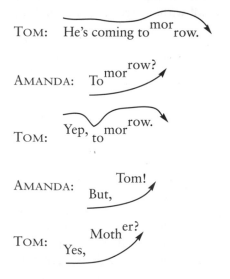

Tom's "Yep" suggests his excitement at having fulfilled her command, forcing her to deal with the immediacy of his action, forcing her to deal with him on his own terms. (Williams's use of the slang *yep* also suggests this.) Tom's "Yes," however, in response to her implied criticism ("But, Tom!") might begin on a low-pitched attack, perhaps in conscious self-mockery of his subservience.

Sometimes the lines call for a playful attack in your follow-through. For example:

AMANDA: Tomorrow gives me no time!

TOM: Time for what?

Tom's repetition of Amanda's follow-through words in his attack gives him an opportunity to repronounce her word, perhaps mocking her inflection (or accent, or note of hysteria) as he rephrases the issue. Note, of course, that Tom knows exactly what Amanda means by "no time." His line is only a rhetorical ploy—thus emphasizing the relationship between technical aspects of line linkage and real-life aspects of person-to-person (including child-to-parent) interaction.

Pauses

Pauses play an important role in dialog. The plays of Samuel Beckett and Harold Pinter, for example, have become famous for their pauses. Look at the following scene from Pinter's *Betrayal*:

ROBERT: Speak.

JERRY: Yes.
   [Pause]

ROBERT: You look quite rough.
   [Pause]
      What's the trouble?
   [Pause]
      It's not about you and Emma, is it?
   [Pause]
      I know all about that.

JERRY: Yes. So I've . . . been told.

ROBERT: Ah.
   [Pause]
      Well, it's not very important, is it?

Five stipulated pauses, plus one ellipsis (. . .) indicating a sixth, in a scene of less than three dozen words, clearly demonstrate unusual line linkage. The pauses, however, can be integrated in the scene because of the intense interest each character has in the other's thoughts. The action continues through the silences with the intensity of each character's investigation of the other. Robert still must ask his questions so as to demand answers—that is, with rising inflections—and then Jerry's silences will be answer enough. The pauses that follow are virtually deafening. Even Robert's "Ah" is an invitation for Jerry to speak, and when he doesn't, we know Jerry's extreme discomfort by what he *doesn't* do.

Pauses serve as line linkage when they are not mere lapses or when they are not just a comfortable rest stop that the actor needs to collect his or her thoughts and feelings. Awkward pauses, even momentary ones, become holes in the dialog, where the actor's energy falls out of the scene and where the audience's attention begins to wander. In order to be effective, both for actor and for audience, the pause must be part of the linkage between lines: It must betoken *something that does not happen* instead of just *nothing happening.*

Long Speeches

A long speech in a play also requires good line linkage, but here the linkage is between your first clause or sentence and your second, and so on until the end. A long speech is not simply a series of sentences; it is an integrated expression. If it is to have a lifelike vitality, the components of that expression must develop an integrated momentum.

Rising inflections are generally the means of sustaining a long speech. A rising inflection means that you have something more to say, that you haven't yet completed your thoughts. Falling inflections are idea-enders; they suggest you have come to the end of your thoughts. If you haven't come to the end, then you must start your speech all over again, which causes a break in the audience's attention.*

Look at the following speech from Shaw's *Man and Superman:*

RAMSDEN: I will not allow you or any man to treat me as if I were a
    mere member of the British public. I detest its prejudices; I scorn its
    narrowness: I demand the right to think for myself. You pose as an
    advanced man. Let me tell you that I was an advanced man before you
    were born.

---

* Rising end-inflections are sometimes called "the English secret" (see page 194) because English actors are specifically trained in their use. Apart from their connection with a character's GOTE, however, they are merely an empty technique.

Beginning actors tend to use a falling inflection before every period and every semicolon. This tendency deadens the dialog and requires the beginner's partner to overcome the inertia of fallen inflections after each clause (something like running a 100-yard dash and stopping every ten feet). Try reading the speech aloud with rising inflections on *public, prejudices, narrowness, myself,* and *man;* then with a dramatically falling inflection on the terminal *born.* The speech is much easier to sustain if you can learn to speak it this way.

◆ E X E R C I S E   25–1

Line Linking

Select a six- or seven-line sequence from the Tom–Amanda scene. With a partner, analyze the sequence for line-linkage possibilities. Read through the lines, concentrating on finding the best possible linkings. Don't be afraid to devote your thinking to pure technical analysis. But as you grow comfortable repeating the sequence, try to understand how the inflections relate to the victories sought by your character, and the tactics used. Make the inflections "real" by trying to be yourself. Are these inflections *yours?* They should become yours.

◆ E X E R C I S E   25–2

The Long Speech

Select any long speech from any prose play, preferably a speech that contains a sustained argument or explanation. In your study, try to find clauses or sentences that call for a rising end-inflection. Mark these in the text of the speech. Memorize and practice the speech until you feel comfortable with it. Deliver it. Are you able to sustain the argument or explanation?

Line Linking in Practice

Line linking, like any acting technique, should be learned in the classroom or studio to the point that it becomes an integral part of your acting instrument. During an acting performance, you should not be thinking about attacks, or follow-throughs, or inflections: You should be thinking solely about your goal and your GOTE. By that time, the technique of linking your lines to others should be unconscious and automatic. The better you understand the relationship between line linking onstage and line linking in daily life, the easier this technique will be.

Line linking is rarely addressed in American acting schools, although it is considered a rudiment of actor training in Great Britain. It has obvious dangers: Nothing will make your acting seem more artificial than concentrating on line linking to the exclusion of all other techniques. Expert line linking is the result of the stage intuition and sense of timing that come from experience. The technique is extremely important in the finest acting you will *see,* and it should become part of the finest acting you will *do* as well.

Summary

Line linking is not easily mastered, but some general principles can be understood and put into practice by the beginner: (1) Pauses are generally ineffective line links unless they indicate specific questions not answered or roads not taken. (2) Rising end-inflections provide a springboard for your partner's next line and stimulate energetic dialog exchanges. Rising inflections sustain long speeches by acting as springboards for subsequent sentences. (3) Strong attacks that come in at a higher pitch ("on top" of a cue—particularly a cue that is itself upwardly inflected) are extremely powerful dramatically. (4) Line linkages that are theatrically effective ordinarily reflect the liveliness of real-life conversation or argument; they are rhetorical features of dialog if the play's *characters* use rhetorical devices themselves.

L E S S O N

26

Scene Structure

Breaking Down a Script

Plays, when you see them in print or in manuscript, are customarily divided into acts and scenes, with the acts separated by intermissions and the scenes by brief pauses in the action. But in acting you must divide a play into even smaller units.

French scenes begin with the entrance or exit of each named character. They are called French scenes because in traditional French scripts they are actually so identified and numbered. Even when not so identified in print, however, they are useful in defining a two-person or three-person "scene" to do in acting class.

Subscenes are even more important for actors: They are units of action within a scene, or French scene, in which each character pursues, to some sort of conclusion, one primary goal. The subscene ends when that goal is accomplished, or abandoned, or (as is more common) reassessed and revised. Subscenes can run from a few seconds to several minutes.

Beats were defined first by Stanislavsky as single units of action within a scene or subscene. Persons initially understood Stanislavsky's term as corresponding to beats in a musical measure—although it has subsequently been suggested that Stanislavsky's Russian term was something more like "bits" and took its present English form only as spoken in his heavy Polish accent by the actor Richard Boleslavsky, who first brought Stanislavsky's teachings to America. In any event, the term *beats* has entered the actor's lexicon as representing individual units of action, which, in our terms, means those

225

short units in which the actor employs a single tactic. In a subscene in which you are pursuing one goal, you might play several—or several dozen —individual beats.

Moments are usually construed as silent beats: moments of reflection when your character sizes up a situation before proceeding. "Take a moment here" is not simply a direction to pause, but to regroup for your next active beat.

These terms are not precisely defined, of course, but they are useful in helping you divide any segment of dramatic material into workable units of varying meaning, intensity, and emotional charge.

Choosing a Scene to Do in Class

In choosing a scene for preparation and class presentation, the key criteria should be:

◆ Does the scene contain compelling *goals for each character?*

◆ Does it permit (or better, does it stimulate) varied *tactics* for each character? Tactics that you can do? Tactics that will expand your range?

◆ Does it provide a reasonably intense and important *interaction* between all the characters in it? Involvement with *other* people?

◆ Does it have a clear *structure* of subscenes and beats?

In order to answer this last question, you will have to study elementary dramatic structure.

Structural Characteristics

The basic structure of dramatic action is usually described as an inverted V listing to starboard (to the right). A conflict begins with some sort of incitement, escalates slowly to a peak of intensity, and breaks suddenly into some sort of release. The peak of the intensity—the top of the inverted V—is called the climax; the incitement is called the inciting action; and the release is called the resolution or denouement. The inverted V leans to starboard— that is, the buildup to the climax is slower than the collapse to resolution— because building to climax sustains audience interest almost indefinitely, whereas climax and resolution provide an aesthetic and emotional jolt that is immensely satisfying but essentially short-lived.

The basic structure is characteristic of plays and scenes and of subscenes as well: It is absolutely fundamental to the drama. Thus a play leads up to a climax, but so does every scene and subscene, albeit in a more restrained fashion. You can graph the action of a play thus:

But if you look more closely at the lines in that graph, they are more accurately drawn as:

The climax of a play, or of a scene, is of primary importance to the actor: It is not only the moment of maximum dramatic tension, it is also the moment when the issues of the play are most clearly defined and the emotions of the characters are most nakedly exposed. In classical dramaturgy (the study of dramatic form), the climax may bring about *recognition* (of higher truth or truths), *reversal* (of fortunes or thinking), and a *catharsis* (a profusion of feelings leading finally to their purification or "cleansing"). Climaxes in tragedies have been awesome: Oedipus gouging out his eyes, Hamlet slaying his uncle, Phaedra taking a fatal poison. Climaxes of comedies are more subtle, but they are inevitably present in well-written and well-produced plays.

You must understand that dramatic structure is not merely a creation of the theatre, nor is it an artifice of dramatic writing. It is fundamental to life itself. It can be seen in explicit acts, such as sexual orgasm; in ritual enactments, such as the bullfight; in other aesthetic forms, such as the symphony; and in many public events, such as boxing matches, horse races, and auctions. In the long range the pattern can be seen in the cycle of life, in Shakespeare's "seven ages of man," and T. S. Eliot's "birth, and copulation, and death." That the pattern of life-rhythms can be represented by the aesthetic pattern of drama is one of the reasons the theatre has been such a satisfying art for more than twenty-five hundred years.

Transitions

Transitions are the imaginary lines between scenes, between subscenes, and between the beats of an actor's performance. Transitions are changes: of attitudes, of actions, of understandings. Nothing communicates information about your character so effectively as your transitions, because change is inherently noticeable and meaningful. Frowning conveys concern, for example, but not so vividly, nor so precisely, as a smile that suddenly *turns into* a frown. That process of turning into, or turning, signals what a character is thinking. Frowning, by itself, is merely the exhibition of an attitude: A smile turning into a frown is an action that can be construed as motivated, intended (if not intentional), and meaningful.

Sharp transitions, as a rule, are more dramatically effective than muddy ones, partly because of the theatre's demand for compression and clarity and partly because of the desirability of dramatic variety. The closer you can define the moment in a scene when love turns to hate or the desire to conquer turns to the desire to escape, the more precisely and vividly you can play the actions on either side of the transition and the more exciting you can make the transition itself. Thus defining transitions closely in your performance, and playing them sharply and boldly, is an important aspect of acting technique.

Scene Breakdown

We can study the elements of scene structure by looking at another passage from Williams's *Glass Menagerie:* the French scene in Scene 3 between Tom and Amanda in which Tom argues with his mother about his lack of independence.

Subscene 1

TOM: What in Christ's name am I—

AMANDA *[Shrilly]:*   Don't you use that—

TOM: Supposed to do!

AMANDA: Expression! Not in my—

TOM: Ohhh!

AMANDA: Presence! Have you gone out of your senses?

TOM: I have, that's true, *driven* out!

AMANDA: What is the matter with you, you—big—big—IDIOT!

Subscene 2

TOM: Look!—I've got *no thing,* no single thing—

AMANDA: Lower your voice!

TOM: In my life here that I can call my OWN! Everything is—

AMANDA: Stop that shouting!

TOM: Yesterday you confiscated my books! You had the nerve to—

AMANDA: I took that horrible novel back to the library—yes! That hideous book by that insane Mr. Lawrence. *[Tom laughs wildly.]* I cannot control the output of diseased minds or people who cater to them— *[Tom laughs still more wildly.]* BUT I WON'T ALLOW SUCH FILTH BROUGHT INTO MY HOUSE! No, no, no, no, no!

Subscene 3

TOM: House, house! Who pays rent on it, who makes a slave of himself to—

AMANDA *[Fairly screeching]:*   Don't you DARE to—

TOM: No, no, *I* mustn't say things! *I've* got to just—

AMANDA: Let me tell you—

TOM: I don't want to hear any more! *[He tears the portieres open and goes out, Amanda following.]*

Subscene 4

AMANDA: You *will* hear more, you—

TOM: No, I won't hear more, I'm going out!

AMANDA: You come right back in—

TOM: Out, out, out! Because I'm—

AMANDA: Come back here, Tom Wingfield! I'm not through talking to you!

TOM: Oh, go—*[He is interrupted by Laura's cry from the other room, beginning a new subscene—and French scene.]*

The French scene between Tom and Amanda is divided here into four subscenes. The primary goals for each character in each subscene might be described as follows:

Tom

Subscene 1: Shame Amanda for "expelling" him.

Subscene 2: Get control of his personal property.

Subscene 3: Get credit (and with it, control) for paying the rent.

Subscene 4: Hurt her deeply, so that he can win next time.

Amanda

Subscene 1: Clean up Tom's language.

Subscene 2: Clean up Tom's behavior.

Subscene 3: Get control of her house.

Subscene 4: Get control of her son.

Note that the goals described here are positive and highly interactional. Tom's goal in subscene 4 is not just "to leave." If all he wants is to leave, he would just leave. To say "I'm going out!" is itself an action, independent of going out, and it has a goal beyond merely self-describing one's behavior. If we remember that Tom's father also left Amanda, we realize how threatening and painful his words are to her—wholly apart from his actual departure. Similarly, Amanda's goal in subscene 2 is not "to justify herself," or "to get angry at Tom." She doesn't need justice, and she doesn't want to be angry: What she wants is for her son to be obedient and chaste. You might even say her goal is to make her son an innocent baby.

Each of the subscenes has several beats, approximately two per subscene per character, which can be described by rough identification and a quote or paraphrase of the relevant lines (some of which never get spoken) or actions:

Tom

1. Rhetorical question: What am I supposed to do?

2. Accusation: You're driving me crazy!

3. Abject irony: Nothing here is mine.

4. Mocking *(laughing wildly)*: You are ridiculous!

5. Heroic martyrdom: I pay for this house! I am a slave!

6. Pretend rage *(tearing the portieres)*: I'll destroy this house!

7. Threat of abandonment: I'm going out!

8. Curse: Go to Hell!

Amanda

1. Elegant chiding: Don't use that expression!

2. Rhetorical question: Have you lost your mind?

3. Maternal command: Lower your voice! Stop that shouting!

4. Frighten Tom with ugliness: horrible . . . hideous

5. Frighten Tom with illness: insane . . . diseased

6. Frighten Tom with immorality: Filth!

7. Shame Tom as usurper: Don't you dare!

8. Regain rational authority: You will hear more!

9. Regain maternal authority: Come back here, Tom Wingfield!

A well-orchestrated pattern of beats creates the variety of actions, tactics, and interactions that characterize a good scene or subscene. In such a scene, the acting of each character evolves and changes from moment to moment; it doesn't simply pour out in a single, monolithic (and monotonous) rant or in a tedious whining complaint. Finding, distinguishing, and playing the scene's individual beats, and the structure that organizes them into a dramatic pattern, makes your acting specific rather than generalized and compelling rather than melodramatic.

As to the structure of this scene, notice how Williams has carefully provided each actor with climactic expressions, sometimes with intentionally incorrect grammar, sometimes with capitalized insults, sometimes with a rapid stage cross, and finally with Tom about to swear at his mother, and Laura—a character new to the scene—desperately entering the conflict and raising the level of tension by one full psyche. Each of these climaxes tops the previous one; this is the way arguments—and scenes—are built.

Notice also how Williams, one of the most skilled writers of American stage dialog, builds the rising intensity within the subscenes. Tom first laughs "wildly" and then "still more wildly," thus increasing the level of tension during his mother's speech. Repetitions are used to escalate effect rather than to convey added content. Sometimes the escalation is in the words themselves. Reverse Amanda's "hideous book" with her previous "horrible novel" and you will see that the line loses punch: "Hideous book" is a stronger pejorative because *hideous* is more specific and extreme and *book* has harsh consonants. This intensification is not accidental. More often, however, the escalating repetitions such as Tom's "I'm going out! . . . Out, out out!" and Amanda's "No, no, no, no, no!" demand a buildup in the actor's delivery. The buildup in these repeated words can be developed in many ways, but they must build. Monotonous delivery of any of these lines would defeat the dramatic impact of the argument and destroy its realism.

Transitions occur quite naturally between subscenes. They do not necessarily require pauses, or "moments," but pauses are often effective. In the transition between the first two subscenes, for example:

AMANDA: . . . you—big—big—IDIOT!

TOM: Look!—I've got *no thing* . . .

Amanda's climax, built by the escalating repetition of *big* and the all-capitalized and exclamation-pointed *idiot,* is a terrifying insult when delivered from mother to son. It forces Tom to assess just how deeply he has alienated his mother. He might well take a moment to collect himself, because when he speaks, he introduces a new argument, one perhaps he has not raised before but has ruminated about. Clearly, the pause after "Look!" is an opportunity for Tom to cut back his intensity, to try to speak calmly instead of shouting. That his mother then accuses him of shouting becomes all the more revealing, and poignant, and counterproductive, and soon he is back up there, shouting as before.

Building to a climax, sharpening transitions, and playing beats and moments to their fullest potential is the technical side of good dramatic acting. Technique echoes reality, and it provides a good shape for dramatic dialog: It brings out the structure of well-written plays and even gives a sense of structure to poorly written ones. Finding the structure in a scene is not an easy task, but the ingredients are known and their outline can be traced. Being able to define how a scene is put together is a necessary first step to making the scene *work;* it is necessary, in acting, not merely to know what a scene is about, or what a character is about, but how a scene or a character can be made to reveal what it's about.

◆ E X E R C I S E   26–1

Scene Structure in Action

Learn the *Glass Menagerie* scene with a partner. Follow the breakdown of the scene closely. Subsequently, in class, do the scene in unison: half the class playing Tom, the other half playing Amanda. Try to blend in with the majority in terms of rising and falling intensities, the duration of pauses, and the rising/falling inflections. Repeat three times. Then, with a new partner, play the scene "cold."

Did new structural elements assert themselves from the unison experience? Don't try to copy anyone; do try, however, to come to grips with what seem to be universal structural elements in the dialog.

Summary

Scenes are not monolithic; they are structured dramatic material, and defining the structure is part of the actor's task. Scenes can be divided into French scenes, subscenes, beats, and moments, with transitions defining the beginning and end of each. The orchestration of these into a building and climaxing pattern creates dramatic form, builds and sustains audience interest, and delivers an aesthetic "jolt" that is always satisfying and often cathartic. This structure is inherent in a good dramatic text, but much of it is supported by the actor, and much is created by the actor.

L E S S O N

27

Building a Scene

Building and Topping

A scene is built both by the depth of the interplay between actors and by the incorporation of good structural builds in that playing.

The climax of a scene—and the subclimaxes that precede it—are the focal points of the scene. These are the *highs,* in actor parlance, and it is your job to make the most of them.

But structure demands more than climaxes, and a scene that is simply a series of highs becomes a shouting match and little else. In order to have highs you must have lows, and in order to get from lows to highs and back again you must have builds and cutbacks.

Much of the structuring of a scene will come through improvisation and spontaneous rehearsal. But some of it will come through conscious effort. You must be prepared to make that effort.

A *build* means rising intensity, usually signified by increased volume, increased pitch range (particularly on the high side), and more vigorous physical activity. Building is simply a function of active goal-pursuit and GOTE-pursuit: When you are trying to win, you try harder and harder as the action continues; you escalate your efforts. *Topping* is line-by-line building. A line that tops the previous one is stronger in delivery: usually louder, sharper, angrier (in an argument), and more physical. In a standard build, one line tops another in serial fashion. Actors should feel very comfortable with standard builds, for they are the basic building blocks of most dramatic scenes.

◆ E X E R C I S E   27–1

Standard Build I

Play this scene: You are a boxing referee counting out the champion who has just been knocked out by the challenger. Imagine a crowd cheering you on and the challenger dancing excitedly beside you as you count: "One, two, three, four, five, six, seven, eight, nine, ten—and the winner is [use your own name here]!" Make each number more excited than the last.

◆ E X E R C I S E   27–2

Standard Build II

Play this scene with your partner. You and a partner are bidding at an auction for something you both dearly want. With each bid, you feel you are getting closer to clinching the sale. Try to top your partner with each bid, and try to win the auction each time.

YOU: Ten dollars.

YOUR PARTNER: Twenty dollars!

YOU: Thirty dollars!

YOUR PARTNER: Forty dollars!

Keep bidding to one hundred dollars, topping each line. Try bidding to two hundred dollars.

◆ E X E R C I S E   27–3

Standard Build III

You and a partner exchange the following dialog, topping each other every time.

YOU: Be quiet.

YOUR PARTNER: You be quiet.

YOU: You be quiet.

YOUR PARTNER: You be quiet.

YOU: You be quiet.

YOUR PARTNER: You be quiet!

Try eight exchanges, then ten, then twelve. How far can you go? (But don't destroy your voice!) You can play variations on this build, such as "You will!" "I won't!" or "Yes!" "No!"

In doing those exercises, you quickly see that a straight build cannot go on very long; you quickly reach the top of your vocal range (and in scene acting you would reach the top of an emotional/verbalizing range as well). No further building is possible. There are two techniques to prevent that. The first is to develop more subtle gradations of topping; well-trained actors can "go up the ladder with smaller steps" and can sustain a straight build in finely modulated ways. That ability, of course, requires considerable training and experience. The second technique you can put into practice immediately: cutting back.

Cutting Back

A cutback is a sudden drop in intensity—at least in expressed intensity—which allows you to start building again. The cutback cannot be arbitrary, however; it must come from some change of approach, and usually from some minor subclimax in the action or argument. The four subscenes of *The Glass Menagerie* studied in Lesson 26 show four builds followed by cutbacks, each build reaching a bit higher than the last. On a larger scale, this is the ordinary pattern of drama.

Each cutback must be tied to some sort of realization, or reconsideration, within the scene itself. In the auction exercise, for example, imagine that after "eighty dollars," you stop bidding, pull out your wallet, check the "secret compartment," and then with a smile whisper "ninety dollars." You have de-escalated the intensity in a classic cutback, from which you and your partner can start the build all over again, climaxing at a final sale of "two hundred dollars" without losing the overall build or losing your voices.

Getting on Top

Topping the other actor's line—and topping it while leaving both yourself and your partner with somewhere yet to go—is one of the great skills of acting, as it exemplifies your goal orientation and fulfills—momentarily at least—some of your character's expectations.

Volume and pitch are the first ingredients of getting on top. You can hear this in music, where a composer builds excitement into a score by adding voices, adding instruments, and raising the volume and pitch. Physicalizing is another way: In an American musical, the classic build progresses from solo to chorus to solo plus chorus, to "Everybody dance." Listen to some of the great musical builds in music literature: The "Dies Irae" from Verdi's *Requiem* for its rising and apocalyptic exhilaration; Ravel's *Bolero* for its steadily growing sensuality. An actor who could master such builds would be able to achieve near-miracles onstage.

As an actor you can build an argument by becoming more precise, by lengthening the vowels, by getting more reckless, by risking more tactically, by showing more feeling, by loosening your tie, by grabbing a knife, by standing up, by standing on your toes, by stepping forward, by making a noise, by slamming your fist on the table, by "biting" your words, by turning over a piece of furniture, by smashing your glass in the fireplace. Conversely, you can build a seduction scene by getting sultrier and sultrier, by letting your voice grow more and more liquid, your body more sensual and evocative, and your actions more and more fetching and charming.

Pacing a Build

Line linking is crucial in building, since lines that build *must* be springboards for each other. Look at the exchanges between Tom and Amanda in both Lesson 25 and Lesson 26. See how the builds—fairly obvious in each case—evolved from closely linked lines—indeed, from overlapping lines in the second of those scenes. In general, pauses kill builds, and therefore pauses, again in general, should be reserved for transitions and cutbacks.

Accelerating tempos are characteristic of a build; this occasionally means speeding up line delivery, but more often it means speeding up cue pickups. A scene reaching its climax is like an argument reaching its breaking point: Both people are simply *dying* to speak; they can't wait to be *let* into the conversation—they *break in* instead. This accelerated tempo speeds up the blood and induces a recklessness that is also characteristic of the emotional exuberance of climactic confrontations. Think of a bullfight, which reaches its peak of excitement as the bull gets closer and closer to the matador and passes in shorter and shorter (faster and faster) lunges. So does a scene build to its highest level of intensity.

Cutting back—on pacing, on volume—is, as we have seen, usually necessary between subscenes, following climaxes and subclimaxes, and between some beats; but cutting back too quickly and too often is a trap for the beginning actor. Cutting back is (unfortunately) a comfortable thing to do: It gives you some breathing space and thinking time; it takes the pressure off. But we say "unfortunately" because too much cutting back slackens the dramatic tension of a scene, undercutting its dramatic structure. It may be easy for you, but it's bad for your scene and for your character's goal-oriented attack. So *cut back only for aggressive (goal-oriented, GOTE-oriented) reasons.* Not because you're tired, or under too much pressure from the scene, but because it will help you to win your goal.

And please don't try to "justify" cutting back because "you do it in life." You can find plenty of reasons to be an uninteresting actor if you look hard enough. Remember, if a bull doesn't escalate its anger and intensity during the bullfight, sharpening its tactics and speeding up its charges, the promoter gets a new bull. If an actor fails in the same way—in the professional theatre, at least—the director gets a new actor.

Complex Builds

Straight builds—with escalating volume, rising pitch, and accelerating tempos—cannot be sustained indefinitely, and they cannot simply follow each other like a string of sausages—not even like an ascending string of sausages. In addition to straight builds, the theatre has much more subtle builds that could be called complex.

Complex builds require a change of *tactics* within a build.

◆ E X E R C I S E   27–4

I Detest Monday

Build the following line: "I detest Monday, Tuesday, Wednesday, Thursday, Friday, Saturday, and Sunday!"

Now build this line: "I adore Monday, Tuesday, Wednesday, Thursday, Friday, Saturday, Sunday."

Notice that building the first line requires a growing sense of displeasure, whereas building the second requires an increased sensitivity and enjoyment. Each line heads toward a different climax or end point. As an actor, you should work to differentiate all seven steps—in both directions—by degree of intensity.

◆ E X E R C I S E   27–5

I Detest January

Substitute months of the year for days of the week, increasing the steps of Exercise 27–4 from seven to twelve.

◆ Exercise   27–6

Come Here

With a partner, build the following exchange:

You: Come here.

Your Partner: No.

You: Come here.

Your Partner: No.

You: Come here.

Your Partner: No.

You: Come here.

Your Partner: No.

You can play the "Come here" dialog as a straight build, or you can vary the tactics. In this case, varying the tactics is the best solution if the tactics build. That is, you first invite, then command, then wheedle, then threaten. Or you could invite, wheedle, threaten, and seduce. In either event, the change of tactics permits a varied approach within a straight and continuous build.

Building can also employ a change of rhetoric or tone of voice. A parent arguing with a child will frequently escalate the argument by talking in a louder and lower voice, and by employing the child's full name: "Jonathan Mark Spencer, you come right in here!" Increasing formality, with rising emotional drive, builds a scene. Molière, the French comic dramatist of the seventeenth century (and one of the best dramatic craftsmen of all time), used this device frequently. Look at this straight build of a lovers' quarrel from *The Bourgeois Gentleman* as it shifts from simple banter to the more formal to the overinflated:

Banter: Well, then explain.
   No, I've said enough.
   Tell me.
   No, I have nothing to tell.

More Formal: Have a heart.
   No.
   I beg you.

Leave me alone.
I implore you.
Go away from me.

OVERINFLATED: Speak to me!
Absolutely not!
Enlighten my suspicions!
I can't be bothered.
Ameliorate my anxiety!
I have no wish to do so.

◆ E X E R C I S E   27–7

Building Molière

Use the speeches from *The Bourgeois Gentleman* to practice building dialog exchanges. Involve your movements and expression, not merely your voice.

Once again, building is something that happens in life, not just in the theatre. If you are pursuing a goal, and you find obstacles in your way, you have to work harder to win what you want. If at first you don't succeed— and you won't, or the play will be over after the first line—then you not only have to try, try again, but you have to try *harder*. Try *better*. Arguments escalate precisely because the other person doesn't agree with you. Seductions intensify because the object of your desire doesn't immediately run into your arms.

Whatever you strive for in the theatre, you are bound to encounter resistance (in dramaturgy it's called conflict); your efforts to overcome the resistance are akin to your efforts to top your partner and thereby build your scenes. Building a scene, then, shows most of all that you *care*. A scene that doesn't build not only seems dramatically flat, it seems to be about someone (you, if you're the culprit) who doesn't care whether she or he wins or loses, who doesn't care about the outcome or achieving a goal. The person who cares *will* escalate the arguments and actions, *will* top all objection and counter all resistance, *will* explode right to the climax and catharsis if necessary to get what he or she wants. This intensification is what building requires and what building is; it is not simply a mechanical fact of good dramaturgy, which in this case is only a reflection of deeply felt human interaction.

GET THAT PERSON

The only thing you can bring to the stage is your will to get that other person to do your bidding.

WILLIAM H. MACY

Summary

Scenes don't just happen—they are built. Building means finding the structure of the scene and playing the builds up to the subclimaxes and climaxes. Scenes build by increased volume, raised pitch, increased commitment and concern, and accelerated tempos. Experienced actors can make straight builds of infinitely subtle gradations; beginning actors should start the process of learning how to make those small steps toward climactic heights. No builds can be sustained indefinitely, however, so actors must also learn to cut back from time to time, usually between subscenes, after subclimaxes, or both, to give themselves room to build again. Builds can also be varied and complex, building on tactics and tones and rhetorical formulation rather than straight volume, pitch, and intensity. In addition to matching mechanical matters of dramaturgy, building is lifelike. It conveys the impression of characters who care deeply and are committed to the winning of deeply desired goals.

L E S S O N

28

Creating a Monologue

Going It Alone

There will come a time when you are asked to prepare and present a dramatic monologue. This is a speech from a play, or a collection of dramatic speeches that you can effectively link together, that is performed with nobody else onstage. Sometimes this speech will be an excerpt from a play which, if fully staged, would have other characters onstage at that point. In other cases, the speech was originally meant to be spoken directly to the audience, with no other characters onstage at the time. In this situation it is also called a soliloquy.

Why do actors perform monologues? For one reason, it is a simple way to create an acting exercise without having to involve anyone else. For another, the monologue is the most frequently used form of audition piece, either for actors seeking a role in a play or admission to an acting school. Most graduate acting schools, for example, require at least two contrasting monologues (ordinarily one from a classical play and one from a modern play) as part of the application procedure. And so acting classes often assign monologues as part of the basic training. But monologues are particularly difficult and raise some fundamental acting problems.

The basic problem of the monologue is: To whom is it addressed? Put another way, who is the Other of your character's GOTE; of your "Goal-Other-Tactics-Expectation" formula?

The answer is that in every monologue you *must* identify an Other person or persons to whom you are speaking, and you must then play your monologue to that person or persons. Monologues can never be simply or wholly self-addressed. Even when you are "thinking out loud," you must be thinking out loud "to" or "for" someone else.

The Monologue to Someone Else

In most cases in which you perform, as a monologue, a speech from a play, you should be speaking to persons whose presence you imagine. In this case, it is first necessary to physically "place" the imaginary person or persons in the scene with you as though they were, indeed, "in the scene (scenery) with you." In other words, locate them on the "set."

Second, it is necessary to devise and create specific tactics that you will play to these imaginary people and also to "create," again through your imagination, their reaction to your tactics—so that you will be able to adjust your evolving goals and tactics to their "reactions."

Third, it is necessary, when performing a monologue, to "really try" to win your goals through these imaginary people. To perform your tactics as vigorously, and as passionately, as you would if there were a "real" acting partner responding to you. To look your imaginary partners in the eye, and to stare them down, or to beckon them forward. This, of course, takes sort of a "double imagination," and it requires that you not only act your part but imagine your partner's part. But all of this is completely in line with the nature of acting.

The Soliloquy

A soliloquy, however, does not have any identifiable "other person" to whom you are clearly speaking. Don't think that this is only a problem in Shakespearean acting: The soliloquy has a long history reaching right up to the most modern theatre. Sophocles, Molière, Chekhov, Brecht, Miller, Williams, Beckett, O'Neill, (Lanford) Wilson, and a probable majority of present-day American playwrights employ soliloquies. So you will inevitably have to face the question of whom the soliloquy is addressed to.

In Shakespeare, Brecht, Wilson, and many contemporary authors, the soliloquy may often be addressed directly to the audience, thereby making the audience the Other. In these soliloquies, you can look the audience (singly and collectively) in the eye and employ tactics (charm, threaten, seduce) directly on them just as you would on an acting partner or partners. In these cases the soliloquy may be called a *direct address*. Iago's soliloquies in *Othello* and Richard's in *Richard III,* for example, are clearly meant to be spoken directly to a live audience, and the characters' obvious goals are to solicit audience admiration and support. It is my personal (if admittedly debatable) opinion that *all* of Shakespeare's soliloquies may be so addressed and that Hamlet, for example, is seeking a certain audience feedback in his soliloquies. "To be or not to be, that is the question (don't you think???)." This position, at the least, can make for very active and engaging soliloquies, as the actor can simply play the GOTE directly to the audience and engage in a full range of tactical interactions with audience members.

In more realistic plays like Chekhov's, however, characters are usually not expected to look the audience directly in the eye, and the soliloquies are generally thought of as "thinking out loud." It might be useful in these cases to ponder what reasons people have for thinking out loud—why *you* ever think out loud, if you do.

Sometimes thinking out loud is a form of prayer. In these cases you might be described as speaking to God or to God's representative. Some characters—Konstantine, for example, in Chekhov's *Seagull*—could be said to be soliloquizing to their literary muse. Others could be speaking to ghosts or spirits: to one of their parents in heaven or to their "guardian angel." Most people—and most dramatic characters—can be said to feel themselves at times in the presence of a set of characters from somewhat spiritual worlds: divinities, deceased ancestors, momentarily absent role models and loved ones. Soliloquies can be addressed to these spiritual creatures.

Sometimes thinking out loud is a form of rehearsal. You might be preparing a speech you hope to give to someone sometime: an invitation to a date or the climax of a yet unspoken argument. In this case you are speaking to a real person—who is simply not present.

Sometimes thinking out loud is a trial musing-over of possibilities to see "how they sound." Putting vaguely formed ideas into words, and then into spoken words, can be the process by which we organize our thoughts. In these cases the walls—the environment—can be a sounding board that helps focus your mind. (In Willy Russell's one-woman play *Shirley Valentine,* the sole character directly addresses "wall" in the first act, which takes place in a kitchen, and "rock" in the second act, which takes place on a beach.)

A character's "musings" may be addressed to a pseudo-audience. Chekhov frequently allows characters to soliloquize in the presence of deaf or sleeping characters. Do they hear and understand? We—and the soliloquizing characters—don't know exactly. So the soliloquy is a working out of ideas, posing as a kind of nonsense lullaby to a less than fully perceptive character.

In all cases, however, the soliloquy will take on resonance and dramatic meaning to the extent that it is played *to someone else* (a god, a muse, a wall, a nonpresent loved-one, as a rehearsal to a nonpresent enemy) than just "to yourself." That outside presence will engage your GOTE: It will create an Other, an expectation and a goal for the speech, and it will induce

MONOLOGUES

There is really no such thing as soliloquy, for example, you can't talk to yourself: you talk to the people next to you intensely, and when you've exhausted them you burst into passionate discourse with the audience and worry them silly with the state of mind you're in.

IAN JUDGE

you to employ tactics in the goal's pursuit. No soliloquy or monologue should be simply a meditation or be self-absorbing.

Playing a Monologue or Soliloquy

Choose a monologue in which you can define at least one "other" person or persons to whom you are speaking: persons whose opinions you *care* about; persons whose actions can help you achieve specific goals.

"Place" those persons in specific locations. If you are staging your monologue before an audience, locate the persons between you and the audience, or in the audience, or behind the audience. Make the location very specific; have an exact sight-mark for each character and imagine the sight-mark (an "exit" sign, say) as being (looking like, acting like) the character.

Distinguish the "placed" persons by locating each on a different side of the room. If you are speaking both to the (present) Dauphin and your (spiritual) God (as, for example, in a monologue from *St. Joan*), place "the prince" as seated to your left and place "God" above to your right.

Use the audience as a character only in a soliloquy where you are addressing the audience as themselves. Do not, for example, use members of the audience as actual named characters in the play.

Divide the monologue or soliloquy into subscenes, beats, and transitions, with attention to rising action and climaxes, just as in the scene preparation in the last lesson.

Prepare and perform your monologue or soliloquy as you would a scene, building your tactics, arguments, and appeals as you would with a two-person dialog. Plan to "top" the imagined reactions of your imaginary acting "partners." Don't just act: interact. The authority of your monologue presentation will, in good measure, be a function of how well you can make us believe you are really talking with and listening to "other" people (or gods, or ghosts), and that you are trying to put real pressure on them.

◆ E X E R C I S E   28–1

Prepare a Monologue

Go back to Exercise 7–2. Taking one of the longer speeches, read the play (or at least the scene) it comes from, and prepare it as a class monologue. Follow the principles above.

   Choose a monologue (long speech) from any play; prepare and present it. Choose a soliloquy from any play; prepare and present it.

Summary

Monologues and soliloquies are important acting exercises. In both, it is necessary to identify and create—through your imaginative resources—the "other" person or persons directly or indirectly addressed in the speech. Soliloquies should be interactions with these imaginary "others"; they should convey your character's goals, tactics, and expectations; they should not be merely meditations, no matter how eloquent or articulate.

L'Envoi

L'envoi is a rather quaint literary term for the author's last words—sort of like saying "The ball is now in *your* court." It is also an opportunity for the author to return to the first person, which I now choose to do.

The problems of acting transcend culture, theatrical experience, and educational background; they surface in all actors almost all the time. Good actors lick their problems by training, by craft, by instinct, and by dedication. They put their time where it belongs: in their work. I have never known harder-working actors than veteran professionals. The more experienced they are, the more time and effort they put into their acting, and the more serious they are about matters of craft and technique.

The lessons in this book can be covered in a one-year course. Better, they can be explored in some depth in a one-and-a-half or a two-year course, interspersed with scenework. There are some lessons that actors could return to well into their flourishing careers; without question, areas touched on here will remain problems for some actors throughout their lives.

To study acting as a humanistic activity, as a means of self-expression and of developing self-confidence, to study the art of theatre as exemplified by the actor and by the acting process: These are laudable goals. To a great extent, they are *my* goals. To study acting with the idea of making your livelihood as an actor—an artist of the theatre—is an equally laudable goal but an infinitely more difficult one.

My l'envoi is addressed primarily to those actors who want to go on, beyond *Acting One*, to the possibilities of a professional career. This career requires great dedication and sacrifice. The hours are long, the working

REALLY TRY

Your work should be like a light bulb. You're on your tippy toes trying to screw it into the socket on the ceiling but you can't quite get it all the way. I think it's the same in acting. You've got to be reaching. And it's always got to be imperfect.

DUSTIN HOFFMAN

conditions dreary, the life perplexing, the opportunities few, and the rewards seemingly always around the corner. The pay is bad (when there is pay), and the work is irregular (when there is work). The politics are often pervasive and unfair.

To overcome these conditions you will need a solid acting approach that you can "turn on" in an instant at an audition, a cold reading, an interview, a rehearsal, or as a hurriedly summoned understudy.

You will need working habits that are concentrated and efficient, and you will need the freedom to employ them twenty-four hours a day—*any* day—when necessary.

You will need an instrument that is the world's best: Lacking that, you need one that is very close to being the world's best. There are only a few hundred career actors, after all; there are hundreds of *thousands* of acting students, community actors, and retired football players and rock stars.

You will need a technique that is fully developed, that goes into operation silently and unconsciously and seems unforced, and that clings to your approach like skin to a snake.

You will need to feel comfortable in periods other than your own, and with styles of speaking, moving, gesturing, and behaving that at first sight seem strange, even ridiculous. You will need to feel comfortable performing in forums quite unlike your acting classroom: in big open amphitheatres, cramped television studios, in-the-round experimental theatres, and in a casting director's office.

You will need to understand different sorts of characters: fat people, thin people, scared people, proud people, rulers, slaves, winners, losers, mutes, mutants. And you will have to learn how much of *you* is in them—and how much of them is in you. And you must learn how to show all this without fear of discovery, but rather with joy in the freedom of your fearlessness.

You will have to know how to manage a career and build an art at the same time; how to stay fed and intellectually satisfied on a day-to-day and year-to-year basis.

You will need a love for the theatre: for plays as well as playing, for ideas, for words, for deeply drawn characters and feelings, for the rhythm of dialog, for physical expression, for the human body, for poetry, for nuance, for imagery, and for life itself and all that it can teach us.

You will need the most demanding and most exacting standards—for *yourself*—and a willingness to reach for them always.

If you have these things, and also the ineffables of talent and luck, you may have a chance. If you have them in prodigious quantity, you may have a good chance. I certainly wish you well. This book is dedicated to your success.

A Glossary
of Acting Terms

Note: Not all the following terms are used in this text. They are, however, words you may hear while pursuing studies in acting. All words are described only as they pertain to acting and to the theatre.

action   everything an actor does onstage. Distinguish between outward actions (Romeo kneeling before Juliet) and inner actions (Romeo falling in love with Juliet).

action cue   a word in the speech preceding yours that initially prompts you to speak in response.

arc (of a role)   the overall **action** of a character during a play, and the way in which the character changes and develops during the course of that play.

aside   a character's brief remark, often witty, delivered directly to the audience. Other characters on stage are presumed not to hear it. A **presentational** technique, most common in comedies from the sixteenth to the nineteenth century. See also **soliloquy.**

beat   the smallest unit of action. Said to derive from the classroom teaching of Richard Boleslavsky, a disciple of Stanislavsky's, who, when referring to each little "bit" of an actor's action, pronounced it in his Polish accent. Also, as occasionally seen in stage directions, a short but pregnant pause in the dialog; shorthand for "wait a beat before speaking."

blocking   arranging the major movements of actors on stage, such as entrances, exits, stage crosses, sitting, standing, going up and down stairs. In full play productions, this is often initiated by a director.

business or **stage business**   hand or other small movements that actors make, often with props, that although normally incidental to the plot convey lifelike behavior. Examples include putting on reading glasses, lighting and smoking a cigarette, and dusting bookshelves. Initiated by both actors and directors to add texture and detail to performance.

cheating out (or **cheating**)   angling the body partly toward the audience, while still presuming to face the character you are in conversation with. "Cheat out a bit," a director might say so that the audience can see your face better. Though a common staging technique, it may seriously inhibit the intensity of personal interaction between actors.

communion   to Stanislavsky, the desirable state of full emotional rapport among actors in a play.

cue   in general, the line preceding your own that "cues" you to speak. See also **action cue** and **line cue.**

downstage   the front of the stage in a proscenium theatre; that part nearest the audience. "Cross downstage" is the director's instruction to move forward.

emotional memory   reliving situations in your own life while performing, often with the aid of **substitution,** in the hope of arousing your own emotions while acting a role. An age-old technique, made prominent by Stanislavsky in his early writing, but later discarded by him. Also known as *affective memory* and *emotional recall.*

empathy   the sense of personal identification the audience may develop with one or more characters in a play. The capacity of the audience to share feelings with, care for, and root for a dramatic character—in the person of an actor.

end-inflection   the inflection at the end of a line or word. Rising end-inflections tend to propel action and ideas forward, falling end-inflections tend to conclude them.

expectation   as used in this book, the actor's assumption of his or her character's belief that victory is possible (even when the actor knows, from reading the script, that failure will be the result). A technique that energizes the actor during the performance and tends to create **empathy** in the audience.

eye contact   two actors looking into each other's eyes.

goal   as used in this book, the character's quest at any given moment; what the character wants to achieve. In the conventional translation of Stanislavsky, the **objective.** Also sometimes called the *intention* or the intended *victory.*

improvisation   acting without a fixed text; playing a character's actions but with your own spontaneously invented words. Often used as a rehearsal technique; sometimes used as a theatre form in itself.

indicating   displaying, rather than experiencing, emotion onstage. Considered an acting flaw, as the audience can see that the emotion does not derive from the action of the play, but simply from the actor's desire to emote, to simply "indicate," in a mechanical fashion, the feelings of her or his character.

inductive tactic   an interactive tactic intended to induce a change in another character's (actor's) behavior. Smiling, befriending, seducing, and charming are all inductive (as opposed to **threatening**) **tactics.**

indulging   when in the grip of an emotion, in performance, sustaining it purely for its presumed dramatic impact on the audience. Considered an acting flaw as it does not advance or contribute to the action of the play. "Don't indulge it," a director might say.

inflection   the change in pitch within a spoken line. See **end-inflection.**

inner action   the action of a play that cannot be described simply by recounting the actor's words or outward movements, but are internal shifts: mental decisions, mood swings, emotional upheavals, and so on.

intention   see **goal**

lift   in speech delivery, to raise the pitch of a specific syllable.

line cue   specifically, the last syllable of the last line preceding your own.

"Magic If"   Stanislavsky's invention: The actor plays "as if" he or she were in the character's situation. Playing Juliet, you play "as if" you were in love with the actor playing Romeo. Playing Hamlet, you play "as if" the actress across from you was your mother and she wanted you to drop out of school and stay home.

moment-to-moment   the action of a scene or play in each individual moment, plus the minute changes in situation that occur from "moment to moment." Generally used in contrast to more general, unchanging emotional states, or relatively static character attitudes.

naturalistic   a dramatic (and acting) style that seeks, as much as possible, to represent ordinary life onstage.

objective   the best-known translation of Stanislavsky's term *zadacha* (problem). See **goal.**

pointing   physically pointing, with a finger, open hand, head toss, or other gesture, at a person (place, object) to indicate, often with emphasis, the person (place, object) intended.

practical props   props that actually have to work during performance; for example, a television set or cell phone that is seen to operate during the play.

presentational   acting that is openly "presented" to the audience without the illusion that the dialog is simply a conversation between the characters. Normally considered an acting flaw in naturalism, but not necessarily in other forms of drama. **Soliloquies, asides, takes,** and many musical numbers are openly presentational to the audience.

prima donna   an actor, female or male, whose arrogance and selfishness breed resentment among fellow workers. Literally, "first lady," and originally derived from certain overly demanding opera stars.

props or **properties**   small and usually hand-carried objects—for example, combs, pistols, pocket watches, telephones—used by actors during performance.

proscenium theatre   technically, a theatre that has a proscenium arch dividing the audience from the stage; used more generally, and in this glossary, to describe a staging orientation that has the audience on one side of the action only.

"real"   acting that convinces the audience it is genuine human behavior, performed on the stage but fully experienced by the actors. Placed in quotation marks here because acting is always, in fact, at least partly an illusion, and the "reality" of acting, no matter how spontaneous it seems, is always in part contrived. That the actors show up at the theatre at the same time the audience does is, in fact, the beginning of the contrivance of drama. Still, "Be more real" is a frequent directorial command, meaning, among other things: "Experience this more personally" or "Put more of yourself into it." (Or, as some cynics might say, "Seem to be more real.")

realistic   generally, but not uniformly, **naturalistic.** Acting (and drama) that is like ordinary life in most respects, though occasionally presentational.

representational   used as the opposite of **presentational,** and referring to acting that fundamentally seeks to humanly represent, rather than theatrically present, a dramatic character. The difference, however, is generally a matter of degree rather than pure opposition.

resonance   the voice's quality of "re-sounding" through the throat and nasal passages. Resonance amplifies the vocal sound and gives it strength, tone, timbre, and personal quality.

result   often used to indicate the outcome of a drama and what the actor should avoid playing before it occurs. "Don't play the result" means to play like you're going to win (see **expectation**) even if the play dictates that you will eventually fail. "Play the action, not the result," is a common director's instruction.

soliloquy   a speech given directly to the audience, ordinarily with no one else onstage. Common in ancient and Elizabethan drama and in modern drama as well. Usually played as a direct address to the audience, sometimes played as a character thinking aloud in the audience's presence.

spine   see **superobjective**

stage left   in a **proscenium theatre,** the actor's left, while facing the audience. "Cross left," when said by the director to the actor on such a stage, means cross to *your* (the actor's) left.

stage right   the actor's right. See above.

stakes   The emotional level of an acting performance. As in poker, where the term originated, "raising the stakes" in acting means that you have more to lose and more to win; thus you will be led to a greater emotional commitment to achieving your goals.

Stanislavsky   Konstantin   Stanislavsky   (also   spelled   Stanislavski), 1863–1938. Russian co-founder/director of the Moscow Art Theatre in 1897, creator of the world's first and best known systematized study of the acting art.

Strasberg   Lee Strasberg (1901–1982). Austrian-born acting teacher, artistic director of the Actors Studio, and developer of what came to be known as "Method acting," an approach based on the early teachings of **Stanislavsky.**

substitution   consciously imagining a person or event from your real life in the place of your actual acting partner, or the situation of the play, in order to stimulate real emotion. Often used in the **emotional memory** technique.

subtext   the hidden meanings of a dramatic text, comprising its **inner actions** and the unstated **goals** of the characters.

superobjective   Stanislavsky's term (actually *sverkhzadacha*, or "super-problem") that represents the character's long-range **goal** for the entire play. Also sometimes called the *spine* of the role.

tactics   in this book, the means by which a character seeks to achieve his or her **goal.** Tactics can be **inductive** or **threatening.**

take   as a noun, a quick, quizzical, or comical look at the audience or another actor. A **presentational** technique, often used in farce and commedia dell'arte.

targets of attention   persons, places, or objects the character focuses on.

threatening tactics   tactics a character may use to achieve a **goal** by implying force, violence, intimidation. Almost all characters can be seen to use threatening tactics at some point, although **inductive tactics** are more commonly used by most characters.

three-quarters   a stage position in a **proscenium theatre,** where the actor is facing halfway toward the actor to her or his side and halfway toward the audience. Thus the audience is essentially seeing a three-quarter view of the actor. See **cheating out.**

upstage   the opposite of **downstage;** the back part of the stage in a **proscenium theatre;** the part farthest from the audience. Derives from the eighteenth century, when the stage was slanted ("raked") toward the audience, with the rear of the stage higher than the front.

upstaging   to deliberately go upstage of an actor with whom you are sharing a scene, in order to make that actor face upstage to maintain the illusion of **eye contact,** or even a genuine conversation. Considered —if done for this purpose—selfish behavior worthy only of a **prima donna.**

virtuosity   great technical skill, in acting or any performing art.

vocal fold/vocal cord   interchangeable terms referring to the organs in the throat that, under the proper stimulus, generate sound.

I N D E X